Praise for S

THE GAME WARDEN'S SON

"I am happy to report that I have read *The Game Warden's Son* and that I enjoyed it very much. *The Game Warden's Son* holds the reader's attention with interesting narration of a variety of hunting and fishing violations in the deserts, valleys, mountains, and coastal areas of California. It has lively character portrayal and good insight into human nature, especially the crass disregard that many people have toward wildlife. Even more, this book is a wonderful tribute to the legacy of a father, a son, and many other wildlife professionals dedicated to protecting all of California's natural resources."
—John D. Nesbitt, award-winning author of *Field Work* and *Dark Prairie*

"What a great book! *The Game Warden's Son* not only captures the essence of the adventures of being a game warden, it sets the groundwork on how the passion to protect the wildlife resources can be inspired in a young person's upbringing! Steve does a wonderful job of re-creating the stories so others can enjoy the adventure. I was impressed by the fact that the stories from the 1950s have changed very little over the past 60 years. I was entertained and reminded of the many stories I was lucky enough to have experienced myself during my career as a game warden."
—Michael P. Carion, retired Deputy Director/Chief of the Law Enforcement Division of the California Department of Fish and Wildlife

"After two and a half decades as a California game warden myself, and nearing the end of my career, my desire to continue the same battles protecting fish and wildlife has been rejuvenated by reading Steve's book. It's as if I were a brand new warden just out of the academy! I just can't get enough of it and know how important our role is. I'm pleased to see Steve's true accounts again shine a light on what it takes to wear the badge on behalf of wildlife."
—Jerry Karnow, Jr., Past President of the California Fish and Game Wardens Association

"You might have thought the Wild West was tamed 150 years ago. Not so. In recounting stories from his real action-packed life growing up as a game warden's son and his own career as a California Fish and Game warden, Steve

Callan will keep you on the edge of your seat and show you that law and order comes in many guises."
—Patricia Lawrence, executive producer, Travel Radio International and reporter for the *Palo Cedro East Valley Times*

BADGES, BEARS, AND EAGLES

"This engrossing memoir by debut author Callan lets readers in on highlights of his 30-year career as a California wildlife officer. With a healthy dose of bravado, he always gets his perps, though he credits his fellow officers, like long-time partner Dave Szody, and the roles they've played in cases brought against poachers and other law-breakers. He recalls stories from back into the 1970's, his memory matched by a knack for pacing and recognition of how much information readers need to understand the dynamics of the cases. From beer-swilling poacher flunkies to 'entrepreneurs' dealing in black bear gall bladder for use in Chinese medicine, Callan and his partner sent a lot of wild characters to jail. The vignettes are jaw-dropping, funny, tragic, enraging, exciting, and hopeful—sometimes all at once. An avid outdoorsman with respect for the land and its inhabitants, Callan shares some of the ecological and social history of each California region he's worked; while those without knowledge of hunting will soon learn the intricacies of California's byzantine regulations. Never wavering from his ideals, Callan demonstrates an enviable love of his life's work and has plenty of adventure stories to share."
—*Publishers Weekly*

"Exceptionally well-written…. The writing style is almost flawless, and reading this gem is pure effortless joy."
—Gerry Lister, *International Game Warden* magazine

"A thrilling ride into the heart of bad guy country. Which is pretty much anywhere in the state, any place that people can abuse wildlife and habitats for a profit…. The author has reconstructed his and other cases from memory, interviews and court documents. The result is a series of suspenseful, well-written procedurals in which good triumphs, but not without a lot of foot work and tense dealings with well armed scofflaws…. It's compelling reading about true public service."
—Dan Barnett, *Chico Enterprise-Record*

"Steve Callan has written an honest and compelling memoir of his career as a warden for the California Department of Fish & Game. Game wardens usually work alone, rarely with backup, and often must deal with men carrying

loaded firearms. It's not a calling for the faint of heart, but one requiring high intelligence, tact, and insight into human nature. Californians are fortunate to have wardens of Callan's distinguished character protecting their wildlife."
—Boyd Gibbons, former Director of the California Department of Fish & Game, retired President of The Johnson Foundation and former U.S. Deputy Under Secretary of the Interior

"Most people do not think of a game warden as a detective. In *Badges, Bears, and Eagles*, Steve Callan—Californian, detective, environmentalist, wildlife protection officer, and outdoorsman—takes the reader on a thrilling adventure, providing an inside look at what a dedicated game warden truly does."
—Randal Hendricks, sports agent, attorney, and award-winning author of *Inside the Strike Zone*

"Always alone, with backup (if any) an hour and a half away, the game warden is usually dealing with people carrying guns. This book is a genuine chronicle of the very unusual and exciting life of a California game warden. Steve Callan always managed to bring me the most unusual cases any prosecutor would ever see."
—Larry Allen, District Attorney, Sierra County, CA, and former Shasta County Deputy DA and Environmental Prosecutor

"Callan is John Grisham for the Outdoorsman. Conservationists will applaud his sometimes 'unique' efforts to protect our natural resources from those who would abuse them. Whoever knew there was so much intrigue in Fish and Game cases?"
—McGregor Scott, former Shasta County District Attorney and former United States Attorney-Sacramento

"Callan's chronicle of the life of a California Fish and Game warden stands out because in addition to the typical illegal hunting and fishing cases, he provides the reader with real life examples of wardens protecting wildlife habitat and conducting exhaustive undercover operations. I thoroughly enjoyed reading this book."
—Donald Koch, retired Director of the California Department of Fish and Game

THE
GAME
WARDEN'S
SON

THE GAME WARDEN'S SON

Steven T. Callan

Seattle, WA

coffeetownpress

Coffeetown Press
PO Box 70515
Seattle, WA 98127

For more information go to: www.coffeetownpress.com
www.steventcallan.com

The following is a work of nonfiction. Names and identifying details have been changed, except when used by permission.

Cover design by Sabrina Sun
Cover photograph of migratory birds by Steven T. Callan

The Game Warden's Son

ISBN: 978-1-60381-345-7 (Trade Paper)
ISBN: 978-1-60381-346-4 (eBook)

Library of Congress Control Number: 2015945718

Printed in the United States of America

10 9 8 7 6 5 4 3 2 1

For my brother

Kenneth Wallace Callan

1949–2010

Acknowledgments

———————◆———————

I WOULD LIKE TO thank Catherine Treadgold and Jennifer McCord at Coffeetown Press for their professional advice, constant encouragement, and continued confidence in my writing.

The Game Warden's Son could not have been written without the support of my wife and best friend, Kathy. Her proofreading skills, encouragement, and unfailing patience proved invaluable.

I'm indebted to the following current and retired state and federal officers for providing priceless information: 90-year-old retired Fish and Game Patrol Lieutenant Gil Berg, 89-year-old retired Fish and Game Chief of Patrol Ned Dollahite, retired Fish and Game Lieutenant Dave Szody, retired Fish and Game Patrol Captain Nick Albert, retired Fish and Game Warden Bob Prosser, retired Fish and Game Patrol Captain Mike Wade, retired Fish and Game Warden Jon Dunn, Fish and Wildlife Patrol Captain Rick Banko, retired U.S. Fish and Wildlife Special Agent Joe Sandberg, retired Fish and Game Patrol Captain Ed Degraffenreid, retired California Highway Patrolman George Whitmer, retired Fish and Game Warden Al McDermott, retired Fish and Game Lieutenant Don Jacobs, retired Fish and Game Warden Ken Taylor, retired Fish and Game Warden Larry Bruckenstein, and Fish and Wildlife Warden Ryan Hanson.

Thank you to photographer Steve Guill for contributing valuable information and a photograph.

For their kind words, I am so grateful to award-winning author John D. Nesbitt, retired California Department of Fish and Wildlife Deputy Director/Chief of Law Enforcement Division Michael P. Carion, Past President of the

California Fish and Game Wardens Association Jerry Karnow, Jr., and Executive Producer of Travel Radio International and *Palo Cedro East Valley Times* reporter Patricia Lawrence.

Finally, I would like to thank my father, 89-year-old retired California Department of Fish and Game Patrol Inspector Wallace Callan, for inspiring me to make wildlife protection my life's work.

Table of Contents

—◆—

Introduction

———◆———

I WAS THUMBING THROUGH an old photograph album when I came across a small, black-and-white picture of my brother and me, dated May 1955. I had just turned seven and Kenny was five. We were standing at the edge of a grass-covered canyon, with a dry streambed, a row of oak trees, and a herd of grazing Black Angus cattle at the bottom. With the exception of a narrow dirt road leading off into the horizon, there were no signs of human habitation as far as the eye could see.

That photograph was taken from our backyard in San Diego, California. For a brief moment in time, before developers turned it all into houses and shopping centers, this was our playground—miles of canyons, distant mesas, and undiscovered farm ponds to explore. It was there—in that wondrous world of horny toads, blue-bellied lizards, and giant pollywogs—that my love of nature and insatiable interest in wildlife blossomed.

***

THE GAME WARDEN'S SON details over a half century of wildlife adventures and investigations, beginning with my storybook childhood as the son of a California Fish and Game warden. Inspired by my father, I would eventually pursue my own career in wildlife law enforcement—a dream come true. I invite you to follow my father, me, and other dedicated state and federal wildlife officers from the early 1950s all the way into the twenty-first century.

Writing this follow-up to *Badges, Bears, and Eagles* has been a labor of love, involving countless hours of research, reconnection with old friends and associates, and endless hours of writing and rewriting. During the process, I called to mind a lifetime of unforgettable experiences, a treasure trove of fond memories, and more than a few laughs.

The stories in this book are based on actual events. Some scenes involving perpetrators have been dramatically enhanced in a way that fits the available information. The dialogue has been reconstructed from my memory, from interviews with current and retired officers, and from officers' records, transcripts, and written accounts. The names of violators, witnesses, and certain other individuals have been changed.

I wrote *The Game Warden's Son* for those who love the outdoors, are passionate about our precious natural resources, or simply relish a good story. I hope you enjoy it.

THE EARLY YEARS

1948–1960

San Diego

———◆———

E VEN AT THE YOUNG age of nine, I was fiercely protective of wildlife. One afternoon, my neighbor Johnny Annaloro and I were playing down in the canyon behind my house in the North Clairemont neighborhood of San Diego, California. We had flattened out several cardboard boxes and were using them as makeshift sleds on the weed-strewn hillside. Fifty yards away, two kids were throwing rocks at something crawling across the ground.

"What are they trying to hit?" asked Johnny.

"Let's go see," I replied, sprinting in that direction.

We were about halfway to our destination when I recognized the rock throwers as Darrell Matousek and Randy Parsons, two troublemakers from up the street. Darrell was large for his age—a head taller than I—and known as the neighborhood bully. He enjoyed picking on the smaller kids when grownups weren't around. Darrell's only friend was a devious little sycophant named Randy Parsons. Randy liked to instigate fights, but he never seemed to participate himself.

"Don't hurt that lizard!" I shouted.

"Mind your own business," said Darrell, picking up another rock and preparing to throw it at the foot-long San Diego alligator lizard. The lizard had already lost its tail and was scampering across the ground toward a patch of ice plant.

"I said, leave that lizard alone!"

"What are you gonna do about it?" challenged Darrell. I looked back at my friend, who averted his gaze and obviously had no interest in a fist fight with a boy of Darrell's size.

"I'm waiting," taunted Darrell, his threatening mug now inches from my face.

My stomach churned and my heart pounded furiously as adrenaline coursed through my body. I had painted myself into a corner. The question crossed my mind: Was I willing to get beaten up for trying to protect a lizard? While Darrell and Randy laughed at me, I remembered something my father had said. Never start a fight, but the best way to end one is to hit the other kid in the nose as hard as you can.

"Come on, you little—" Before Darrell could finish his sentence, I doubled up my fist, hauled off, and punched him right on the end of his nose. Darrell just stood there, shocked and dumbfounded, with blood dripping down his chin and onto his clean white T-shirt.

"Hit him back!" shouted Randy. "Don't let him get away with that."

Darrell stepped forward and doubled his fists. With no other options, I released a flurry of right and left punches, landing at least one on Darrell's lower lip. The others completely missed or hit the side of his incredibly hard head.

"Come on, Darrell, hit him!" shouted Randy.

Darrell either didn't want to fight or didn't know how. I guessed that he had bluffed his way through the first ten years of his life, relying entirely on his exceptional size.

"Are you gonna let him get away with that?" shouted Randy.

"Shut up, Randy," replied Darrell. "If you want to fight over that lizard, go ahead."

Randy didn't say another word. He followed Darrell back up the hill and over the rise. Darrell didn't give me any more trouble after that. We never became friends, but he would wave to me sometimes when I saw him at school. As for the lizard, it disappeared into the ice plant on the upper canyon wall, leaving a writhing section of its long tail behind.

That was probably the first time I had engaged in the act of protecting wildlife, and it wouldn't be the last.

***

MY GRANDMOTHER ANNE INSPIRED my early interest in nature. Born in 1895 to Norwegian immigrants, she had an eventful childhood, to say the least. Her father, six-foot-four-inch entrepreneur and adventurer Thomas Wilson, left Norway and came to America in 1893, using his savings from a successful herring catch. While living in Vancouver, Washington, he invested in a stagecoach line before turning to gold mining in 1905. By the age of thirty, Wilson had made a small fortune gold mining near Tonopah, Nevada. He and a partner discovered what became known as the Round Mountain Placer

Fields and formed the Round Mountain Mining Company. With water scarce, Thomas Wilson invented a method of separating gold from sand and rock without using water; in the annals of Nevada mining history he was known as "Dry Wash Wilson." My great-grandfather would spend the fortune he amassed in the mining business on San Diego oceanfront property and a date palm ranch near Indio. He lost the bulk of his assets during the Great Depression.

Anne stayed in San Diego, married, and raised three boys: David, my father Wallace, and John. When I came along, Anne was in her fifties and could out-walk anyone half her age. I remember my grandmother as tall and slender, with beautiful snow-white hair.

Grandma Anne was well-read, musically talented, artistic, and opinionated. The original hippie, she was not shy about expressing her progressive views to anyone who would listen. Anne became a vegetarian long before it was popular and grew nearly everything she ate in her own backyard in San Diego.

My grandmother loved nature. In spite of her paltry income, she maintained a lifelong membership in the San Diego Zoological Society. Whenever my younger brother Kenny and I came for a visit, she'd march us down to the bus stop and off we'd go to the San Diego Zoo for a day of high adventure.

The three of us would explore every nook and cranny of that fascinating place, seeking out hard-to-find areas near the back of the zoo where few ventured. It was there on those distant hillsides that I as an eight-year-old first witnessed the ungulates: deer, elk, moose, bighorn sheep, and antelope. When we tired, Grandma would sit us down on a nearby bench and entertain us with stories of earlier times.

Knowing how much I loved baseball, Grandma Anne sometimes mentioned her longtime friend and bus-riding companion, May Williams. May worked for the Salvation Army, the source of many of the family's clothes during the Depression. Grandma said that May frequently talked about her son Teddy during their bus rides together. "That skinny young man used to walk down the street in front of our house, throwing rocks in the air and batting them with a stick," said Grandma. "I always worried about him breaking somebody's window." Teddy went on to become the legendary Boston Red Sox slugger Ted Williams.

Before I could ask a question, Grandma would spot an interesting animal and change the subject. "Do you see that large bird over there?"

"Yes, Grandma. That's a cassowary, isn't it?"

"Very good, Steven! Your father had an encounter with a bird just like that when he was about sixteen years old."

"Tell me about it, Grandma."

"Well, in those days Wallace and his friend Richard Haack would hitchhike all over San Diego. Sometimes they'd go clear out to the beach in La Jolla, and other times they'd go to the zoo in Balboa Park. Did you ever wonder about all those empty pens in my backyard?"

"What about them, Grandma?"

"They used to be filled with birds."

"Where did the birds come from?"

"Sometimes Wallace and Richard would come home from the zoo with an egg. We had an old laying hen that would incubate the egg and the boys would wait to see what hatched out. Most of the time it was a banty chicken or a turkey, but we had a few strange birds running around in the backyard for a while."

"Tell me about the cassowary, Grandma."

"One day your father saw this large green egg sitting next to the edge of a bird cage here at the zoo. He'd reached through the fence to snatch it when a bird just like that one over there charged him. Wallace pulled his hand back just in time but cut it pretty badly on the wire fence."

"What happened then, Grandma?"

"Your father learned a valuable lesson and never brought home another egg. With the war going on and Wallace determined to do his part, he enlisted in the Navy a year later. I had to go down and sign for him because he was only seventeen."

"Was it dangerous, Grandma?"

"Your grandfather and I were very worried during those years. Wallace would write letters home, telling us about the battles they had fought out in the Pacific Ocean. He was on a battleship. When your father finally came home, he finished high school and eventually became a fireman here in San Diego."

"Grandma, Kenny's way over there."

"Kenneth, you come back here! We'll buy you an ice cream when we get to the top of the hill."

***

My father, Wallace J. Callan, known to his friends as Wally, was a San Diego fireman during the 1950s. A fireman's work schedule consisted of twenty-four-hour shifts at various assigned fire stations throughout the city, followed by twenty-four hours off. During the summer months, we spent most of those days off at the beach.

La Jolla's Casa Cove was one of our favorite beaches. The old concrete seawall offered shelter from oncoming waves, creating an ideal place for kids to safely swim and practice their snorkeling skills. Mothers generally kept an eye on the kids while the fathers, most of them off-duty firemen, swam out to sea and dove for abalone. Each diver would tie a gunny sack to the inside of an inflated inner tube and hang on as he paddled out past the seawall and into the open ocean. Sometimes they paddled out so far that we lost sight of them. Abalones were plentiful in those days, and limiting out was the rule, rather than the exception. Occasionally, one of the divers would take a recently harvested abalone out of his gunny sack and hide it under a rocky ledge near shore. We kids would take turns diving seven or eight feet down to find the hidden treasure. For those of us between eight and ten years old, this was not an easy task. First we needed to locate the abalone, which was firmly fastened to a rock. Then we had to hold our breath long enough to slip an iron between the abalone and the rock, all the time being thrown back and forth by the incoming and outgoing surge. What a thrill when the reluctant mollusk finally popped loose!

One summer's day at Casa Cove, we were all sitting on the beach when a man emerged from the water carrying his fins, mask, and snorkel. He ventured to the back of the cove, asking if anyone had a spear gun he could borrow. Having no luck, the would-be spear fisherman walked up the steep hill to the street and out of sight. A half hour later, the same gentleman returned, carrying a spear gun. We watched, spellbound, as he and a companion put on their diving gear and entered the water. Within minutes, they swam around the outer edge of the seawall and disappeared.

An hour had gone by when my younger brother Kenny shouted, "There's those two guys with the spear gun!" We could see the divers working their way around the outer edge of the seawall and into the cove. By that time in the afternoon, the wind had come up and the once-calm ocean was becoming rougher by the minute. Pounding waves were knocking the two men about and making their exit quite difficult. Waves were also battering the seawall, sending sprays of white foam high into the air.

"It looks like they're towing something," I shouted from my windy vantage point atop the seawall. I jumped down and raced my brother and Timmy McCoy to the water's edge. The two spear fishermen had finally made it inside the cove but were struggling fiercely to reach the shallows with whatever it was they had in tow. Holding a spear gun in one hand, the lead swimmer was pulling a towline with the other and kicking frantically. His partner was doing a sidestroke, submerging himself in the foamy surf with every forward thrust. Each time a wave reached shore and retreated, an enormous dark gray object popped to the surface.

"It's huge!" shouted Timmy, as my father and Timmy's dad, Bernie McCoy, walked up behind us. Exhausted, the two spear fishermen finally touched bottom and sloshed their way toward shore. Now at a depth of three feet, a massive, deep-bodied fish was exposed; it floated motionless in the foamy water. "That's a black sea bass," my father said.

The sight of such an extraordinary animal was almost more than my excited heart could handle—its tail was the size of a truck tire, and its cavernous jaws fell open with each outgoing wave. I heard Bernie McCoy say that the gigantic grouper must have weighed five or six hundred pounds. We watched several men drag the colossal fish across the beach and up the hill to a waiting truck.

For the rest of the day I felt sad that such a magnificent creature had been killed and removed from the ocean. The incident spurred my passion for fish and wildlife, but what happened next turned this ten-year-old kid into a nature lover for life.

EARLY ONE MORNING, a week or so after the giant sea bass episode, we headed for the beach. Our favorite 1950s-era San Diego radio station, KCBQ, was playing "I Was a Big Man Yesterday," by the Four Preps. I remember singing along from the backseat.

"Steve, we're here," my father broke in. "Come help me unload the car."

We had arrived at Casa Cove about 8:30. Arriving early was essential if you wanted a parking spot anywhere near the beach, even in those days. As we pulled in, several of my father's firemen/diving buddies began to show up: Bernie McCoy and his eight-year-old son Tim, Dave Peter and his two boys Mike and Joey, and Bill Chilcote.

My father was thirty-two years old in 1958. At five-foot-eight, he had remained muscular and physically fit from his years as a member of the USS Alabama boxing team. Prior to World War II, Dad and his younger brother, John, would show off their gymnastic talents by performing handstands from the top rail of the Casa Cove seawall—not exactly a wise thing to do, but they performed some pretty crazy stunts in those days.

Bill Chilcote was my father's closest friend. One or two years older than my father, Bill was the original beach bum. He stayed in good physical condition by skin diving whenever he wasn't on duty at the fire station. Fast talking and always looking for a way to get rich, Bill once talked my dad into partnering with him on the purchase of an old commercial fishing boat called the *Gracy*. During lobster season, Bill and my father would charge their firemen friends five dollars each for a night dive off beautiful Coronado Island. Using long underwear for wet suits and household flashlights wrapped with sections of inner tube for dive lights, they brought home some gargantuan lobsters. The would-be entrepreneurs never made a nickel and sold the boat a few years later.

My father used to say that you could count on one hand the number of days in a year when the ocean near San Diego was calm and free of groundswells.

This turned out to be one of those days at Casa Cove. Kenny and I jumped out of the car and rushed to the edge of the retaining wall that overlooked the cove. "Dad, you should see this!" I shouted. "It's flat as a pancake."

"You guys, don't run off," said my father. "Help me carry this stuff down to the beach."

It was too late. Kenny and Timmy McCoy had run ahead and were already racing across the sand below. Always eager to please, I helped my father carry beach towels and a large gray bag full of diving gear.

"We're the first ones here," I said, as our group walked down the steep hill and made our way across the sand to the upper edge of the seawall. Six-inch waves rolled in and lapped gently against the shore, each time making a soft gasping sound.

"I'll keep an eye on the boys if you guys want to go out first," offered Bernie. Mike asked his father if he could go along. At age eleven, he was the oldest boy in the group. A year younger than Mike, I seized the opportunity and reminded my father of his promise to let me go on a dive if there were ever a calm day. Both fathers eventually gave in, and Mike and I excitedly prepared our diving gear.

I was sitting at the outer edge of the seawall, clearing my dive mask and putting on my fins, when I heard the splat of Bill Chilcote's inner tube hitting the water. "I'll look around here until you guys are ready," said Chilcote, as he stepped off the edge of the seawall into ten feet of water.

Dave and Mike were next, followed by my father and me. With heads down and snorkels skyward, three adults and two very excited apprentices calmly paddled out past the seawall and into the open ocean.

This was no swimming pool—it was the endless Pacific Ocean. With every kick of my fins, the shore got farther away and so did the ocean floor. I was a confident swimmer, but in spite of my father's reassurances, I worried about running into the ocean's most infamous predator. My father had encountered harmless leopard sharks, smoothhounds, dogfish, small hammerheads, and even a few twenty-foot basking sharks while diving off the San Diego coast; I wondered if it were only a matter of time before we came face-to-face with a potentially dangerous shark, like a great white or mako. Years later, I would relish my sightings of these magnificent creatures while scuba diving in the Florida Keys, Bonaire, and Little Cayman.

As we continued out to sea, we bobbed like corks on the intermittent groundswells. Forests of sienna-colored kelp reached up from the reefs below, waving back and forth in the gentle current. Brilliant orange garibaldis darted about, chasing other fish from their rocky crevices. Senoritas and yellow kelpfish swam in the upper reaches of the kelp forest, while a four-foot leopard shark cruised the sandy bottom. With every fish sighting, I became less apprehensive and more comfortable in my surroundings.

Bill Chilcote had gone ahead and was already diving. I could see the tips of his fins as he tucked his body and disappeared.

"Wally!" shouted Chilcote, popping to the surface. "Bring the boys over here." When we reached Chilcote, he explained that the upper edge of an underwater cave was fifteen feet below. "Just under the ledge is a monster grouper," said Chilcote. I was thrilled by the possibility of seeing my second giant sea bass in a week's time. This one would be alive.

"Make sure you keep clearing your ears as you go down," instructed my father. Breathing through my snorkel, I watched from the surface as Dave and Mike made their first attempt. Mike couldn't quite make it and returned to the surface. "Take a couple of deep breaths and let's go," said my father. "If your ears start hurting, hold your nose and blow gently. Don't force it."

Taking a healthy gulp of air, I tucked my upper body, straightened my legs, and headed for the reef below. At twelve feet, my ears screamed with pain so I slowed down and began the clearing process. By the time I was able to clear my ears, I was out of breath and had to return to the surface. Thirty seconds later, my father popped up beside me.

"Did you see it?" I asked. "Is it still down there?"

"Yeah, it's just under the ledge."

"How big is it?"

"About the size of your Uncle Mel's Volkswagen."

Again I headed down. This time I made it to the top of the ledge before my ears began to hurt. I treaded water for a few seconds, rising slightly in the water column. My ears finally cleared, but once again I was out of breath and forced to surface. This was the most exciting thing I had ever done, and I wasn't about to give up before getting a glimpse of that enormous fish.

Down I went, eventually reaching my father. Staring back at me through his dive mask, he pointed to a spot just under the ledge. My eardrums were uncomfortable, but this time I was able to peer into the underwater cavern. The walls were covered with blue-green sea anemones, abalones, and starfish so plentiful they were stacked on top of each other. Lobsters peeked from every crack and crevice. As the air in my lungs dwindled, I became anxious and almost panicked. *Where is this monster fish? Dad's pointing at it, but I can't see anything but rock.* Bubbles spewed from the edges of my mouth and out the side of my snorkel. I couldn't hold my breath much longer. Finally, I saw something move. It was a pectoral fin slowly pulsating up and down in the dark shadow beneath the ledge. I had mistaken the seven-foot behemoth's dark gray body for part of the rocky outcropping. Built like a half-grown steer and perched at the top of the food chain, this massive predator exhibited no fear. Hovering motionless and serene, it seemed completely unfazed by all the attention it was receiving. Surfacing, we left the colossal fish alone and headed back to the beach. Not until forty years later, while photographing a goliath grouper off Key Largo, Florida, would I again have such an exhilarating and unforgettable underwater experience.

IT WAS 1958 WHEN my father was notified that he had passed the examination to become a California Fish and Game warden. After completing his required law enforcement training, he was assigned to the patrol boat *Marlin*, out of Seal Beach, a few miles south of Los Angeles. Our family bought a house in nearby Westminster, a semirural community located a bike ride away from Knott's Berry Farm and a short drive from a recently built amusement park called Disneyland.

I became a Dodgers fan and followed Walter Alston and the "Boys of Summer" all the way to the 1959 World Series. Our Little League team even attended one of their regular season games at the Los Angeles Coliseum. That night, the entire stadium was filled with Little League teams from all over Los Angeles.

My days in Westminster would mark the beginning of my storybook childhood as the game warden's son.

A Trip to the Islands

————◆————

I FIRST EXPERIENCED CALIFORNIA's Channel Islands in 1959, as an excited eleven-year-old passenger aboard the Fish and Game patrol boat *Marlin*. My father, California Fish and Game Warden Wally Callan, was the *Marlin*'s rookie boarding officer, responsible for patrolling California's offshore waters from the Mexican border to Point Conception.

It was 6:00 a.m. in mid-October when we parked at the Seal Beach Marina and I followed my father down the dock to the Department of Fish and Game boat slip. After almost a year of begging to come along, I was finally getting my chance. My head was filled with stories that my father had told about seeing whales and dolphins on his patrols to the Channel Islands. Now it was my turn, and I couldn't wait. We were about to set out on a three-day, two-night ocean adventure I would remember for the rest of my life.

"Where's the boat?" I asked, rushing ahead.

"Slow down and wait for me," said my father. "Be careful you don't trip and drop your suitcase in the water."

The wooden dock squeaked and groaned under our feet as we passed row after row of incredibly expensive yachts.

"Do these boats all belong to movie stars?" I asked. "Look at the size of that one!"

"Quiet down. Ours is the big gray one up there on the right."

"Wow, is that a PT boat?"

Still painted Navy gray, the *Marlin* was a sixty-five-foot converted U.S. Navy LST boat, with an engine capable of accelerating from eight to forty knots in a matter of seconds. Would-be violators had little chance of outrunning this old girl.

As my father and I climbed a ladder to the deck, we saw a burly, dark-haired man in his mid-thirties. Wearing a long-sleeved khaki shirt, khaki pants, and a big smile, Deckhand Paul Barrens welcomed us aboard.

"Paul, this is my oldest son, Steve."

"Here, let me help you with that," said Barrens, taking my suitcase. "Follow me and I'll show you the rest of the boat."

Barrens led me to the galley below, where a balding, middle-aged gentleman was sitting at the table, sipping coffee.

"Steve, this is Captain Bill Plett."

"Good morning, young man," said Plett. "How old are you?"

"Eleven."

"I have two boys about your age. They live in Avalon, out on Catalina Island."

I imagined how much fun it must be growing up on an island where you could fish and swim in the ocean every day. My father had regaled me with stories of Avalon boys swimming out to the incoming tourist boats as they arrived from the mainland and diving for coins in the incredibly clear water.

"She sounds good now," came a shout from the nearby engine room. Out stepped Engineer Hal Seals, the fourth and last member of the *Marlin*'s crew. He appeared to be about my father's age, tall, thin, and a bit glassy-eyed. Seals was more reserved than the rest of the crew, but he and I would become good friends before the trip was over.

"Are you guys ready to shove off?" asked Plett. "After we gas up, we have to pull into Long Beach and pick up those two VIPs from National Parks."

Our first order of business was transporting two upper-level National Park officials to Santa Barbara Island. The smallest of California's Channel Islands, this archipelago had been home to ranching and farming activity for much of the previous century. Domestic cats were brought in, along with rabbits, sheep, goats, and an assortment of invasive weeds. Their presence proved disastrous for native wildlife and vegetation. The cats multiplied, became established in the wild, and killed off a subspecies of song sparrow found nowhere else on Earth. Exotic rabbits had all but wiped out the giant sunflower, a species of *Coreopsis* that once blanketed the tiny island with magnificent yellow flowers. Human interference had left the island brown and virtually barren. The slow road to recovery began in 1938, when President Franklin Roosevelt designated Santa Barbara Island and Anacapa Island as national monuments.

It was after 8:00 a.m. when the two middle-aged National Park officials stepped aboard the *Marlin* and we began our thirty-eight mile voyage to Santa Barbara Island. Both men carried cased rifles, backpacks, and enough camping equipment for two nights.

Impressed with the park officials' status and intensely interested in their agenda, I shouted questions over the resounding roar of the engine, all the way across the channel.

"What are the guns for?" I asked.

"When the ranchers vacated Santa Barbara Island, they left behind the nonnative animals they had brought in over the years," said the gray-haired leader of the team. "One of those animals is a reddish-colored rabbit from New Zealand that has multiplied and destroyed much of the native vegetation. We've been trying to rid the island of these rabbits for several years now, so we brought the rifles along in case we see any."

That conversation, fifty-five years ago, was my first lesson on the subject of ecology. Unbeknownst to me at the time, my instructor was one of the U.S. National Park System's most famous naturalists and the author of several books on the subject. I learned a valuable lesson on just how damaging the introduction of exotic plant and animal species can be to fragile ecosystems like the one on isolated Santa Barbara Island.

During the trip across the channel, my father schooled me on the workings of the boat's compass and showed me how to navigate while traveling across vast expanses of ocean with no visible landmarks. We were about halfway across the channel to Santa Barbara Island when he suddenly pulled back on the throttle and brought the boat to a slow idle.

"What do you see, Dad?" He pointed to a dark gray fish basking at the surface. The tips of its huge tail and dorsal fins were protruding from the water.

"Looks like a big broadbill, Wally," shouted Paul Barrens.

"That's what it is," my father shouted back.

Everyone rushed to the starboard side of the boat. "Wow! It must be ten feet long," I said, impressed by its characteristic three-foot saber and those silver-dollar-sized eyes. But what I remember most about that incredible fish was the metallic blue sheen across the length of its back when the sun hit it just right.

We anchored about three hundred yards off what they now call the Landing Cove, on the eastern side of the island. From my vantage point on the deck of the *Marlin*, I looked across the turquoise water at a coastline of fifty-foot rock cliffs guarding a bone-dry mountain the shape of a whale's back. Knowing that my father was an experienced skin diver with a current fishing license, Captain Plett asked if he would mind harvesting a couple abalones. "Hal will put together a nice lunch for our National Park guests before they go ashore," said Plett.

My father kept his old gray dive bag on board, the same one he had carried to the beach many times during his fireman days in San Diego. He agreed to make the dive, wearing nothing but swim trunks, a dive mask, a snorkel, and a pair of fins. Within minutes he was climbing down the ladder into sixty-five degree water.

"Everything okay, Wally?" asked Barrens.

"The water's a little cold, but other than that I'm all right," said my father, peering up at us through his dive mask. "Could one of you hand me my abalone iron?"

With an abalone iron in his right hand for prying the tasty morsels from the rocks, my father placed the snorkel in his mouth, took a deep breath, tucked his body forward, and straightened his legs. Like a human torpedo, he descended to the bottom with one kick of his fins. We all watched from the deck as this incredibly skilled skin diver disappeared beneath a rocky ledge thirty feet below.

"Did you find any abalone?" I said, as my father popped to the surface.

Hanging onto the ladder, he handed his mask, snorkel, and fins to Barrens. Reaching inside his swimsuit, my father pulled out two legal-sized abalones, one green and one pink. "Will these do?" he said.

Abalone were still plentiful in the clear waters off Santa Barbara Island during the 1950s and early 1960s. Greens and pinks, like the two specimens we ate for lunch that day, could be found clinging to the undersides of just about every submerged rock. Since that time, abalone numbers have continued to dwindle, some species to the point of near extinction, thanks to excessive commercial exploitation, illegal take, warming water temperatures, and disease. Today, all species of abalone in Southern California waters are protected and may not be taken at any time.

After lunch, Paul Barrens lowered the skiff and transported the National Park scientists to shore. Excited to ride along, I continued to be impressed by the unbelievable clarity of the water. When we reached shore, we were met by two more scientists. The taller of the two, a shirtless beanpole wearing an Army green canvas backpack, couldn't wait to tell Barrens about a possible violation he had witnessed.

"I was up on the mesa overlooking Shag Rock when I saw this boat," said the scientist, obviously excited. "I know it was a lobster boat because there were lobster traps stacked on the stern."

Barrens had recently passed the warden's exam and was anxious to get his feet wet, so he diligently listened to everything the young scientist had to say. "Go on," he said.

"I sat down behind a *Coreopsis* bush and began watching them with my binoculars," said the scientist. "These two guys hoisted a trap and pulled it on board. When the trap came out of the water, I could see all these lobsters flopping around inside. There had to be at least ten or twelve in the trap. All but two or three looked quite small."

"How far away were you?"

"Maybe fifty yards or so, but I could see everything with my binoculars."

"Then what happened? Did you see them measuring any of the lobsters?"

"No. I figured they would keep the big ones and throw the little ones back, but the larger lobsterman walked back to the cabin and returned with a burlap sack. One by one, they ripped the tails off the small lobsters and threw the bodies in the water. It looked like they put the tails in the sack and the two or three larger lobsters in a holding tank."

Under California law at that time, no lobster with a carapace under three and a quarter inches in length could be possessed. Commercial lobster fishermen were required to return the undersized lobsters—shorts—to the water, unharmed. Any lobsters found on board had to be whole, with their tails intact.

"Could you identify the boat?" said Barrens.

"I couldn't make out any numbers—the stern was facing me. But I wrote down the name."

"You did?" said Barrens, surprised. "What was it?"

"The *Rascal*."

"Really?" said Barrens, holding back a chuckle.

"Do you know them?" asked the informant.

"Yeah, we know 'em," said Barrens, a smile on his face. "Was one of the fishermen short and stocky, with a scrubby gray beard? And the other a big, heavyset loudmouth, with a cigarette hanging out the side of his mouth? He was probably wearing an old, faded red baseball cap."

"That's them! I could hear that one guy's booming voice from way up on the bluff."

"When did this happen?"

"Yesterday, about five in the evening."

Barrens wasn't wearing a shirt, and he didn't have anything to write with, so one of the National Park employees loaned him a pencil and a piece of paper from his backpack. While Barrens jotted down notes regarding the lobster incident, my curiosity was getting the best of me. "Did you shoot any rabbits?" I asked.

"No, we didn't even see any," replied the shirtless National Park official. "And that's a good thing. We're hoping those long-eared eating machines have finally been eradicated."

When Barrens and I returned to the patrol boat, we found that the crew was taking a break before rounding the north side of the island. Barrens filled my father and Captain Plett in on the reported lobster violations.

"That doesn't surprise me," said Captain Plett. "I've suspected Jack

Dykstra, the *Rascal*'s owner, for years. We've never managed to catch him with anything illegal."

"Next time we run into those guys, we'll have to take a closer look," said my father.

"Excuse me," I interjected. "I saw a rod and reel leaning against the wall down in the galley. Would it be all right if I fish while you guys take a break?"

"Sure," said Captain Plett. If you hook into a marlin, give us a shout. We'll be down below."

"What should I use for bait?"

"I think there's a little chunk of abalone left in the ice box," said Seals. "I'll get it for you."

I baited a number-two-sized silver hook with a chunk of abalone and dropped my offering over the side. Four-inch perch darted from the nearby kelp and immediately began nibbling at the bait as it plummeted downward, eventually out of sight. A slight breeze had come up, riffling the water's surface, so I could no longer see all the way to the bottom.

"My sinker just hit bottom, Dad. Now what do I do?"

"Just be patient and wait. You never know what you might catch."

I don't think anyone really expected me to catch anything. My father watched for five or ten minutes, then went below to get a cup of coffee. I was standing on deck, daydreaming about the giant marlin I was going to hook, when something took hold of my line and slowly began to run with it. No customary nibbles or quick tugs this time—just a steady, rapidly increasing flow of fishing line spinning from my reel spool.

Clutching the rod handle against my side and up under my right arm, I pulled the rod tip upward and began reeling with all my might. At the age of eleven, I had no idea how to set the drag on the old deep-sea casting reel. It didn't take me long to figure out that if I didn't slow the fish down, I would soon be out of fishing line.

Five minutes had gone by when my father returned to the deck. I hadn't made any progress and seemed to be losing the battle. Each time I tried to reel, the incredibly strong fish would take out more line.

"Try to keep the rod tip up," said my father.

"It keeps taking my line out, Dad. What happens if I get to the end?"

"Whatever it is will tire eventually. If you feel it let up a little, reel as fast as you can. Get some of that line back and make sure you keep the rod tip up."

"I'm trying, Dad, I'm trying!"

Almost an hour had gone by when the crew heard all the commotion and returned to the deck. By then, my back was giving out and my arms ached. I had retrieved some of the line, but every time I managed to maneuver the powerful fish close to the boat, it would take off again.

"What's he got, Wally?" asked Barrens.

"I'm not sure. I thought it might be a sheephead, but it's too big for that."

"It's fighting like a shark," added Plett.

"Hang in there, Steve," said my father. "It's bound to get tired."

"I'm the one who's tired, Dad."

"You want some help?"

"Not a chance," I said, grimacing. "I just wish this thing would give up."

My ninety-eight pound frame was about to give out when the monster on the other end of my line finally quit struggling. Its sheer bulk was almost more than I could handle, but I kept on reeling until the massive fish broke the surface. Like something out of a science fiction movie, it had wing-like pectoral fins, a protruding Roman nose, unusually large eyes, and a whip-like tail with a sharp spine at the end.

"It's a damn bat ray," said Barrens, laughing. "The biggest one I've ever seen."

"We're gonna have to cut the line," said my father. "We can't bring that thing on board."

Seconds later, our problem was solved. The enormous ray lifted one of its three-foot pectoral fins into the air, twisted its body, and with a splash, threw the hook. We all watched as my worthy opponent glided across the surface, eventually caught its wind, and bolted for the bottom. To this day, if someone asks about the biggest fish I've ever caught, I tell them it wasn't a marlin, a tuna, or even a salmon. It was a hundred-and-fifty-pound bat ray.

Late that afternoon, we pulled up anchor and began a slow patrol around the north side of Santa Barbara Island, keeping a close eye out for any sign of a lobster boat. Just beyond Shag Rock, Paul Barrens spotted a red float.

"That's attached to one of Dykstra's traps," said Barrens. "It's probably the one our informant saw from the bluff."

"I see another float," said Captain Plett, sitting at the helm and scanning the coastline ahead with binoculars. "It's near the cove where the elephant seals hang out."

"Elephant seals?" I blurted.

My father had returned from a patrol to San Nicolas Island and Santa Barbara Island the previous summer and told me about seeing elephant seals hauled up on some of the isolated beaches. Excited about the prospect of seeing these behemoths myself, I had read up on the subject.

Northern elephant seals were once abundant on California's Channel Islands. By the late 1800s, whalers had mercilessly slaughtered the entire world's northern elephant seal population to the brink of extinction. Fewer than one hundred animals remained in 1920, all of them on Mexico's Guadalupe Island. The Mexican government protected them in 1922, and the United States followed suit shortly thereafter. Northern elephant seals numbered approximately 14,000 in 1959, all of them descendants of the handful that had survived on Guadalupe Island in 1920.

"Don't get excited," said my father. "They're all out at sea this time of year. You'll get your chance to see them next summer."

That night we anchored in the cove where we had dropped off the National Park scientists. Hal Seals made a big pot of spaghetti for dinner. Every fifteen minutes or so, I watched him pour a small glass of red wine into the pot. I'm not sure if it was my hearty appetite or Hal's cooking, but that was the best spaghetti I've ever eaten.

The next morning, just after daylight, we slowly cruised around the south end of the island. The ocean was quiet and motionless. With no waves pounding against the rocks, the only sounds we heard were the cries of a few gulls overhead and sea lions barking in the distance. The farther south we ventured, the louder the barking became, until it was almost deafening. Thousands of the raucous pinnipeds were resting on the rocks, darting beneath the boat, and porpoising in and out of the water. Early morning sunlight beamed across the water's surface, working its way up the rocks and bathing the resting sea lions in soft, warming sunlight. Right before my eyes, their dull brown and gray coats turned bright shades of red and gold.

Leaving the sea lions behind, we rounded the south end of Santa Barbara Island and spotted a towering rock formation jutting out of the water. "That's Sutil Island," said Plett. "If I remember correctly, Dykstra and his loud-mouthed buddy had a couple traps out on the backside of that point."

As we approached Sutil Island, my father turned to me and said, "If we run into these guys, I want you to go below and stay there."

"Okay, I will," I said, not really expecting to see anyone.

Suddenly, another boat came into view. It was the *Rascal*. Jack Dykstra and his partner, Nate Arnold, were out on deck. Dykstra immediately spotted us and tossed something overboard. Without looking back, he bolted straight for the cabin and disappeared from sight.

"Did you see that?" said my father, watching with binoculars from the pilot's seat.

"It looked like he threw some kind of bag over the side," said Plett. Swinging the wheel around, he pushed the throttle forward and brought the *Marlin* up on plane.

Within seconds, we crossed a quarter-mile stretch of placid water and cut the engine. The *Rascal* bobbed up and down like a cork as we came to a stop on her starboard side and waited for the wake to subside.

"Good to see you guys out here," shouted Dykstra, reappearing from the cabin. "How's the family, Bill? Are you still livin' in Avalon?"

Busy jockeying the *Marlin* into position, Plett did not respond to Dykstra's question. When the water finally settled and bumper pads were in place, Plett barked out a greeting. "How's it going, Jack?"

"Is there some kind of problem, Bill?" said Dykstra.

Arnold remained uncharacteristically silent.

"Warden Callan is going to come aboard," announced Plett.

Arnold had been silent long enough. He let out with a bellow, his voice so loud it flushed a congregation of gulls and cormorants that were perched on the rocky cliffs above. "What the hell does he need to come aboard for? We ain't done nothin'."

Hearing all the clamor and my father's name mentioned, I climbed the steps and peeked out from below deck. Concerned for my father's safety, I watched as he climbed down from the *Marlin* and boarded the decrepit old lobster boat.

"We received information that you gentlemen have been taking short lobsters," said my father. "Do you have any short lobsters or unattached lobster tails on board?"

"Hell no, we ain't got no—"

"Easy, Nate," interrupted Dykstra. "They can search all they want. We've got nothin' to hide."

Dad walked past Dykstra and Arnold, headed straight for the cabin entrance. The two lobster fishermen whipped their heads around, slack-jawed and obviously concerned. Arnold must have caught a glimpse of me, because he did a double take and turned his head back in my direction. I quickly ducked below deck.

Meanwhile, my father began his search by opening a small ice box in the *Rascal's* galley. The box was conspicuously empty. After examining every possible hiding place in the galley, he proceeded to the bunk area. Checking under each mattress, he found nothing but candy wrappers and empty cigarette packages.

About to give up and return to the upper deck, the determined warden noticed a scrap of hinged plywood where the door to the head had once hung. The so-called head was such a tight squeeze, it was difficult to imagine how anyone as large as Nate Arnold could fit inside. The paint was peeling off the walls and the toilet paper holder was a rusty shark hook. Lying on the floor, next to the toilet, was an eighteen-inch stack of tattered magazines.

What attracted my father's attention was the toilet seat: it was down and so was the seat cover. "How many men put the seats down unless their wives tell them to?" my father would later ask the crew. With the toe of his shoe, Dad carefully lifted the seat. Inside the bowl were enough undersized lobster tails for a gourmet dinner. Needless to say, these specimens would never see the inside of a boiling pot.

Returning to the upper deck, my father asked for a pair of gloves, a plastic bag, and an implement he could use to fish the lobster tails out of the *Rascal*'s toilet. He was immediately sidetracked by Barrens and Seals, who pointed toward something submerged beneath the patrol boat.

No other location in the Channel Islands hosted a healthier kelp forest than Sutil Island. Whatever it was that Dykstra had thrown overboard had apparently become caught on a kelp frond.

"Wally, there's a brown object hung up in the kelp about twenty feet down," said Barrens.

"As soon as I take care of this, I'll take a look," said my father.

For the first time in his life, Nate Arnold was speechless. Dykstra, on the other hand, couldn't have been more apologetic. Over and over, he repeated, "Please don't pull my lobster permit." Ignoring Dykstra's pleadings, my father climbed down the ladder into the water.

"Let's get this over with," my father said, donning his face mask. "This water's cold!"

Pushing a length of kelp aside, my father tucked his body forward, straightened his legs, and headed downward. Thirty seconds later, he rose to the surface holding a dark brown burlap bag. A few of the lobster tails had fallen out and disappeared into the depths, but a dozen or so remained inside.

Dykstra and Arnold lost their lobster permit for one year. I never heard how much their fines were, but I'm sure it wasn't nearly enough. Back in those days, a conviction of any kind was considered a success.

Later that afternoon, Paul Barrens and I took the skiff back to the original cove and picked up the two National Park scientists we had dropped off a few days earlier. My father snapped our photograph as we returned to the *Marlin*. Dad took several photographs on that trip. I still enjoy setting up the old slide projector and looking at them every once in a while.

Paul Barrens later became a warden and eventually a boat captain like Bill Plett. Bill remained on Catalina until he retired. Twenty years after my eventful trip to the islands, I walked into the Long Beach Regional Office as a patrol lieutenant for the Department of Fish and Game. Whom did I see but my old friend Hal Seals? He'd become a warden and spent his enforcement career working in Southern California. No longer the skinny eleven-year-old, I asked Hal if he remembered me. "Of course I do," he said. "How could I forget that big bat ray you caught?" Bill Plett, Paul Barrens, and Hal Seals are all gone now, but I will never forget my old friends and the great time we had.

WESTMINSTER AND THE SURROUNDING Southern California area were growing by leaps and bounds. My parents had always wanted to get away from the big city and raise their three boys in a rural, small-town atmosphere. In 1960, my father transferred to the Northern California farm town of Orland. Orland had everything my family had been looking for: friendly people, good schools, a prominent state college twenty miles away, and seemingly endless miles of farm fields, streams, mountains, and open space. With an abundance of wildlife and every freshwater fish species imaginable, it was paradise for the game warden and his son.

The Road Hunter

---◆---

"**T**HAT'S STRANGE," SAID BERG, pulling to a stop and reaching for his binoculars. "What's that fancy new car doing out here in the middle of all these rice fields?" It was mid-morning in early August 1954, and the enthusiastic young rookie warden was patrolling for pheasant poachers near the Northern California farming community of Biggs.

Born in 1925, Berg had enlisted in the U.S. Marines at seventeen and become a World War II veteran by the ripe old age of twenty-one. After completing high school and working for several years at various state jobs, five-foot-nine-inch, 175-pound Gilbert Joseph Berg began what was to be his life's work as a warden for the California Department of Fish and Game.

I asked Berg, now eighty-nine, about the men he worked with in those days.

"Well," said Berg, "Don Davison was the captain in 1954. Gene Mercer was in Chico, Jim Hiller was in Willows, Will Payne was in Oroville, and Lloyd Booth was in Orland. Old Lloyd was a few years from retirement and used to sleep through all the squad meetings and training sessions. We all thought that was pretty funny. Dave Nelson didn't become captain until just before your dad took over the Orland position in 1960. I had so much fun in those days, I was disappointed when my days off rolled around."

"Tell me about your district," I said, eager to know what being a warden in the Northern Sacramento Valley was like during the early 1950s.

"The Feather River and lower Butte Creek ran through my district, so there was plenty of salmon poaching activity during the fall spawning season," said Berg. "During the winter months, you might see a million ducks rise up in the evenings and head out to the rice fields. Most of the commercial duck poachers were down in the Butte Sink and around Gray Lodge Wildlife Area. We worked damn long hours but loved every minute of it. And pheasants… boy, did we have pheasants! The road hunters out of Chico, Oroville, and Gridley kept us busy all year 'round."

Speaking of road hunters, Berg segued to the Willie Ray Slack case he had made sixty years before. The Slacks were a large family of outlaws and ne'er-do-wells out of Chico. They didn't believe in laws, particularly game laws, and had been thorns in the sides of area Fish and Game wardens for many years.

Bill Slack, known to his friends and family members as Willie Ray, was forty years old, six feet tall, and heavy around the middle. An obnoxious braggart, he liked driving fancy cars and was seldom seen without a stogie in his mouth. Willie Ray was a building contractor, specializing in barns, sheds, and horse corals. Everyone who worked for him was a cousin or shirttail relative. The area Fish and Game wardens used to say, "When the Slacks aren't pounding nails, they're usually out killing something."

On that memorable day in early August 1954, Willie Ray Slack was driving his pride and joy, a brand-new baby blue Plymouth Belvedere, through the rice fields of western Butte County. Berg had received reports of closed-season pheasant poaching in the area and was staked out at the west end of the field behind a pump shed, a patch of tall weeds, and a rusted-out tractor with three flat tires. Sitting in the driver's seat of his 1952 Ford sedan patrol car, he watched as the out-of-place automobile, a trail of dust billowing behind it, meandered eastward toward Biggs.

The mid-morning temperature was well on its way to ninety degrees, and the humidity among thousands of acres of flooded rice fields was stifling. Sweat poured from Warden Berg's forehead into his eyes as he tried to focus his binoculars on the Plymouth sedan. Each time he saw the suspicious car's brake lights come on, Berg would climb from his patrol car and position himself to see what the driver was doing.

"I stayed about a half mile away so he wouldn't spot me," said Berg. "The car would stop, and seconds later I'd see a rifle barrel pop out the driver's-side window. The driver would walk out and pick something up, fool around at the back of his car, and close the trunk. I found it puzzling that I could hear the trunk slam shut but never heard a gunshot. When the suspect sped up and began to drive away, I decided it was time to make a stop."

Jumping back into his patrol car, Warden Berg raced after the speeding Plymouth. Approaching from behind, he reached up with his left hand and switched on the red spotlight. Unfortunately, the suspect couldn't see the red light through the cloud of dust in his rearview mirror. Choking on the dust, Berg rolled up his window and depressed the short-cycle siren button mounted on a metal plate beneath his dash. Startled by the ear-piercing blast from Berg's siren, the suspect swerved to the right, continued for another quarter mile, and rolled to a stop.

Walking up to the car, Warden Berg could see the driver frantically moving around inside. New on the job, Berg had heard stories about the Slacks and their poaching but had not yet encountered a member of the clan in the field.

"How ya doing?" said Berg, standing a few feet behind the driver's open window. "I see you have a fishing rod in back. Have you been fishing?" Berg couldn't have cared less about the fishing rod. His friendly greeting was simply a way to defuse any tension resulting from the car stop.

"No," mumbled the driver, reaching for the cigar butt in his ashtray. "Just looking around."

"Please place your hands on the wheel where I can see them."

The pheasant poaching suspect looked over his left shoulder at the uniformed officer. He seemed to be sizing him up and wondering why he hadn't seen him before. The Slacks had familiarized themselves with most of the wardens in the area, keeping track of their assigned days off and learning their normal patrol habits. As has always been the case, there were dedicated wardens who worked long and unpredictable hours, and there were semi-retired "good ol' boys" an outlaw could pretty much set his clock by.

"What's your name?" asked the suspect, placing his visibly shaking hands on the steering wheel.

"I'm Warden Berg."

"How long have you been around here?"

"Almost a year now. Please step out of the car."

"What's this about?" asked the suspect, stepping from the car and quickly closing the door behind him.

"May I see some identification?"

"Can't a man take a drive in the country without being harassed?" said the suspect, handing Berg his California Driver's License.

Warden Berg immediately recognized the name William Ray Slack, having heard the other wardens mention it several times. "Do you still live at this Chico address, Mr. Slack?"

"Same address," replied Slack. "Why did you stop me?"

"Where do you work?"

"I'm self-employed. Where the hell is Mercer? He can tell you who I am. I want to know why you stopped me."

Without responding to Slack's protests, the warden opened the suspect's car door and reached for the gun he had spotted when Slack exited the car. The .22 caliber bolt-action rifle was lying between the door jam and the driver's seat. Immediately noticeable was an eight-inch metal cylinder attached to the end of the rifle barrel. *That explains not being able to hear gunshots,* thought

Berg. *He's been using a silencer.* Warden Berg pointed to the silencer and asked, "Where did you get this?"

Hemming and hawing, Slack finally replied, "I made it."

"Have you shot anything with it?" asked Berg, pulling the bolt back on the .22 rifle and removing a live round from the chamber.

Sweating profusely and shifting his feet, the normally confident and overbearing Slack replied, "I might have used it to shoot a rabbit now and then."

"Do you have a hunting license, Mr. Slack?"

"Of course I've got a damn hunting license," said Slack, his tone becoming increasingly belligerent, "but I ain't been hunting."

Warden Berg opened his hand, displaying the live .22 cartridge that he had just removed from the chamber of Slack's rifle. "Your rifle was loaded," said Berg, calmly.

"That's in case I see a coyote," said Slack.

"Well, you can't have a loaded rifle in your vehicle when you're out here on a public road," said Berg. "Would you please pop open your trunk?"

It was as if someone had drenched Slack with a bucket of ice-cold water. His leathery, rust-colored skin turned bright red, his jaw dropped, and the veins in his forehead began to throb. Slack had long been suspected of taking overlimits of ducks, failing to tag his deer, and shooting pheasants from his car window, but so far no warden had been able to catch him in the act. He knew he was about to get busted, but what had to bother Willie Ray most was the ridicule he would receive from his outlaw friends and relatives. How could he explain being arrested by a pistol-assed, rookie game warden with less than a year on the job?

"What gives you the right to search my car?" demanded Slack, in a last-ditch effort to intimidate the young officer and prevent him from opening the trunk.

Having watched Slack shoot from his car window, Warden Berg was confident that he had all the probable cause in the world to make the car stop and search the vehicle. "I've been watching you for the last forty-five minutes," said Berg, finally at the end of his patience. "You can open the trunk or I'll do it."

Slack reluctantly opened the trunk, revealing an adult rooster pheasant and a turkey vulture. "How did you happen to shoot the turkey vulture?" asked Berg.

"You mean *that* buzzard?" said Slack. "It was feeding on a dead skunk in the middle of the road. I just wanted to see if I could hit it."

"You hit it all right. What did you intend to do with it?"

"I don't know, maybe have it mounted. What's the difference? It's a damn buzzard."

"Those 'buzzards,' as you call them, do a great deal of good. We'd have dead animals smelling up the whole countryside if it weren't for those birds. Didn't you just say it was feeding on a dead skunk when you shot it? In any case, turkey vultures are protected by state and federal law."

Warden Berg's words were obviously falling on deaf ears. Slack had been shooting hawks, owls, and vultures out of trees and off power lines for years. They were nothing more than convenient targets for this habitual violator. "So what's gonna happen?" said Slack.

"The judge will answer your questions when you appear in court. Between the loaded rifle, the closed-season pheasant, and the silencer, you've got some explaining to do."

Warden Berg seized the rifle, ammunition, and the two illegally taken birds into evidence.

Several weeks later, William Raymond Slack appeared in the Biggs Justice Court and was found guilty of five Fish and Game violations: take and possession of a protected nongame bird (turkey vulture), take and possession of a pheasant during closed season, shooting game from a vehicle, using an illegal weapon to take pheasants, and possessing a loaded rifle in a vehicle. He was fined $1,250, which was unheard of in 1954. Unfortunately for Slack, that was just the beginning. Warden Berg had delivered the rifle and silencer, along with a copy of his arrest report, to the Federal Bureau of Alcohol, Tobacco, and Firearms (ATF). After testing the rifle and silencer, ATF filed felony charges against Slack for making, possessing, and using a silencer. Slack pleaded guilty in front of the federal magistrate in Sacramento. He was fined $2,000 and ordered to forfeit his Plymouth Belvedere. Rumor has it, Slack left the federal courthouse with tears in his eyes.

Gil Berg would go on to enjoy a long and productive career, working in Santa Barbara, Calpine, and eventually retiring as a patrol lieutenant in 1980. He and my father remain lifelong friends.

Sage Advice

———◆———

T HE FIRST CALIFORNIA FISH and Game wardens were called deputy
Fish and Game commissioners.

COURAGEOUS, but courteous, is a qualification which goes far
in making a good officer. A timid man can accomplish little; an
overbearing one can do more harm than good. Clothed with all the
power and authority of the highest peace officer in the State, there
is no call for harshness on the part of the deputy fish and game
commissioner. Direct, orderly but firm, should be the methods of an
arresting officer. A bullying attitude provokes resistance. Not every
offender of the game laws is a disreputable character or a dangerous
citizen. Many game law violators are the result of thoughtless disregard
rather than willful lawlessness. And while forcible resistance on the
part of a prisoner may be overcome with force, the deputy can well
be courteous to the last possible extremity. There may be times when
swift, sure, and forceful must be the actions of a deputy, in which event
a reputation for tact and courtesy will sustain him if criticized.

—From the *Manual for Deputies,* issued by the California Fish and
Game Commission, May 1, 1914

***

NED DOLLAHITE WAS BORN in 1926 and raised in San Diego, California.
My father, Wallace Callan, was also born in 1926 and raised in San Diego,
California. Both boys attended Hoover High School, both men served in the

U.S. Navy during World War II, and both men completed highly successful careers working for the California Department of Fish and Game. Ned and my father did not meet or become acquainted until well into their Fish and Game careers. That's when they learned that they had grown up two blocks from each other. Remarkably, the one-time neighbors both chose to retire in Redding.

I frequently cross paths with retired Patrol Chief Dollahite. When I do, we usually have plenty to talk about. Now eighty-eight, Dollahite remains vital and still very much interested in the condition of California's natural resources. I recently asked the man who led the department's law enforcement division from 1978 to 1983 if he had any advice for today's dynamic young Fish and Wildlife wardens.

"If you have a few minutes," he said, "I'll tell you a little story about something that happened to me back in December of 1958."

Ned Dollahite's first assignment was the Tulelake Patrol District, named after the tiny northeastern California town of Tulelake. The town is located in the Tule Lake Basin—thousands of acres of intermittent wetlands and farmlands, frequented by millions of migrating waterfowl during the fall and winter months. Known best for its world-renowned duck and goose hunting, Dollahite's patrol district also abounded with deer, antelope, pheasants, and grouse. Today, it is a mecca for birders, who flock there from all over the world to photograph incredible congregations of eagles, hawks, and waterbirds.

On that eventful night in 1958, young Warden Dollahite was looking for spotlighters on a lonely mountain road in Modoc County, fifty unpaved miles from the nearest backup. Wardens were few and far between in those days. Being pretty much on your own most of the time, you needed to use good common sense, and as Dollahite put it, "keep your wits about you." Unlike the four-wheel-drive pickups that today's wardens are equipped with, our hero's patrol car was a two-wheel-drive 1955 Ford sedan with 110,000 dusty miles recorded on its odometer.

It was about 1:30 in the morning when Warden Dollahite noticed beams of flickering light bouncing off the trees overhead. What sounded like an older-model pickup was rattling up the mountain in his direction. The young warden didn't like making head-on car stops, but under the circumstances he had no choice: there was no time to turn around and the suspected violators were coming right at him. When the pickup topped the hill, Dollahite lit it up with his headlights and turned on his red spotlight.

A rusted-out, primer-gray 1954 Chevy pickup came to a sudden stop directly in front of Warden Dollahite's patrol car. Walking up to the driver's-side window, Dollahite immediately recognized the occupants as Virgil "Three Fingers" Dobbs, a wood cutter and well-known violator out of Alturas, and his foulmouthed wife, Della, a waitress at one of the greasy spoons along the highway.

"You folks are out kind of late, aren't you?" said Dollahite.

Temporarily blinded by the beam of Dollahite's flashlight, Dobbs squinted and stared back at the lean, five-foot-ten-inch warden. "It's a free country, ain't it?" replied Dobbs, displaying two missing front teeth. Della sat there quietly, mouth agape. Lying in the seat between Virgil and Della was a lever-action 30-30 rifle.

"I would like to make a safety check of your rifle," said Dollahite, continuing to shine his flashlight through the open window. "Mr. Dobbs, would you please carefully hand it to me?"

Neither subject responded. Virgil sat motionless, ignoring the warden's request. The normally loquacious Della looked like a cat ready to pounce. Warden Dollahite knew the wheels were turning in Virgil's and Della's brains as they tried to figure a way out of their predicament.

Glancing in Della's direction, Virgil suddenly opened the driver's-side door and climbed out of the pickup, forcing Warden Dollahite to step back. At the same time, Della grabbed the rifle, jumped out through the passenger-side door, and disappeared into the darkness. Now on high alert, the anxious warden could hear Della working the action on the rifle. Was she jacking a round out of the chamber in a clumsy attempt to avoid being cited or jacking a round into the chamber, with more sinister intentions in mind? The safety-conscious officer chose to believe the latter.

"Please make your wife hand over the rifle," said Dollahite, sternly. Virgil refused and Della stood her ground. Keeping a close eye on Virgil, Warden Dollahite stepped forward and shined his flashlight into the bed of Dobbs's pickup. The bed contained a chainsaw, a wooden box, a gas can, a splitting maul, and two wedges. He found no blood or other evidence of a deer having been taken.

"I'm disappointed that you've chosen not to cooperate," said Dollahite. "You are both in violation for failure to exhibit your firearm upon demand and for resisting a peace officer in the performance of his duties. I'll give you one more opportunity to reconsider and peacefully turn over the rifle."

Virgil remained silent, and Della stayed hidden in the darkness. Warden Dollahite took a notepad from his shirt pocket and jotted down the license number of the Dobbses' pickup. "Mr. and Mrs. Dobbs," said Dollahite, "I'll be contacting you again later this morning." With that, the young Fish and Game warden climbed into his patrol car and drove down the mountain.

The next morning, Warden Dollahite secured arrest warrants for Virgil and Della Dobbs. He contacted Del Baxter, the warden in Alturas, and a female sheriff's deputy. The officers drove to the Dobbs residence, arrested both subjects, and delivered them to Judge Heathcliff Beal, at the Modoc County Courthouse. The frail, gray-haired old judge had been on the bench for over forty years. During that time, he'd heard every excuse in the book.

"Virgil and Della Dobbs, you're each being charged with Section 2012 of the California Fish and Game Code—failure to exhibit your firearm upon demand—and Section 148 of the California Penal Code—resisting a peace officer in the discharge of his duties," said the judge. "How do you plead?"

"I guess we's guilty, Your Honor," said Virgil.

"Della, how do you plead?"

"Guilty, Your Honor."

The judge took a few minutes to read Warden Dollahite's arrest report. "I believe I know why you committed this dangerous and foolish act," he said. "Before I pronounce sentence, would you like to tell me what you were doing driving around on that mountain at 1:30 in the morning?"

"We was lost, Your Honor," said Virgil.

"Lost!" shouted the judge. "Virgil, you've been cutting timber in those woods for the last twenty years. Do you really expect me to believe you were lost? That will be five days in the county jail. What about you, Della? Do you have anything to say?"

"Well, Your Honor, I figured if I could get the bullet outta the gun, Virgil wouldn't get a ticket. Trouble was, when I racked one bullet out, another one went in. I guess that weren't the right thing to do."

"Della, you should be sittin' in that jail next to your husband. Instead, I'm going to place you on six months' summary probation. The rifle will be immediately turned over to Fish and Game and forfeited. Make sure it's not loaded. If I see either of you back in my courtroom, I won't be so lenient. Next case."

Warden Dollahite's calm demeanor and skillful handling of this potentially volatile situation make him an excellent role model for wardens today. In the end, Virgil and Della Dobbs were arrested for their crimes and had their day in court. More importantly, no one was hurt tussling over a rifle in the middle of the night or engaging in a needless shootout.

Ned Dollahite had a long and productive career as a patrol captain, a regional inspector, and finally, the chief wildlife protection officer for the entire State of California.

A few days after my conversation with Ned, I received a letter in the mail:

> I would like to say that during those years of my youth in San Diego, another young man my age, named Wally Callan, lived just around the corner from my home. Although we never knew each other during those years, it seems that we both chose California Fish and

Game warden as our occupation. We did meet many times during our working years and remain good friends to this day.

—Ned Dollahite

My brother Kenny and I watch cattle in the canyon behind our home
in San Diego (1955).

Proudly displaying Dad's bass catch beside my dad and Kenny (San Diego, 1952).

San Diego Fireman Wallace Callan in his dress uniform (1955).

Grandma Anne at the San Diego Zoo (circa 1955).

While working for the San Diego Fire Department, my father and his diving buddy
Bill Chilcote bought the *Gracy* (1955).

Wally Callan on the deck of the *Gracy* with a giant lobster, circa 1956. Lobsters of
this size were not uncommon in San Diego waters back in those days.

Bill Chilcote and Wally Callan on the *Gracy* with part of the night's catch
(circa 1956).

My pal Johnny Annaloro and me in our North Clairemont Little League T-shirts,
back in 1956. This was my first year in Little League.

My great-grandfather Thomas "Dry Wash" Wilson (circa 1916).

A new addition to our family in 1958: I was proud to hold little Matthew while
sitting on our San Diego front porch with my mother, Doris, and my brother Kenny.

Casa Cove, La Jolla, California: the site of many boyhood adventures. I took this photo many years later, in 1985.

Me at the helm of the Fish and game patrol Boat *Marlin* (1959).

Bill Plett, Hal Seals, and Paul Barrens look on as I wait for a big one off the coast of Santa Barbara Island (1959).

Fighting the monster fish in the waters off Santa Barbara Island (1959).

Paul Barrens and I transport the National Park Service VIPs from Santa Barbara Island back to the patrol boat *Marlin* (1959).

SMALL-TOWN WARDEN

1960–1970

Greenheads and Muddy Sneakers

And here again the white man did what he has so often done in other times, and other places, and other circumstances: he acted like an irresponsible, thoughtless, viciously spoiled child: and instead of conserving this beneficent gift of nature, he hastened with all speed to destroy it and put an end to it.
—From the *History of Colusa and Glenn Counties* by Charles McComish and Rebecca Lambert, 1918

Throughout America's relatively short history, there have been many examples of people commercializing wildlife until the species became threatened, endangered, or in some cases, extinct. The American bison, the California tule elk, the southern sea otter, the northern elephant seal, and the passenger pigeon are prime examples, not to mention several of our great whales.

During the mid-to-late 1800s, San Francisco and Sacramento became stopping-off places for multitudes of fortune seekers headed for the California gold fields. Markets, restaurants, hotels, brothels, and saloons sprang up, creating an enormous demand for fresh meat. Up from the depths of hell came a faction of opportunists so greedy and so lacking in moral character, they would do anything for a fast buck. That included decimating entire populations of wildlife.

Under the cover of darkness, so-called "duck draggers" slithered and belly crawled up on feeding waterfowl. *Boom, boom-boom-boom-boom, boom-boom!* Volleys of shotgun pellets rocketed along the ground, killing dozens, sometimes hundreds of birds at a time. Immense flocks of ducks and geese filled the sky, their distress calls so deafening they drowned out the continued thunder of shotgun blasts: b*oom-boom, boom, boom-boom-boom.* Birds fell like rain, tumbling and fluttering to the ground.

Market hunters slaughtered and sold ducks, geese, swans, and shorebirds. Even songbirds like robins, warblers, finches, and meadowlarks were killed and thrown on the pile. Most sought after were the greenheads (drake mallards), and cans (canvasbacks), but sprig (pintails), speckle-bellies (white-fronted geese), butterballs (buffleheads), and honkers (Canada geese) were also loaded onto wagons and hauled off to waiting markets.

This despicable activity continued unabated until the early 1900s, when state and federal laws were finally established and officers were hired to enforce those laws. The federal Lacey Act was passed by Congress in 1900, banning the interstate commerce of unlawfully taken plants and wildlife. Widespread market hunting effectively came to an end, but state and federal officers continued to arrest smaller numbers of these unscrupulous outlaws into the 1950s and early 1960s. Occasional "duck dragging" cases are still being made today.

***

"I'LL PROBABLY BE GONE all night," announced my father, opening the closet door and reaching for his uniform coat. "I'm meeting Jim Hiller and Gene Mercer down in Willows about ten o'clock. Hiller's been getting reports of late night duck shooting out east of the refuge."

It was a Saturday evening in late November 1962. The weather was clear and calm. We had finished dinner and my mother was busy washing dishes. Fish and Game Warden Wally Callan, my father, was thirty-six at the time. Two years earlier, he had transferred from Marine Patrol, out of Seal Beach, to Orland, a sparsely populated farming community at the north end of California's Central Valley. Our home was a modest, single-story house at the east end of Colusa Street.

"Dad, can I go with you?" I pleaded. "There's no school tomorrow." I enjoyed riding on patrol, weekends and sometimes after school—whenever I didn't have baseball or basketball practice. Soon after moving to Northern California, I'd been given a copy of Francis Kortright's classic, *The Ducks, Geese and Swans of North America,* and had become fascinated with waterfowl—so much so that at age fourteen I could identify just about every duck and goose in the Pacific Flyway.

"I might not be back until after daylight. You better stay home."

"I won't fall asleep. Besides, I can help you stay awake."

"Mercer will be there. He's sure to say something if I bring you along."

Gene Mercer was my father's neighboring warden, out of Chico. A year or so away from retirement, Mercer had been wearing a Fish and Game warden's badge since the days when wardens drove Model Ts. He was a sharp-tongued, gruff old codger who never passed up an opportunity to express his opinion.

"I won't be any trouble."

"All right, but if Mercer says anything, you just keep quiet and be respectful."

"Does that mean I get to go?"

"Yeah. Put your boots on and get your coat. No whining about how sleepy you are."

There had been a steady stream of ducks and geese migrating south all day, headed for the Willows rice fields. It was about 9:00 p.m. when we reached Willows and turned off onto one of the many county roads that crisscrossed the valley. The moon was coming up and I could see silhouettes of ducks and geese in the night sky. It would be a while before the other wardens joined us, so our plan was to find a good spot out west of the Sacramento National Wildlife Refuge and listen for shots.

During the rainy season there was always a risk of getting stuck in the mud when driving a two-wheel-drive sedan off the pavement. The department's remedy was a Handy Man jack, found in the trunk of every patrol car. It hadn't rained for several weeks, so we turned off the county road and proceeded at a snail's pace down a narrow levee that led into one of a hundred flooded rice fields.

"Let's park here and see if we hear anything," said my father, as he turned off the motor and opened his driver's-side door. I climbed out the passenger side and was greeted by a symphony of waterfowl sounds. Ducks whistled and whirred overhead as we quietly walked out on the levee under the dim light of a half-moon. Unaware of our presence, birds flew so close I could feel the wind from their wingbeats on the back of my neck. There were widgeons, lots of widgeons. Stately pintails swooped in from out of nowhere and speedy little green-winged teal darted back and forth in every direction. What I remember most vividly was a pair of mallards splashing down not fifteen yards from where I was standing—*quaaack, quack-quack-quack-quack-quack*. The raucous hen was announcing her arrival. Suddenly there rose a thunderous, ear-splitting clamor, as thousands of ravenous snows and white-fronted geese burst into the air, their shrill honks and repeated cackles—*wah, wah-wah-wah*—music to this impressionable teenager's ears. Having rested within the safe confines of the refuge all day, every web-footed wonder in the Pacific Flyway knew it was feeding time and was coming to the party.

"Dad, how do you catch these duck draggers?" I asked.

"It's not easy," he said. "Most of 'em are young guys, nineteen or twenty years old, wearing sneakers. They usually have lookouts who warn them if there's any sign of a game warden. Then they run like hell."

"What about their cars? Can't you find their cars?"

"Somebody usually drops 'em off and picks 'em up later."

"If I see one of those guys running away, I'll chase him down and tackle him for you."

Though he had a slight grin on his face, my father resisted the urge to laugh. "You just stay with me and do what I tell you."

"Two five five–two five four," the radio blared.

My father reached into the patrol car and grabbed the microphone. "Two five five, go ahead."

"My ETA is about fifteen," said Warden Hiller.

"Come on, get in," said my father, as he flopped into the driver's seat and turned the key in the ignition. I jumped in and away we went, back down the levee and out to the county road.

It took us about ten minutes to reach an intersection northeast of the Sacramento National Wildlife Refuge. My father turned off the headlights, reached under the steering wheel, and flipped a hidden toggle switch. With windows rolled down and only a tiny "sneak light" to illuminate our path, we slowly headed eastward.

We had driven about two miles when my father pulled his patrol car to the left and brought us to a stop behind an old barn and some scattered farm equipment. Warden Mercer was already there, standing next to a dark green Ford sedan, hands resting on his slender hips. Before the sneak light was turned off, I caught a glimpse of the usual glower on Mercer's gaunt face.

Gene Mercer stood about five-nine and might have weighed 165 pounds, soaking wet. Narrow at the shoulders, he wore glasses and usually covered his hairless head with a Stetson.

My father stepped out and quietly closed his door. I was about to reach for my door handle when I heard Mercer say, "I see you brought your kid along." With feelings a little hurt by Mercer's comment, I was hesitant to leave the safe confines of my father's patrol car. My mind flashed back to the previous summer, when Mercer had joined us on a trout fishing trip into Grindstone Creek.

All the way down the rugged jeep trail into Grindstone Canyon, my younger brother Kenny and I had listened from the backseat as Mercer regaled the three of us with stories about all the outlaws he had apprehended over the years. Since my father was the youngest and least-experienced member of Dave Nelson's captain's squad, Mercer was never shy about offering his "sage" advice.

Mercer and I fished upstream that sultry July day, while my father and Kenny fished down. With not even a slight breeze to stir them, the alder leaves that shaded the stream hung limp and motionless. During the years before the big flood scoured the canyon and washed away all the riparian vegetation, Grindstone Creek was one of the premier trout streams in California, teeming with eight-to-fourteen-inch native rainbows—all of them eager to attack an artificial fly or lure.

We had agreed to meet back in three hours, so I headed downstream about noon. By then, the temperature had climbed into the nineties and my full-length rubber hip boots were stiflingly hot. I dared not fold them down, for fear of exposing my legs to one of the many rattlesnakes that dwelled near the large rocks bordering the stream.

Mercer had already caught his limit and was waiting in the shade when I returned to camp. The first thing I did was fold down my hip boots to cool off. I decided to clean the three or four trout I'd kept, so I pulled out my pocket knife, and without thinking, waded up to my waist in the stream. Ice cold water immediately rushed down my legs and filled my boots.

"I knew you were gonna do that," shouted Mercer, his words barely audible over the roar of rushing water.

"Well, why didn't you say something?" I shouted back, embarrassed and feeling foolish. I don't think he heard me, which was probably a good thing.

MY THOUGHTS OF THE previous summer were suddenly interrupted by the sound of another patrol car pulling in behind the barn, with sneak light on and headlights turned off. It was Jim Hiller, the middle-aged warden out of Willows. Hiller was tall and dark-haired, with a Tuffy-style uniform jacket warming his slender frame.

Still sitting in the front seat of my father's patrol car, I listened from an open window as the evening's plans were discussed. During the conversation, a volley of shotgun blasts came from the adjacent rice field, a half mile away. Ten shots were fired in rapid succession.

The suddenly accelerated plan was for Mercer to drive a mile east to the next levee and walk in from there. Hiller and my father would immediately approach, on foot, from the adjacent levee. With flashlight in hand and a look of unbridled enthusiasm on my face, I quietly locked my door and prepared to follow.

"Why don't you come with me?" proposed Mercer, as he opened his car door.

Is he talking to me? I wondered. I stopped and looked over my shoulder.

"Come on," said Mercer. "I could use the company."

Not knowing what to say, I glanced over at my father. There was just enough ambient light to make out the puzzled look on his face.

"Go ahead and go with Gene, if you want to," he whispered.

I would have preferred to follow my father, but I didn't want to hurt Mercer's feelings. "Okay." Maybe the old curmudgeon wasn't so bad after all.

I climbed inside Mercer's patrol car, and away we went. With headlights off and sneak light on, Mercer steered us eastward toward the next levee. We finally came to a stop on the north side of the county road, behind a gnarled old willow tree. Mercer turned off the ignition and quietly stepped out of the patrol car. Opening the back door, he reached inside and retrieved a pair of rubber hip boots. After donning the hip boots, he slipped the car keys into his pocket, grabbed his flashlight, hung a pair of binoculars around his neck, and began to leave. I was already wearing hip boots, so I grabbed my flashlight and prepared to follow.

"No, I want you to stay here and watch my car," said Mercer, sternly.

I stared back at the seasoned old veteran with a look of complete surprise on my face. *Did I hear correctly? He invited me to come along so I could sit here and watch his car?* In the blink of an eye, my previous enthusiasm had been snuffed out, thrown to the ground, and stomped on.

"You want me to stay here?" I asked sheepishly.

"You just sit here in the car until I get back," repeated Mercer, as he quietly closed his driver's-side door, walked toward the levee, and disappeared into the darkness.

I sat quietly in the passenger seat of Mercer's patrol car, fretting and fuming about how I'd been deceived. *What a dirty trick. If I'm going to watch anyone's car, it will be my dad's!* I shined my flashlight on a notepad attached to Mercer's dashboard. Shielding the beam with my right hand, I jotted down the following short message with my left:

> Walked back to the barn.
> —Steve

Quietly locking both doors, I walked out to the paved county road and headed west. With a half-moon that night, there was just enough natural light to make the one-mile hike back to the old barn without using my flashlight and possibly alerting the duck poachers.

All I heard for the first half mile or so were flocks of geese chattering in the distance. Every so often, a drake mallard would pass overhead, wings whistling and quietly communicating his presence with a guttural *kwek— kwek—kwek—kwek.*

As I shuffled up the road, still agonizing over my decision to abandon Mercer's car, my thoughts were suddenly interrupted by the faint din of human voices. *What's that?* I asked myself. *Did I hear someone talking?* I stopped and listened. Nothing. I took a few more steps. *There it is again.* Standing perfectly still, I listened for the sound emanating from the rice field at the north side of the road. The voices stopped, but now I could clearly hear footsteps: someone was sloshing through the mud in my direction. I hunched down behind a patch of tules. The footsteps grew louder and I heard voices again. *They're headed right toward me!* I dropped to the prone position and quietly crawled inside the tule patch.

Two men, not more than twenty feet away, reached the county road. Any closer and they could have stepped on me. Just like my father had said, they were wearing sneakers; I could tell by the squeaking sound their wet tennis shoes made as the men traversed the hard pavement.

From my hidden vantage point, I was able to see the shotguns the men were carrying and what appeared to be gunny sacks slung over their shoulders. As quickly as they had come, the suspected duck poachers reached the opposite side of the road and dropped out of sight.

Where did those guys go? They couldn't have just vanished. I lay in the tules for ten or fifteen minutes, wondering what I should do next. Raising my head once or twice, I peered across the road. Nothing. Finally convinced that the two men had gone, I rolled out of my hiding place and stood up. I had taken one or two steps onto the asphalt when I saw headlights in the distance and heard the roar of a car speeding in my direction.

Could this be my dad? Maybe Mercer radioed him and told him what I'd done. Not knowing for sure, I ducked back in the tules. The headlights were alternating back and forth from high beam to low beam, in rapid succession. *Is that some kind of signal?* I wondered. Two human silhouettes suddenly appeared in the road, fifty yards ahead. Backlit in the rapidly approaching headlights, both subjects waved their arms in the air, bringing the car to a sudden stop. I heard two doors open and slam shut. Turning around in the middle of the road, the car sped away in the same direction from whence it had come.

I climbed out of my hiding place and watched the car's taillights until they were nothing but tiny red dots. The taillights finally disappeared and the whir of rubber pounding against the distant pavement gradually faded to complete silence. There I was, standing in the middle of the county road, pondering what I had just witnessed. *Those must have been the duck poachers who fired the shots earlier. Now they've gotten away.* Head down and despondent, I shuffled westward, in the direction of the old barn.

"Wait a minute!" I said, stopping suddenly and thinking aloud. "How could those guys have waved their arms in the air if they were carrying shotguns and gunny sacks? I didn't see them pick up anything or hear the trunk open and slam shut. They just jumped in the car and took off." I turned and walked back to the point where I had first seen the two men scurry across the road and drop out of sight. Shining my flashlight into the high grass at the south side of the road, I searched for indications of where they might have walked. "Here we go!" I said, still talking to myself. Two foot trails, side-by-side, led through the trampled grass and into a dry ditch bottom.

I climbed into the ditch and immediately spotted two sets of footprints. Following the footprints for about fifty yards, I came to a corrugated metal culvert. The old rusted-out culvert was about four feet in diameter—not wide enough to walk through—so I bent down and shined my light inside. "Anyone in here?" My voice echoed back at me. Something caught my eye at midpoint, but my two-cell flashlight was too weak to shed enough light on the subject. "Now what am I gonna do?" I said. "No telling what's hiding in that old culvert."

The rice fields near the town of Willows provided ideal habitat for every nocturnal animal in the Central Valley, and most of them liked to dwell in old culverts. I slowly crawled inside, anticipating a face-to-face encounter with a rat or a skunk. Crawling past a desiccated carp skeleton, several rusted beer cans, and a wad of bunched up willow branches, I finally found what I was looking for—two gunny sacks, bound tightly with twine. Hidden under the sacks were two 12-gauge pump shotguns. Both shotguns had camouflaged stocks and were heavily splattered with mud. I felt the outside of each sack and confirmed my suspicions: they contained freshly killed ducks, and lots of them.

Excited about what I had discovered, I quickly crawled out of the culvert and hot-footed it up the ditch bank to the road. With only a half mile to go, I sprinted back to the barn in record time. Jim Hiller and my father had just walked out of the field and were standing next to their patrol cars when I walked around the corner of the barn and met up with them.

"What are you doing here?" said my father. "Why aren't you with Mercer?"

"I need to tell you something," I replied.

"Where's Mercer?"

"He told me to stay and watch his car."

"What are you talking about?"

I spotted a grin on Hiller's face. He knew Gene Mercer all too well.

"I got tired of just sitting in his car, so I decided to walk back here. I need to tell you something. I—"

Just then Mercer drove up next to the barn. Stepping from his patrol car, he immediately directed his attention to me.

"Young man, you have some explaining to do," he said. "I told you to stay and watch my car."

"I know where those guys hid the ducks," I replied, looking back at my father and ignoring Mercer's attempts to reprimand me.

"What are you talking about?" repeated my father.

"The guys who fired the shots we heard... I saw where they hid their ducks... and their shotguns."

Leaning against one of the patrol cars, I described what I had just witnessed.

"Wally, I think he's making the whole thing up to get out of trouble," interjected Mercer.

"I'll deal with that later," said my father. "Show us where these ducks are supposed to be."

My father and Jim Hiller followed me back down the road to the cache of ducks. They decided we should go on foot, in case my story turned out to be true and the duck poachers returned.

"I think this is it," I said.

"This is what?" said my father.

"Where the culvert is. We have to climb down into the irrigation ditch."

My father directed the beam of his flashlight into a steep, six-foot chasm, bordered on both sides by high grass and tules.

"Jim, you might as well stay up here," said my father. "No sense in both of us getting dirty."

My father followed, as I carefully negotiated the ditch bank and made my way to the bottom.

"The ducks and the shotguns are in there," I said, pointing to the culvert entrance.

"All right. You lead the way."

I showed my father the two gunny sacks full of ducks and the two shotguns lying underneath. Without saying a word, he shined his flashlight back in the direction of the culvert entrance.

"See that tree branch?" he said. "Go break a twig off and hand it to me."

"What for?"

"Don't ask questions. Just do it."

I crawled to the tree branch, broke off a small section, and crawled back.

"Now you go first," instructed my father. "I'll be right behind you. I'm gonna swish this sand around a little bit, so it doesn't look like an army has been crawling around in here."

Before leaving the ditch, we covered our own tracks the best we could and hightailed it back to the barn.

"Well, what did you find?" said Mercer.

"It's just like he says," replied my father. "Two gunny sacks full of ducks and two shotguns."

"My guess is they'll come back right after daylight," said Hiller. "Steve, did you get a look at the car?"

"I couldn't see it from where I was hiding," I said. "I'm pretty sure it was a car and not a pickup. I remember hearing a loud muffler when they took off."

My father instructed me to wait in his patrol car while he and the others discussed what to do next. In spite of what I'd found, I was still in trouble for not following Mercer's instructions. A few minutes later, my father entered the car and started the engine.

"Where we going?" I asked.

"You're going home. You've done enough for one night."

I had received my share of lectures while growing up, but this one hurt the most. Every time I began to nod off on the thirty-minute drive back to Orland, my father would say, "Wake up and listen to me when I'm talking to you." He made it clear that I wouldn't be going on patrol again anytime soon. I wanted to participate in the stakeout, but that was not to be.

It was nearly 2:00 a.m. when we reached home.

"Tell your mother I'll be home sometime after daylight."

"Okay, I will," I replied, as I closed the door and watched my dream of participating in a real stakeout vanish with my father's patrol car.

My mother had left the porch light on and the door unlocked, as was our custom in those days. I had hoped to sneak in quietly, without waking everyone, but our dachshund had other ideas.

Yip, yip, yip-yip-yip.

"Where's your father?" my mother asked, walking up the hallway.

Yip-yip.

"He's on his way back to Willows. They're on a stakeout, waiting for some duck poachers to—"

Yip, yip-yip.

"Heidi, be quiet!"

"Mommy, I'm thirsty." My brother Matt, who was only four at the time, came walking out of the bedroom, dragging his favorite blanket.

"I'm sorry I woke everybody up."

"I think Kenny's still asleep," said my mother, handing Matt a glass of water. "I hope your father's all right."

"Mercer and Jim Hiller are with him."

"Let's all go back to bed. You can tell me all about it in the morning."

"Come on, Heidi," I said. "You get back in your basket."

It was Sunday afternoon when my father finally pulled into the driveway.

"Did ya catch 'em, Dad, did ya catch 'em?" I asked.

"Yeah, we caught 'em."

"Tell me what happened."

Sleepy eyed and obviously in no mood to talk, my father mumbled, "It's a long story. I'll tell you after I get some sleep." He kissed my mom and closed the bedroom door behind him.

The rest of us were clearing the dinner table and preparing to wash dishes when the bedroom door reopened and my father appeared.

"Doris, did you pick up beer today?" he asked.

"It's in the refrigerator. Are you ready to eat something?"

"Where's the can opener?"

"It's in the drawer where it always is."

Popping open a can of Oly, my father sat down in his usual chair at the end of the kitchen table. My patience was running thin, but I had the good sense to let him take a few slugs before pestering him with questions.

"So, Dad, what happened?"

"Sit down and I'll tell you all about it."

After dropping me off at home Saturday night, my father had returned to Willows and hidden his patrol car behind the grain silos, two miles west of our stakeout site. Mercer had driven east from the barn and hidden his patrol car near the next intersection. Jim Hiller had parked his patrol car inside the barn so there was no chance of it being seen by the duck poachers. He found a place to hide outside, behind an old tractor. California Fish and Game wardens didn't have hand-held radios in those days, so it was essential to have a radio-equipped car nearby.

With the aid of binoculars, Warden Hiller kept a close eye on the area where the ducks and shotguns had been stashed. A few pickups drove by about 4:00 a.m., en route to their respective duck clubs, but no other vehicles passed during the cold hours of darkness. At approximately 7:15 a.m., a cream-colored 1950 Mercury sedan slowed at the railroad tracks near the grain silo and proceeded eastward. My father was suddenly alerted by the louder-than-normal sound of the car's muffler.

"Two five four—two five five, car-to-car," said my father.

It took Hiller a minute or two to run back into the barn and answer: "Go ahead, two five five."

"Be advised, a possible suspect vehicle is headed your way. It's a light-colored Mercury sedan."

"Ten-four," said Hiller.

"Two five one, copy," said Mercer.

Keeping to the shadows, Hiller ran back to his hidden vantage point and waited. The cream-colored Mercury raced by, passing the culvert without even slowing down. Hiller ran back to the barn, reached into his patrol car, and grabbed the microphone. "The suspects went right on by," he said. Fortunately Warden Mercer's patrol car was well hidden. He watched from a distance as the suspect vehicle approached the intersection.

"They're turning around and heading back your way," announced Mercer, shouting into his microphone. Hiller quickly assumed his original hidden position at the side of the road. The Mercury sedan sped westward, muffler popping and smoke belching from its exhaust pipe.

Hiller watched as the front end of the suspect vehicle lunged downward, indicating that the brakes had been applied and the car was coming to a sudden stop. Out they came: two men ran across the road and disappeared into the adjacent irrigation ditch, while the driver ran back and opened the trunk. Just then a pickup passed Hiller's position, headed east. Hiller recognized the driver as Hector Castillo, a middle-aged work foreman who managed the irrigation system on the adjacent rice farm.

Warden Hiller watched the pickup's brake lights come on as it approached the poaching suspects' car. "No, Hector!" whined the sleep-deprived warden. "Don't stop and talk to 'em!" The driver of the suspect vehicle quickly closed the trunk as the pickup came to a stop in the road next to him. Whatever the ruse, it worked: Castillo's brake lights went off and the pickup continued down the road. When it was clearly out of sight, two men scampered out of the ditch and ran back across the road, each carrying a shotgun and a heavily-laden gunny sack. Hiller heard the faint sound of a trunk slamming and watched all three suspects jump back into the car.

Warden Hiller remained hidden until the suspects had passed. Throwing open the barn door, he jumped into his patrol car and reached for the radio microphone. "They picked up the ducks and they're headed west."

"Ten-four," replied my father. "I'll make the stop."

Hiller had closed the barn door and was about to pull onto the county road when Warden Mercer roared by, his red light in the forward position.

The suspects must have been slapping each other on the back when they noticed the Fish and Game warden coming up behind them and another just ahead. They pulled to the side of the road and stopped. Jim Hiller arrived just behind Mercer, who was already out of his car. My father parked directly in front of the Mercury sedan, blocking any chance of the suspects making a run for it.

Warden Hiller immediately recognized the driver as twenty-two-year-old Scott Schumacher, a local grocery clerk. Schumacher was a tall, blond, good-looking kid with a gift for charming the ladies. "Such a polite young man," the women shoppers would say. Hiller knew Schumacher as a sneaky little con artist who'd been up to no good since he was fourteen years old, shooting at ducks with a .22 rifle from his rooftop and killing songbirds with a pellet gun in his backyard.

Also in their early twenties were Schumacher's accomplices, Rick Beasley and Lenny Small, two laid-off mill workers out of Maxwell. Beasley and Small reeked of alcohol. They hadn't shaved in two days and were still wearing muddy clothes from the previous night's romp through the rice fields.

"Let's have a look in the trunk," said Mercer, standing at the rear of the suspect vehicle. Hiller held out his hand and Schumacher handed him the keys. While all three suspects sat in the car, Hiller walked to the rear and popped the trunk. Just as expected, he found two mud-splattered shotguns and two completely full gunny sacks inside. While my father kept an eye on the suspects, Hiller and Mercer checked the shotguns at the side of the road. Both guns were empty, but the plugs had been removed.

One by one, each suspect was ordered out of the vehicle, checked for weapons, and told to provide identification. All three were led to a spot at the side of the road and instructed to sit down. The two gunny sacks were opened and the contents poured onto the ground. Each bag contained over thirty ducks—an assortment of mallards, pintails, widgeons, gadwalls, and green-winged teal.

After thoroughly searching the vehicle and finding no other evidence, the wardens questioned all three men about the illegal ducks and their intended destination. "I didn't even know those were ducks they put in my trunk," claimed Schumacher, the consummate liar. The other two men, more street savvy, refused to talk at all. Since all three individuals were able to provide valid identification and a work address, they were not booked into the county jail. Instead, they were advised that formal criminal complaints would be filed with the Glenn County District Attorney for joint possession of over sixty unlawfully taken ducks. Both shotguns and all of the ducks were seized into evidence.

"That Schumacher kid has always been trouble," said Warden Hiller, after the three poaching suspects had driven away.

"Did he say he works at a grocery store?" asked my father.

"Yeah, he works at the market in town."

"Do they have a walk-in freezer?"

"I believe they do."

"Why don't we pay them a visit just in case this Schumacher kid has any ducks stashed there?"

"That's not a bad idea, Wally."

"You guys go ahead," said Mercer. "I'm gonna head back to Chico and get some sleep."

My father followed Warden Hiller to the market where Schumacher worked. One of the meat cutters led them to the walk-in freezer. In the back corner, on an upper shelf, was a cardboard box with Schumacher's name scribbled on the front. Inside the box were over two dozen ducks, all mallards and all individually wrapped in freezer paper. Mallards are easily identified by their larger size and by sections of orange skin left at the leg joints. Neatly handwritten on the face of each package was the word "Greenhead."

Warden Hiller had been hearing rumors of Schumacher illegally selling wild ducks out the back door of the store for some time. An investigation by Hiller and my father revealed that the young scoundrel had worked out a deal with Beasley and Small: he would drop them off and pick them up in return for his choice of the plunder. Plump, rice-fed drake mallards (greenheads) were considered best of the best by connoisseurs of wild duck.

I wish I could tell you that all three outlaws came clean, gave up the identities of their illegal duck buyers, and spent the next year behind bars. Unfortunately, that wasn't the case. Beasley and Small were sentenced to serve thirty days in the Glenn County Jail. Schumacher got forty-five days but was released after thirty for good behavior. He was fired from the grocery store and eventually left town. Beasley and Small were never heard from again.

As for me, I had learned my lesson about following instructions and was back riding along with my father in a few weeks.

The Road to Plaskett Meadows

———————— ◆ ————————

I AWAKENED TO THE SOUND of hard-soled work boots clomping down the hallway toward the kitchen. "You better get up if you're going with me," said my father, pushing open the bedroom door.

"I'm awake, Dad," I replied, throwing back the bed sheet and jumping to my feet. It was 5:00 a.m. on a Saturday morning in mid-May, 1963. I had just turned fifteen, and we had been living in Orland for nearly three years. The snow had finally cleared on the mountain road into Plaskett Meadows, and I was excited about our first trip of the year to one of my favorite lakes.

For a few days every season, just after the ice on the water's surface began to melt, Plaskett Lake came alive with eighteen-to-twenty-inch rainbows. The trout were ravenous after the long winter and eager to strike anything that looked like food: a fly, a lure, or a four-inch night crawler. In a week or two, the excitement would all be over. An angler could offer everything in his tackle box and fail to entice a fish into taking a single bite.

The sun was just coming up as we pulled away from the curb and headed west on Colusa Street. Coming to a stop at the intersection of East and Walker, I pointed across the road to a 1910-era Craftsman house, the front yard completely overgrown with trees and shrubbery.

"See that old house, Dad?"

"That's quite a house—what I can see of it."

"Old Doc Bihler lives there. He donated the land for our baseball field back in 1930. Dr. Bihler used to wave to us when we'd walk by on our way to school. I haven't seen him for a while. I hope he's all right."

"Why don't you knock on his door sometime and ask if he needs any yard work done?"

"It's sure quiet this early in the morning," I said, changing the subject. "I haven't seen anyone since we left the house."

"That's one of the reasons we moved here—to get away from all the people and the traffic."

"Dad, is it true Orland has the most churches and the most bars, per capita, of any town in the United States?"

"Who told you that?" asked my father, laughing.

"Some kid at school. I thought it was kinda funny. Look, there's four churches right there, one on each corner.... Dad, why don't you say something?"

"I'm figuring up how many bars there are—the Orlando, Dalton's, Boje's, The Richelieu, The Lariat, Shady Oaks—"

"I did go into Sprouse-Reitz and ask about a part-time job. Hey, there's the Holvick's milkman! At least somebody else is up."

"Wha'd they say?"

"Who?"

"Sprouse-Reitz."

"Oh, they said they didn't need anybody right now."

"I always had a part-time job of some kind when I was your age. Why don't you go see Al Vanosek at the 76 Station?"

"Dad, I'm only fifteen, and I still have sports after school."

"No reason you couldn't work on weekends."

"Okay, I'll go see him."

Leaving town, we patrolled west on Newville Road. Passing the newly constructed Black Butte Dam, I reflected on the approaching summer. The surrounding foothills of brilliant green grass, blue oaks, and gray pines would soon be changing color. In a few weeks, the wildflowers would disappear and the landscape would morph into a dull shade of brown.

Fifteen miles out, we crossed the Burris Creek Bridge and entered Glenn County's western foothills. Majestic three-hundred-year-old valley oaks adorned the riparian zone bordering the meandering streambed. I noticed a light on at the Hamm place.

"Dad, you haven't had any late-night calls from the Hamms lately."

"Most of the deer have moved up-range. This fall I'll start getting those spotlighting calls again. By the way, I talked to Brewster Cushman the other day. He said he might need a couple boys to pull weeds out here at the Newville Cemetery. I told him you and your friend Paul would be interested."

"Gee thanks, Dad. Pulling weeds is one of my favorite things to do, especially in cemeteries. I bet Paul will appreciate it, too."

"Okay, that's enough. You need to find something for this summer, even if it's pulling weeds."

Five more miles up the road, we passed Leo Flood's ranch. I peeked over at my father, hoping he wouldn't spot Leo out in the yard and decide to stop and talk. At the age of fifteen, I had not yet learned the art of patience and didn't enjoy sitting in the passenger seat of the patrol car while my father chewed the fat for an hour. I would later learn that a good wildlife officer should make a point of getting to know the ranchers and landowners in his patrol district. Gaining their confidence is essential if the officer expects to hear about any violations that occur when he's not around. Warden Wally Callan had not only become acquainted with the landowners in his district, he had forged friendships with most of them. Seldom did my father patrol through the Newville area without being invited in for coffee. Needless to say, if a shot rang out after dark, he could count on a phone call from one of the ranchers soon after.

Leo Flood's son Lyle lived a half mile west of him. Lyle Flood was my father's age and had become one of Dad's close friends. Lyle's ranch was located a rock's throw from the ghost town of Newville, from which the road got its name. A self-taught historian, Lyle had collected guns and other memorabilia from Newville's heyday and enjoyed telling stories about Glenn County's pioneer settlers and what life was like in those days. Once, while showing my father and me his Old West gun collection, Lyle surprised us with his extensive knowledge of early Glenn County.

"What we now know as Glenn County was actually part of Colusa County during the 1850s," said Lyle.

"I didn't know that," said my father.

"Newville was a thriving little town in those days," said Lyle.

"What happened to it?" I asked.

"The whole town burned to the ground in 1929. All that's left is that falling-down hotel over there and part of the filling station."

Knowing about my interest in wildlife, Lyle began talking about the animals that once existed in the county. "Not just deer and mountain lions," he said. "When the first settlers arrived, there were antelope, elk, and even grizzly bears."

"What happened to 'em?" I asked.

"They shot all the grizzlies because they were a threat to the livestock. The elk and antelope were killed for food and probably just for the fun of it. I don't think anyone even thought about conservation in those days. There weren't any game wardens like your dad around. If there had been, they'd a probably shot them, too."

TURNING SOUTH FROM LYLE'S ranch, we passed the Cushman Ranch, Hull Road, and the confluence of Grindstone and Stony Creeks, before heading west again. The U.S. Forest Service road sign told us it was thirty miles to Plaskett Meadows, but with all the switchbacks and bumpy caterpillar tracks, it seemed more like sixty.

A few miles east of Plaskett Meadows was Cold Creek Campground. We entered the campground about 8:30 a.m. and pulled in behind a grove of towering pines.

"It looks like we've got three or four camps," said my father. "Let's give the people up at Plaskett Lake another hour or so to catch some fish, while I see what's going on here."

"Is it okay if I fish upstream while you check the camps, Dad?"

"Yeah, go ahead. I'll catch up with you in a little while."

My father stepped from the patrol car and reached back for his uniform jacket.

"Is it cold out there, Dad? Should I wear my jacket?"

"I would if I were you. Keep your voice down and don't slam the door when you get out."

"What kind of lure do you think I should use?"

"The stream is pretty small. Figure it out for yourself. Do you have a little Mepps spinner?"

"I think I do. After this we're still going up to Plaskett, aren't we?"

"We'll even try to make it up to Keller Lake if the road's open. Lock the door when you leave. I'll see you in a half hour or so."

"Remember that nice brookie I caught at Keller Lake last year?"

There was no response. My father had already left and was walking downstream toward the north end of the campground.

I quietly locked the car door. With a cloth creel draped over my shoulder and a gold number-one Mepps spinner attached to the end of my line, I headed upstream in the opposite direction.

Although Cold Creek was quite small—probably ten feet across at its widest point—it contained a healthy population of six-to-eight-inch native rainbows. During the early season, some of the old timers from the valley liked to camp in the campground and take advantage of the good fishing. The daily bag limit was ten trout, and no individual was allowed to possess more than ten, regardless of how long he camped there.

I found a three-foot-deep pool about fifty yards upstream from the last campsite and flipped my spinner toward the downstream end. The second my spinner hit the water, a flash of silver appeared just below the water's surface and my rod jerked forward. "I got one already!" I said, laughing aloud. "This guy's a fighter." Around the pool my scrappy opponent raced, darting back and forth until I lifted the tip of my rod and brought the wriggling fish to my waiting left hand. I carefully removed the hook from its lower lip, bent over, and gently placed the eight-inch rainbow back in the water. In the blink of an eye, it was gone.

My father approached from thirty yards downstream, with several nearby campers watching his every move. Distracted, I cast my lure and snagged it on a submerged tree root.

"Dad," I said, "could you reach down and unhook my spinner?"

"Where is it?"

"It's hooked on a tree root just below you."

Removing his jacket, my father rolled up his right shirtsleeve. Dropping to his knees, he reached under the water in an attempt to retrieve the gold-colored lure. The hook had apparently dug in deeper than I thought, because I noticed a grimace on my father's face. As he changed positions, I heard him mumble, "I should make you do this yourself." Just then, my father's left hand slipped, and down he went, headfirst into the icy cold water.

"Oh no!" I blurted.

Up he came, every inch of his uniform, including holster and sidearm, thoroughly drenched. "Come on, let's go," was all my father said as he climbed out of the water and began walking toward the patrol car.

With no further interest in saving my spinner, I snapped off my line and followed. Walking back, I couldn't help noticing that several of the campers had witnessed the embarrassing spectacle and were laughing. I probably would have laughed myself, had it been anyone other than my father. My earlier visions of catching a twenty-inch rainbow in Plaskett Lake were fading fast.

When I reached the patrol car, I found my father standing at the trunk with water dripping from his forehead and an angry scowl on his face. I stood there waiting for a well-deserved tongue lashing, when something wonderful and completely unexpected happened. The morning sun peeked from behind a giant thunderhead and bathed my father in warming sunlight. Suddenly things didn't seem so bad after all. I actually spotted a slight grin on my father's face. As if on cue, we both burst out laughing.

"Next time, unhook your own damn lure," he said, still laughing.

"I'm sorry, Dad," I said, roaring with laughter. "I can't get that image out of my head."

"It's not that funny. Help me get this box out of the trunk."

I have never met a person more resourceful and better prepared for any eventuality than Warden Wally Callan. Inside a wooden box that he kept in his trunk was not only a week's supply of C-rations, but a complete change of uniform: pants, shirt, underwear, and socks. There was even a neatly folded towel.

Operating the pedals in his stocking feet, my father maneuvered his patrol car out of Cold Creek Campground and back on the road to Plaskett Meadows. "That'll give those campers something to talk about for a while," he said.

"I hope the insides of your boots dry before we get there, Dad."

"You better hope so, or I'll be wearing yours. Hold 'em up close to the heater vent so the hot air can get inside."

Plaskett Lake was really two lakes, with each being two, three, or four acres in size, depending on the time of year and the amount of snowfall. The upper lake, where most people fished, sat at the west end of a beautiful meadow with a mountain spring running down the middle. It wasn't unusual to find half of the upper lake still frozen over during the early season.

We arrived a little before noon and slowly headed down the hill toward the campground. To avoid being seen, we turned off on a side road that circled above the upper lake and came out on the south side. With the insides of my father's boots dry enough to wear, he put them on and explained his plan.

"I'm going to slip down through the trees and find a good vantage point from up here on the hill. It might be better if you stay with me until we see if anything suspicious is going on."

"Okay, Dad. Just let me know what you want me to do."

"For now, just keep out of sight and stay behind me."

As we made our way down the hill toward the lake, the first sound I heard was an adult male voice shouting, "Fish on!"

"Dad, did you hear that?"

"Yeah, I heard it. Keep your voice down. Sound carries up here."

From our hiding place behind a large fir tree, we immediately spotted a silver-colored aluminum skiff floating in the middle of the upper lake. It was occupied by two male anglers in their mid-to-late thirties. One of the fishermen was wearing blue jeans and a red, long-sleeved plaid shirt. The other wore dark pants and a black sweatshirt.

"The guy in the red shirt is reeling in a fish right now," whispered my father, watching with binoculars. "Looks like a nice one from the way his rod is bent."

The high-altitude afternoon sunlight reflected off the writhing eighteen-inch trout as the fisherman reached into a short-handled dip net and held up his trophy for his friend to see.

"Looks like he's gonna put it on a stringer," said my father. We watched the angler in the red shirt pick up an empty metal stringer from the deck and attach his fish to one of the clips. He proceeded to attach the other end to the boats' gunnel and drop the fish over the side.

"Fish on!" came another shout from the boat.

"Now the other guy has a fish," said my father.

"Is it a big one?"

"It's not quite as big as the last one."

As we watched the fisherman in the black sweatshirt attach his fish to another empty stringer, his partner hooked yet another fish.

"Fish on!" shouted the first fisherman.

"Dad, do these guys think they're fishing for marlin?"

"They seem to be having a good time," said my father.

My father took a small notepad from his shirt pocket and began tallying the number of fish each fisherman had caught and placed on a stringer. Every time a trout was attached to one of the stringers, he would place a hash mark by that fisherman's name. For the sake of identification, he referred to the first fisherman as Red Shirt and the second fisherman as Black Shirt. At this point, Red Shirt had two fish and Black Shirt had one. For the next two hours, my father and I documented every fish that the two men in the boat had caught and placed on their stringers. According to our tally, Red Shirt had caught and kept nine trout, and Black Shirt had caught and kept eight. Neither angler had thrown a single fish back.

It was about 2:30 p.m. when an ominous-looking black cloud blocked out the warm afternoon sunlight and cast a dark shadow over the lake.

"Dad, I think it's gonna rain."

"I see that," said my father, preoccupied with the actions of the two boat fishermen. "Red Shirt needs to catch one more fish and he'll have his limit. Uh-oh, Black Shirt just hooked another one! That makes nine for him, if he keeps it."

"They must be getting tired," I said. "They're not yelling 'Fish on!' anymore."

At exactly 3:05, Black Shirt caught and kept his tenth trout. We watched carefully to see if he continued fishing. With it now raining a little harder, he re-baited his hook and wasted no time casting his line into the water.

"Dad, we're getting soaked,"

"Yeah. I see these guys have coats on now, but they're not showing any signs of quitting."

"Look, Red Shirt's got another fish!"

"I'll watch to see if he keeps it. You run up to the car and bring back our raincoats. Here's the keys." When I returned with the raincoats, I learned that Red Shirt had placed his tenth fish on the stringer. In spite of the rain, which was now coming down pretty hard, both men continued fishing.

"These guys are hard core, aren't they, Dad?"

"I can't believe they're still fishing. "We'll let them each catch one more fish, then I'll contact them."

About that time, the sky opened up. It was a mid-afternoon mountain gully washer—a cloudburst the likes of which I had never seen. Rivulets of water rushed between our legs and down the hill toward the lake. With their boat quickly filling with water, the two fishermen finally gave up and began rowing frantically toward shore.

"Dad, I don't think those guys would have ever quit fishing if the rain hadn't come," I said, as we ran up the hill toward the patrol car.

"I don't think so either. Do you still have my keys?"

"I think they're in my pocket."

"They better be!"

Reaching the patrol car, my father turned on the motor and ran the heater full blast so we could warm up and attempt to dry our wet clothes. I tried to warm my cold hands by holding them next to the heater vent.

"Now what are we gonna do, Dad?"

"This storm will pass in a few minutes. We'll see if these guys come back out. If they don't, we'll drive over to the campground."

"Do you think they have more fish?"

"It depends on how long they've been here. There might be other people with them, which could complicate things. Why don't you reach back and get that bag in the backseat? We'll eat a peanut butter sandwich while we dry off."

"Do we have anything to drink?"

"I told you to fill up that thermos before we left. You did, didn't you?"

"I was just kidding. It's right here. I even brought some paper cups."

"Do you remember my old friend Bill Chilcote from San Diego?"

"Of course I do. Have you heard from him since we moved to Orland?"

"He called last night and wants me to go to Australia with him."

"Are you gonna go?"

"I wouldn't mind going diving over there. The Great Barrier Reef is supposed to be incredible, but we can't afford that."

The storm passed as quickly as it had come. By four o'clock, the sun was again shining, and people returned to the lake—including our two boat fishermen. We watched them dump the water out of their boat, row out to their previous fishing spot, and continue where they had left off. Their lines hadn't been in the water five minutes before both men again began shouting, "Fish on!"

"Here's what I want you to do," said my father. "Take your fishing rod, walk across the dam, and make your way over to the campground. Figure out which camp belongs to these guys and see if there are any other people with them. You should see a trailer or some type of boat rack attached to their rig."

I casually walked across the dam, as my father had instructed, and made my way up the hill toward the Plaskett Meadows Campground. Reaching the campground, I immediately spotted a pickup parked at the lower end, with a walk-in camper in the bed and a small boat trailer attached. The door to the camper was closed and there appeared to be no other people around. I noticed a swarm of yellow jackets a short distance from the pickup and walked over to investigate. "This must be where they buried their fish guts," I said aloud. Several more bees were milling around a shovel leaning against the pickup.

Hiking down the hill to the upper lake, I noticed a tall, gray-haired man standing on one of the sawed-off tree stumps dotting the shoreline. He was casting a silver spinner into the water and retrieving it. Knowing that my dad would be watching from the hill on the other side of the lake, I stopped to talk. "Hi. Have you caught any fish?" I asked.

"Oh, hello there, young man. You snuck up on me."

"I was just wondering if you had caught any fish."

"I've got a couple there."

"That one's a beauty. Did you catch it on a spinner?"

"No, I caught that big one with worms. I saw those guys in the boat cleaning their fish, so I asked them what they used for bait. They told me they were using worms, with a marshmallow to keep the hook up off the bottom. I didn't have any marshmallows, but I tried a worm and caught that big one."

"Why aren't you using worms now?"

"I only keep enough fish to eat. If I use bait, they swallow the hook and I can't throw 'em back. Those two on the stringer are enough for my wife and me to eat for dinner."

"I like that," I said, walking away.

As I walked back across the dam, I began thinking how refreshing it was to meet a person who appreciated the resource and only took what he needed. Being young and impressionable, I might easily have developed an attitude that all people were opportunists like the two fishermen in the boat. That clearly wasn't the case.

It was about five o'clock or a little after when I reached my father. He was still watching the boat fishermen and tallying the number of fish they'd taken. Red Shirt had caught and kept four more trout since I'd left, giving him a total of fourteen. Black Shirt had caught and kept three more trout, for a total of thirteen. We still had no idea how many additional fish they had back at the camp.

"Now what are we gonna do, Dad?"

"I've seen enough. I'm debating whether to call out to these guys and have them bring the boat ashore, or keep watching."

"Are you worried about them dumping their stringers overboard?"

"Yeah. No telling what kind of games these guys might play. I think we'll just have to wait them out."

We watched for another half hour or so, until a cold wind came up and blew ripples across the once-placid lake. Both fishermen put their coats on, reeled in their lines, and began moving things around. Red Shirt pulled up their makeshift cement-block anchor and Black Shirt began rowing toward the north shore. When the boat reached shore, we watched the two anglers unhook their stringers, grab their fishing rods, and walk uphill toward the campground. My father and I quickly returned to the patrol car and drove over to meet them on the north side of the lake.

"When we get there, I want you to stay in the car and keep your eyes open," said my father. "Let me know if you see anything suspicious."

"I will. Hey, there's nobody else here. That guy I talked to earlier must have left."

"Our boys are walking into their camp now."

"Did you see the look on Red Shirt's face when he saw us coming, Dad?"

As my father stepped from the car, I rolled down my window so I could hear what was being said. Both fishermen were standing at the entrance to the camper, each of them holding a fishing rod and stringer. The angler we had named Red Shirt stood about five-eight and might have weighed a hundred and seventy pounds. He sported a flattop butch haircut and still wore the red plaid, long-sleeved shirt under his jacket. Leaning his fishing rod up against the pickup, he began walking toward my father. Black Shirt, who was slightly taller than his partner and had short dark hair, just stood there. The dark sweatshirt he wore was actually navy blue, with a fireman's insignia on the front.

"How are you guys doing?" asked my father.

"We're doing fine," said the man in the red shirt.

"Looks like you've had some luck. I see a couple nice ones there."

"Yeah, we caught a few," said Red Shirt.

"I'd like to take a look at all your fish."

"Sure," said Red Shirt, throwing his stringer across a nearby picnic table. Black Shirt did the same.

As my father counted four trout on one stringer and three on the other, he asked to see the men's fishing licenses. Both produced current California fishing licenses. Red Shirt was identified as James William Applewhite, out of Richmond, California. Black Shirt was identified as Clyde David Drummond, from Berkeley. I anxiously waited for my father to lower the boom on these two fish hogs and tell them what he had witnessed, but he continued to take his time.

"You guys are a long way from home," said my father. "What do you do?"

"We're both firemen," answered Applewhite.

"Oh yeah," said my father, staring at Applewhite's fishing license. "I used to be a fireman."

"What city?" asked Drummond.

"San Diego. Do you fellas have any more fish you'd like to show me?"

Neither man answered. Drummond looked at the ground and began shuffling his feet. Applewhite fiddled with the keys in his pocket. My father patiently waited for someone to answer his question. With no answer forthcoming, he asked who owned the pickup. Applewhite said it was his. "Would you please open your camper?" said my father. Realizing this backwoods game warden wasn't born yesterday, Applewhite admitted that they had a few more fish inside the camper.

"But we've been here for two days," offered Drummond. Without responding, my father waited for Applewhite to open the door. Inside, he found thirty-two more trout. Counting the fish on the outside stringers, Applewhite and Drummond possessed a total of forty-three trout, all twelve-to-eighteen-inch rainbows.

Applewhite and Drummond were charged with joint possession of twenty-three trout over the legal limit. I heard one of them whining about coming all that way and going home with only ten fish each. My father explained that it was a small lake and if everyone took as many fish as they had, it would soon be fished out. They had caught some beautiful fish and should have been satisfied with that. I was surprised, because I had never heard my father lecture a violator or provide an explanation for the law. On the way home, I asked why.

"I was a fireman," he said. "Those guys are expected to respect the law, not break it. That responsibility doesn't end when they leave the fire station."

"I guess they should have known better, huh, Dad?"

"You bet they should have!"

"I'm hungry. Do we have anything else to eat?"

"You're always hungry. There's some C-rations in the trunk."

"No thanks. I can wait until we get home."

Game Wardens and Ghost Towns

————— ◆ —————

WHEN THE WHISTLE BLEW at 5:00 p.m. on Friday, November 12, 1965, Frank Heise, Ricky Dupree, and Dale Blunt walked off work at a timber mill near Elk Creek, California. All three men were in their mid-twenties at the time.

Sporting a butch haircut, Frank Heise was a husky five-nine, his arms well-muscled from pulling green chain for the past five years. Ricky Dupree stood four or five inches taller than his cousin Frank and was noticeably thinner. He wore black, horn-rimmed glasses with a strip of faded white surgical tape over the nose piece. Dupree had wandered aimlessly after barely graduating from Orland High School, so Frank got him a job at the mill, sweeping up.

Dale Blunt had grown up on a run-down dairy farm outside Willows. Tired of milking cows at four in the morning, he secured a job at the same mill where Heise and Dupree worked. Blunt was a hefty, boisterous man, six feet tall and weighing well over two hundred and fifty pounds. He claimed to get the energy he needed for pulling green chain from all the beer he drank after work and on weekends.

Heise and Dupree lived together in a single-wide mobile home out on Road M, south of Orland. Dupree's car was broken down and up on blocks most of the time, so he traveled to and from work in Heise's 1958 maroon-and-primer-gray Dodge Coronet with the right front bumper bashed in.

Walking out to the parking lot, Heise began talking about all the deer they'd been seeing while driving to and from work.

"Why don't we pick up a couple six packs and do a little huntin' tonight?" suggested Heise. "That skinny little forky I shot during deer season didn't last very long."

"I'm in," said Dupree, opening the passenger door of Heise's car.

"You better be in," quipped Heise. "You ate more of that deer than I did. How about you, Dale?"

Blunt was just about to climb into his souped-up, red-and-white 1955 Chevy. "As long as you're buyin' the beer," he replied.

"Let's hang out at my place until about midnight," said Heise. "We'll stop at Graham Brothers to pick up beer and a couple TV dinners on the way through town. Just follow us."

All three men hung around Heise's trailer, drinking beer and smoking cigarettes until after 11:00 p.m. They didn't have to work the next day, so sleep was not a concern. Preparing for the night's hunt, Heise popped open his trunk and placed a hand-held spotlight inside. Blunt walked out and asked what kind of rifle they were going to use.

"This little beauty never misses," said Heise, half smashed and full of bravado. He unzipped a leather gun case and pulled out a Marlin/Glenfield Model 60, semiautomatic .22 rifle, with scope attached. "I just put the crosshairs between those shinin' green eyes and down they go." Heise placed his rifle inside the trunk, next to the spotlight and three six-packs of beer. He climbed into the driver's seat and started the engine. Blunt jumped into the backseat. "Let's go, Ricky," shouted Heise.

Dupree came running out of the trailer with a beer in his hand. "I was lookin' for my cigarettes."

"Chug that beer and leave the can here," said Heise. "Wait till we get through town before opening another one. Moranville or one of his boys is liable to be out prowling around and I don't want another open container ticket."

The three would-be deer poachers slowly cruised through downtown Orland and headed out Road 200. They passed Black Butte Dam and continued west on Newville Road. Arriving at the Newville Cemetery about midnight, Heise pulled to the side of the road, walked to the rear of the car, and opened the trunk. All three men grabbed a beer. Heise removed his rifle from the case, cocked a live round into the firing chamber, and placed the rifle in the front seat next to him. Dupree, who had obviously been spotlighting before and knew the drill, removed the spotlight from the trunk and inserted the cord into the car's cigarette lighter receptacle.

Passing the Flood Ranch, Blunt commented on how many deer they were seeing in the car's headlights. Heise and Dupree explained that they didn't want to shoot too close to any of the ranch houses, for fear of someone hearing the shot and calling the game warden. Reaching the intersection of Newville Road and Road 306, Heise turned south toward Elk Creek. When he had gone a mile or so, he lifted his foot from the accelerator and slowed the car to five miles per hour. Dupree rolled down his window and began shining the spotlight into the adjacent field.

"There's a couple right there," said Dupree, quickly turning the light off. As Heise stopped the car, Dupree again turned the light on and lit up three deer—a full-grown doe and two smaller yearlings.

"Let's find something a little closer," said Heise.

Continuing south, they turned west onto Hull Road. Rolling his window down, Heise began shining the spotlight out the driver's-side window. Blunt spotted two deer in the headlights up ahead. "There's a couple crossing the road," he said. "Let me take a shot."

Dupree handed the rifle to Blunt. Blunt rolled down the back window as Heise held the spotlight on a healthy-looking doe that had just jumped the fence. Heise whistled softly, attempting to attract the deer's attention, while Blunt steadied his left arm on the window frame. Curious about the whistle, the deer stopped, stood motionless, and stared back at the light. "Put one right between those green eyes," instructed Heise. Blunt squeezed off the trigger, hitting the deer between the eyes and killing it instantly.

"Nice shot," said Dupree. "You look like you've done this before."

"My brother and I used to spotlight deer out by Stoneyford Reservoir," said Blunt. "Hiller once came to our house looking for a deer we'd killed, but it was hidden out in the hayloft and he never found it."

Heise turned off the ignition. All three men straddled the barbed wire fence and walked out to the deer that Blunt had killed. With Dupree holding the flashlight, Heise took his hunting knife and carefully sliced through the deer's abdominal wall. Pulling up on the deer's hide so as not to puncture any organs, he opened it up and emptied the abdominal cavity. "That's enough for now," said Heise, wiping his hands on a rag. "Let's get this thing in the trunk before anyone comes along."

Heise walked back to the fence and climbed over. Using the same rag, he wiped blood from his knife blade. Dupree grabbed the deer's back legs and dragged it to the fence. With Blunt taking the front legs, he and Dupree swung the seventy-five-pound deer over the fence and dropped it to the ground. Heise popped open the trunk as the other men straddled the fence and stepped over. Dupree and Blunt again lifted the deer and prepared to swing it into the trunk. One of the legs slipped from Dupree's hand, causing the deer's hindquarters to fall and skid across the back bumper. "Come on," complained Heise. "Get it in there." With the deer safely hidden inside the trunk, the three men jumped back into the car and continued hunting.

It was approaching 1:00 a.m. when Dupree fired a shot just south of the Cushman Ranch. The deer ran off and wasn't seen again. Heise had promised

Blunt the doe he'd killed, so Dupree and Heise were determined to bag a deer for themselves before heading back to town.

Out of beer and three sheets to the wind, the three deer poachers turned west on Newville Road and headed northeast toward Paskenta. Rounding the first bend, they passed the ghost town of Newville. Newville had thrived from the early 1850s until 1929, when all but a few buildings burned to the ground. During its heyday, the little pioneer town boasted a general store, two livery stables, two saloons, a blacksmith shop, two hotels, a post office, a race track, and a service station. Now only the ramshackle, two-story Newville Hotel and the falling-down service station remained.

"That place is spooky," said Dupree. "A bunch of us came out here on Halloween night when I was in high school."

"Did you go inside?" asked Blunt.

"I started to go upstairs in the hotel, but I heard a strange noise and chickened out. Most of the steps were broken, anyway."

"What did the noise sound like?" asked Heise, holding back a chuckle.

"It sounded like a voice coming from one of the rooms, saying, 'Go away.'"

Heise couldn't hold it in any longer and began laughing hysterically. "That was me, you jackass!"

ABOUT 1:15 A.M., I was awakened by the familiar sound of telephones ringing in the middle of the night, one coming from my parents' bedroom and the other from the kitchen wall. Everyone in the house had come to expect these calls during the winter months. That's when deer ventured out of the mountains and congregated in the foothills west of Orland.

Minutes after the phones rang, my parents' bedroom door opened and I heard my father's work boots stomping down the hall toward the kitchen. Dialing the kitchen telephone, he soon had Harold Erwick on the line. As big as a house, Warden Erwick had occupied the adjoining Corning Position for many years. The gray-haired veteran wore wire-rimmed glasses and looked exceptionally neat in his uniform. "Harold always looks like he just climbed out of a band box," my father would say. A man of many talents, Warden Erwick sang opera and photographed weddings in his spare time.

"Hi, Harold. Sorry to wake you. Shots were fired just south of Fred Cushman's place. I'll head out from here and meet you at the intersection."

Warden Wally Callan quietly closed the front door, jumped into his patrol car, and sped away. He drove through the deserted streets of Orland, reached Road 200, and raced west. The weather was calm and partly cloudy, with the temperature down in the mid-forties. Erwick left Corning a few minutes later, reached Black Butte Road, and raced southwest.

***

OUR THREE DEER POACHERS had driven about two miles farther west on Newville Road, when Frank Heise glanced at his fuel gauge. "Damn!" he shouted. "I meant to stop at King Dollar for gas and cigarettes on the way through town."

Dupree leaned over and peeked at the gas gauge. "It's below the empty line. We must be running on fumes!"

Heise turned the car around and gently accelerated back toward Orland. As they crossed the old cement bridge and once again approached the Newville ghost town, Heise's car sputtered, lunged forward a few times, and chugged to a stop.

"Now we're screwed!" said Heise. "Help me push this thing off the road."

"What are we gonna do?" asked Dupree.

"Jimmy Rodriguez, from work, lives a few miles south of here. He'll give us enough gas to get back to town."

"WHICH PLACE IS JIMMY'S?" asked Blunt.

"It's that trailer on the left side of the road, with all the junk cars in back and the chickens running around."

"That's quite a walk," said Dupree, questioning Heise's idea.

"I guess we could sit here and wait for the game warden to come along," said Heise.

"Are we gonna leave that deer in the car?" asked Dupree.

"No," said Heise. "Let's get it out of the trunk and hide it somewhere."

"How about over there, in that old gas station?" suggested Dupree.

"Come on," said Heise, opening the trunk. "Give me a hand with this thing."

Heise and Blunt dragged the deer across the road, into some tall weeds, and up to the old service station. Dupree shined his flashlight inside.

"I don't want to go in there," said Heise. "Too many nails sticking up. Let's just drop it over in the creek bed."

Blunt and Dupree dragged the carcass to a location ten yards west of the old service station and dropped it off a steep embankment, into the dry streambed. Once back at the car, Heise lifted an empty five-gallon gas can from the trunk, locked his rifle inside, and began walking south toward the tiny community of Chrome. Dupree and Blunt reluctantly followed.

***

IT WAS ALMOST 2:00 a.m. when Wardens Wally Callan and Harold Erwick met at the intersection of Black Butte Road and Newville Road. In tandem, with headlights off and sneak lights on, they slowly proceeded west on Newville Road. When they came to the intersection of Newville Road and Road 306,

Erwick continued on Newville Road and Callan headed south on Road 306.

"Two five five, one two two, car-to-car," said Erwick over the radio.

"Go ahead," said Callan.

"Yeah, Wally. Come back to the old ghost town. I think we might have something."

"Ten-four."

Warden Callan turned around and drove back to Newville. As he pulled up, headlights still off and sneak light on, he saw Warden Erwick standing at the rear of an older-model sedan. Callan turned off the ignition and walked over to Erwick.

"What do we have, Harold?"

Erwick pointed his flashlight at the car's rear bumper. "From the looks of this blood and hair, I'd say someone killed a deer."

Warden Callan reached down and picked up a hair fiber stuck to the bumper. Holding it in the light, he bent the fiber until it broke off sharply, an indication that the hair was hollow and had most likely come from a deer. "They must have run out of gas or broken down," said Callan.

"Do you think they were foolish enough to leave the deer in the trunk?" asked Erwick.

"My guess is the deer is hidden around here somewhere and our boys are on foot," said Callan. He walked to the front of the car and placed his open hand on the hood. "They haven't been gone very long. The hood's still warm."

While Warden Erwick searched the area, Warden Callan radioed Sacramento dispatch and ran a check on the license plate. The suspects' car came back registered to a Franklin William Heise, on Road M, in Orland. After writing down the information, Callan walked across the road to a spot where Erwick had obviously discovered something. Erwick pointed to a clear trail of pushed-down wet grass leading in the direction of the old gas station. The two wardens followed the trail, discovering tiny spatters of blood along the way. Reaching the gas station, the wardens discovered a new trail leading west, toward the dry streambed.

"Here it is," said Erwick, directing the beam of his flashlight into the streambed. "Looks like a good-sized doe."

Callan looked down at the deer lying on its side, up against a fallen tree branch. "We didn't see anybody on our way out," said Callan, "so they're probably on foot, somewhere between here and Chrome."

"What do you want to do, Wally?"

"If we catch 'em on foot, we might be able to pin the deer on the car's registered owner, but whoever's with him will claim he didn't have anything to do with it. I think our best bet is to stake this place out until they come back."

"Where we gonna hide the cars?"

"I guess we could hide 'em on the other side of the creek, behind those trees. Hopefully these guys will come back before daylight. We don't want the cars too far away in case we need the radio."

With both cars parked out of sight on the other side of the dry streambed, Wardens Callan and Erwick walked back to the old gas station and found a place to hide. They waited in the cold, early morning air until 4:15 a.m., when the distant sound of an oncoming vehicle captured their attention.

"It's coming from the south," said Erwick.

"I can hear it winding down and shifting gears," said Callan. "Sounds like an old pickup."

Just then a beat-up, rattletrap of a pickup slowed, turned left onto Newville Road, and headed in the wardens' direction. "Here they come," whispered Erwick.

The pickup came to a stop next to Heise's parked car. Someone exited the passenger side and slammed the door. Others were heard jumping down from the bed. "Thanks, Jimmy," came a voice from the darkness. A single flashlight beam appeared as someone walked toward the rear of the suspect vehicle. Jimmy turned his pickup around in the middle of the road, his headlights illuminating the old gas station and causing the two wardens to duck out of sight. By the time he had depressed the clutch and grinded the gears three or four more times, Jimmy was finally out of sight.

"What a piece of junk," said Erwick from his hidden position beside my father. "What do you think they're doing, Wally?"

"They're probably putting gas in the car," whispered my father.

"Do you think they'll come out and get the deer?"

"If these guys couldn't remember to buy gas, they might forget all about that deer."

Just then the suspects' car doors opened and a dome light came on. Two men jumped in the front seat and one in the back. The motor started, and the car began to pull away.

"They're leaving!" said Erwick.

"We'd better run to our cars and stop 'em before they get to the crossroads or we won't know which way they went," said Callan.

Both wardens sprang to their feet and began running through the tall grass toward their patrol cars. Suddenly, the suspect vehicle wheeled around in the middle of the road and headed back in the wardens' direction.

"They're comin' back. Get down, Harold!" Callan ran for the high grass and dove for cover. Erwick's version of a run was actually a fast walk. As he leaned forward and held out his arms in an attempt to lower himself to the ground, he tripped, sending his glasses flying and his enormous body tumbling into the weeds.

"Harold, are you all right?" whispered my father, lying perfectly still in a prone position.

"I think so," whispered Erwick, "but I lost my glasses."

The suspects' car had come to a stop thirty yards away, its headlights pointing in the direction of the hidden deer.

"Wally, can you see them?" whispered Erwick, still sprawled out on the ground. "What are they doing?"

"They're just sitting in the car. It sounds like they're arguing about something."

Suddenly the car doors were flung open and out they came. The driver walked back and opened the trunk. Two men, later identified as Blunt and Dupree, ran to the creek bank, jumped into the ravine, and retrieved the deer. As they dragged it back toward the car, Warden Callan stood up and shouted, "Department of Fish and Game. You boys stay right where you are."

"Damn!" muttered Heise from the rear of the car. "I told those idiots we shoulda' left that deer."

Franklin William Heise, Richard Samuel Dupree, and Donald Dale Blunt were arrested without incident and booked into the Glenn County Jail. The deer, spotlight, and .22 rifle were seized into evidence. Charged with unlawful take and possession of deer during closed season, the three deer poachers were eventually released on their own recognizance and instructed to appear in the local justice court on November 24.

Heise, Dupree, and Blunt appeared in court, as instructed, and pleaded guilty. They each received $200 fines, which was a month's pay in those days. Outside in the parking lot, Heise was overheard reading Dupree and Blunt the riot act: "I told you we should 'a left the deer and gone home. I'm gonna have to work overtime for three months to pay that fine. Remind me never to listen to you two idiots again."

Warden Harold Erwick remained in Corning for the remainder of his thirty-three-year Fish and Game career and retired July 1, 1970.

Wallace Callan, my father, would continue to chase fish and wildlife outlaws around Glenn County until he transferred to Fortuna in 1970. He was promoted to patrol captain in 1973, moving to the San Francisco Bay Area. In 1979, my father became the regional law enforcement supervisor (inspector) in Southern California. He retired from the California Department of Fish and Game in 1982.

Every spring, when the hills turn emerald green, my family and I take a ride out Newville Road to enjoy the scenery, visit the ghost town site, and rekindle old memories.

Downtown Orland, California (circa 1960).

Teaching my brother Matt the fine art of fishing at Cold Creek (circa 1962).

Shivering in the snow near Plaskett Meadows with childhood friend and future warden Larry Bruckenstein and my brother Kenny (circa 1961).

Wally Callan on the porch of the Newville Hotel (circa 1962).

Some of my best childhood memories are of days spent fishing
at Grindstone Creek (circa 1963).

The fish rescue crew: Mike Cauble, Paul Martens, Glenn Tibessart, unidentified
gentleman, Steve Callan, and Kenny Callan, circa 1964. As the Orland Fish and
Game warden, my father had organized this effort to rescue stranded fish
in Stony Creek. What fun we had!

My broken wrist may have prevented me from playing baseball that year, but I could still go on patrol with my father. Here I am sitting on the hood of Dad's patrol car, near Plaskett Meadows (circa 1966).

One of my father's many pheasant cases. Pictured are Warden Wallace Callan, U.S. Fish and Wildlife Agent Bob Norris, and Warden Harold Erwick (1967).

Wardens Wally Callan and Gil Berg in front of our house on Colusa Street in Orland (circa 1962).

The Callan family in 1969: Wallace, Steven, Doris, Kenneth, and Matthew.

THE NEXT GENERATION

1970–1980

River Days

———————◆———————

"Habitat is where it's at," as they say, but the only way to maintain healthy populations of fish and wildlife in a state with thirty-eight million people is by establishing laws and providing dedicated, well-trained officers to enforce those laws.
—*Badges, Bears, and Eagles* (March 2013)

I BEGAN MY OWN CAREER with the California Department of Fish and Game in September of 1974. As I mentioned in my earlier book, *Badges, Bears, and Eagles*, my first assignment was the Earp Patrol District, along the Colorado River. Before assuming my duties as a Fish and Game warden, I was required to complete POST (Peace Officers Standards and Training) at the Riverside Sheriff's Academy in Southern California.

The academy was located at the bottom of a canyon on Box Springs Road, in Riverside, California. It seemed like a peaceful setting for a police academy, with manicured lawns, beige-colored Spanish-style buildings, a shooting range, and an exercise area. What I remember most were the legions of cottontail rabbits that descended upon the lawns every evening when the sun went down.

The afternoon I arrived, I was twenty-six years old, standing six feet tall and weighing a lean but muscular 190 pounds. My academy class included two other newly hired Fish and Game wardens—Len Potter and Tom Lipp. Potter was tall and thin, with dark, receding hair. With a pipe as his constant companion, he portrayed himself as the studious, professorial type. Lipp was also tall and thin. Immediately popular with the other officers, he quickly assumed the role of class clown. The remainder of the academy class was made up of fifty newly hired deputy sheriffs and city police officers from departments all over Southern California.

Half of each training day was spent doing physical training: Mount Rubidoux runs, hand-to-hand combat, cuffing techniques, and firearms. Sergeant Peterson, with the Riverside County Sheriff's Department, was in charge. Friendly and personable off duty, he assumed the role of an iron-handed Marine drill instructor when class was in session.

Sergeant Peterson caught me doing Richard Nixon impressions at the back of formation one morning and ordered me to come up to the cement stage and perform for the entire class. "Now, let's see how well you fish cops do push-ups," said the sergeant, when I had finished my performance. I think I surprised him when I knocked out thirty quick ones on my fingertips. "That'll be enough entertainment for today," said Peterson. "Get back in formation."

The other half of each training day was spent learning the California Penal Code, rules of arrest, constitutional law, and search and seizure. Mr. Dillon's entertaining search and seizure lectures were worth the price of admission. Forty years later, I still remember valuable lessons from that class.

An Inglewood patrolman we all called Animal led the class in physical training. While the rest of us viewed the required run up and down Mount Rubidoux as unmitigated torture, this masochistic street cop seemed to enjoy it.

Warden Potter earned first place in academics. I placed second in both categories—physical training and academics—and was selected by the academy staff as "Best Overall Officer." Potter ranked number two overall and Lipp finished fifth in the class. Fish and Game Training Inspector Ellis Berry drove down from Sacramento headquarters for the graduation ceremony. "Inspector Berry," said Warden Lipp, "are you proud of how well your wardens did?"

"You guys were expected to do better than the cops," answered Berry. "It's a good thing, too. If you hadn't, you'd a been fired."

I always wondered if that gruff old character meant what he said, or if he was only kidding.

***

THE COLORADO RIVER IS on the extreme eastern edge of three California counties: San Bernardino, Riverside, and Imperial. Each county's population center is over a hundred and fifty miles west of the river, across the vast and incredibly hot Mohave Desert. During the 1970s, a small handful of sheriff's officers known as resident deputies were assigned to these outlying areas. Instead of reporting to an office or a substation, some of the deputies in the more isolated areas worked out of their homes, as Fish and Game wardens did.

With this isolation came a certain independence. Independence sometimes led to a form of Old-West-style law enforcement that Wyatt Earp might have enjoyed, but Mr. Dillon, my search and seizure instructor, might have seriously questioned.

***

MICHAEL DAVID SZODY, KNOWN to his friends as Dave, was named the Blythe/Palo Verde Fish and Game warden in 1975 at the age of twenty-nine. Tall and thin, my future working partner was born in Monterey, California. Raised by his grandparents, Dave lived a half-mile from the ocean and spent much of his childhood on or near the water. Smart as a whip, Dave seemed to lose interest sometime between elementary school and high school. In fact, he barely graduated from high school. Having nothing better to do, young Szody halfheartedly entered Monterey Peninsula College. If they had offered courses in softball and partying, this freshman might have done quite well. Unfortunately, they didn't, and school administrators suggested that Mr. Szody leave school until he was more serious about his education.

After working at a number of part-time jobs, Szody decided that he might like law enforcement. He re-entered Monterey Peninsula College with a major in criminal justice. This time around, Dave was more motivated and seemed to have a purpose. His grades improved and he was well on his way to a respectable career. *Not so fast*, said Uncle Sam. *Your name is high on the military draft lottery list and we need fine young men like you in Vietnam.* Szody saw the handwriting on the wall and enlisted in the U.S. Air Force.

While reviewing his background, Air Force personnel learned that Airman Szody had majored in criminal justice. Immediately after completing his basic training, Dave was sent to Colorado Springs to be trained as an air policeman. He did very well and became so enthusiastic about his new position that he actually volunteered to go to Vietnam. The Air Force was happy to oblige, and on December 4, 1966, Air Policeman Szody landed in the middle of an assault on Tan Son Nhut Air Base, just outside of Saigon. A week later, he was shipped north to Phu Yen Province and Tuy Hoa Air Base, which would remain his new home for the next year.

As Airman Szody toured Vietnam, he was struck by the abject poverty that was seemingly everywhere. His own upbringing could have been described as poor by American standards, but the compassionate young man had never seen anything like this. Children with virtually no clothes would run after the military vehicles, begging for food and anything else the soldiers could provide. There was little time for reflection while under the relentless stress of combat, but these scenes became permanently fixed in Dave Szody's mind. He told himself that if he made it through this chaos, he would take life more seriously at home and try to make a difference in the world.

Szody finished his tour of duty in 1970 and went back to Monterey, where he promptly married his high school sweetheart. He and his bride moved to Santa Rosa, where Dave took advantage of the GI Bill and enrolled in Santa Rosa Junior College. Money was tight, so he took a part-time job on a Pacific Gas and Electric construction crew. One crew member, whom Dave described as a "loudmouthed blowhard," made a lasting impression on him. It seems the crew was out in the field eating lunch one day, when the conversation turned to hunting and fishing. Bert, the crew member in question, started bragging about his illegal deer hunting exploits. "If a game warden ever catches me in the woods, only one of us is coming out and it's not going to be the game warden," said Bert, with his usual bluster. Szody didn't say anything at the time. Instead he made up his mind, then and there, to be a Fish and Game warden. He would take great pleasure in throwing outlaws like Bert in jail.

Soon after, Szody moved to Sacramento and enrolled in the Sacramento State University Criminal Justice Program, with a minor in biological science. While attending the same upper-division zoology class at Sacramento State, Dave Szody and I discussed our career plans: we both wanted to be Fish and Game wardens but would seek park ranger positions if that didn't materialize. This is where it gets interesting: I was hired as a park ranger for Sacramento County, and a short time later, Dave was hired as a park ranger for Monterey County. I was hired by the Department of Fish and Game in 1974 and assigned to the Earp Patrol District, while Szody was hired by the Department of Fish and Game six months later and assigned to the adjoining Blythe/Palo Verde District. We became lifelong friends and ended up working and solving wildlife crimes together for most of the next thirty years.

***

CALVIN LEMASTER WAS IMPERIAL County's resident deputy sheriff for an isolated area along the Colorado River that stretched from the Riverside County Line to the Mexican border. With the exception of one or two California Highway Patrolmen, LeMaster and Fish and Game Warden Dave Szody were the only enforcement officers in this fifty-mile expanse of scorching desert. They relied on each other for backup from time to time, whether it was a Fish and Game matter or a bar fight.

"Wade, I can't find the Zingers," grumbled Deputy LeMaster. Calvin LeMaster loved those bite-sized morsels of sugar-coated goodness and seldom finished a patrol without at least one stop at Bowman's Bait and Tackle.

Wade Somers was the proprietor of this four-hundred-square-foot establishment in the heart of downtown Palo Verde—population 123. It was the only store in town and Wade specialized in selling beer, booze, cigarettes, soft drinks, junk food, and fishing tackle. Most of his customers came from the busloads of farm workers who stopped in after a hard day's work. The backroom of this little gold mine was always stacked to the ceiling with cases of beer, which Wade turned over just about every forty-eight hours.

Deputy LeMaster continued to spin the lazy Susan several more times. "We still have cupcakes, Sno Balls, Twinkies, Ho Hos, and fruit pies," said Somers, "but I'm sorry, Calvin, we're out of Zingers. The delivery truck should be here this afternoon. Can you hold out until then?"

Calvin LeMaster was thirty-five years old. He was short and stocky, with forty pounds of excess weight centered between his gun belt and the steering wheel, and wore horn-rimmed glasses held in place by an elastic band. "Okay, I'll be back," said Calvin, as he flopped into the driver's seat of his patrol unit and headed south on Highway 78.

That same morning in late April 1976, Warden Dave Szody and I were patrolling the Colorado River south of Palo Verde. Szody pulled his patrol car off the pavement onto a dusty, unpaved road that meandered a mile or so through a thick forest of mesquite, arrowweed, and tamarisk before finally reaching the river.

"Where does this lead?" I asked, rolling up my passenger-side window to escape the billowing dust.

"There's a little camp spot down here next to the river," said Szody. "A couple weeks ago I caught two guys in here shooting quail out of season. It was also the closest I've ever come to being bitten by a rattlesnake."

"Really? How'd that happen?"

"I was sneaking up on these guys through the salt cedar, when I came face-to-face with this huge diamondback. It must have been seven feet long and as big around as your arm."

"What'd ya do?"

"I didn't know what to do! It was just lying there in the shade. There was a big bulge in its body, like it had just eaten a ground squirrel or something."

"Was it rattling?"

"No, if it had been, I'm sure those two guys would have heard it. I couldn't see 'em through the brush, but I could hear 'em talking."

"Did you know your dashboard panel is about to fall off?"

"Yeah, I'm hoping this Matador will hold together until I get my new truck."

"Anyway, what happened with the snake?"

"I couldn't do anything, so I just stood there, hoping the snake would behave itself and stay curled up against the trunk of that salt cedar."

"Are we gonna be able to make it through this gully without getting stuck?"

"As long as we don't slow down in this soft sand, I think we'll be all right."

"If we get stuck in here, nobody will ever find us," I said.

"Somebody's been in here recently. Those tire tracks look pretty fresh," Szody said.

"So what happened?"

"What were we talking about?"

"The snake and the quail poachers."

"Oh, I could hear this one guy bragging about ground-sluicing a covey of quail and killing six in one shot. After hearing that, I left the snake where it was and walked out in the open."

"Were they camped in here?"

"Yeah, they had been fishing for catfish all night. I found the quail hidden at the bottom of an ice chest, under a pile of fish."

"Something must have died," I said. "Look at all those vultures circling."

"We'll park and walk in from here," said Szody, "in case those are fresh tracks ahead of us."

Taking care not to slam the car doors, Szody and I quietly crept up the trail toward the river. We were nearing the campsite when we rounded a bend and spotted a rusted-out, light blue pickup. Szody pointed to a side trail that led upstream from the camp. We followed it to a point overlooking the river, where we immediately spotted two men fishing from the bank.

With no other enforcement issues demanding our immediate attention, we decided to remain hidden and watch the two fishermen for a while. Both anglers appeared to be in their late fifties or early sixties. Judging from their heavy-duty fishing rods, our subjects were after flatheads or large channel cats. Their intentions became even more evident when one of the fishermen baited his hook with a baseball-sized chunk of red meat and flung it halfway across the river.

"What are these guys using for bait?" I whispered.

"It looked like some kind of red meat," said Szody. "You don't suppose they shot a deer?"

We continued watching for a half hour longer, until the other fisherman baited his hook with an even larger chunk of red meat and cast it into the river. "I've seen enough," said Szody. "Let's go see what these guys are up to."

Warden Szody and I walked into the camp, which was shaded by two large tamarisk trees. Both fishermen were sitting in lawn chairs, facing the river. I noticed fresh ironwood coals in the fire pit and a bloody hunting knife swarming with yellow jackets lying on top of a large ice chest.

"Hello," said Szody. "How's the fishing?"

Startled by the sound of Warden Szody's voice, both fishermen jerked their heads around, looks of utter shock on their grizzled, unshaven faces. I stood in the shadows, monitoring the scene from ten yards away. One of the fishermen finally spotted me and blurted, "Oh, there's two of you."

"Are you catching any fish?" repeated Szody. Neither fisherman immediately responded.

The larger of the two, a roly-poly gray-haired gentleman wearing overalls and a dirt-stained navy-blue T-shirt, finally said, "We caught a couple catfish." His companion stood by silently, stroking his reddish-gray beard.

"Where are the fish?" asked Szody, addressing the bearded fisherman.

The bearded angler turned his head and nodded in the direction of the river. Watching this familiar scene play out, I reflected on a similar incident I had witnessed, many years before, while riding on patrol with my father.

My father had contacted two middle-aged striped bass fishermen downstream from Ord Ferry, on the west bank of the Sacramento River. While I watched from a distance, my father asked if the gentlemen had caught any fish. "No," said the larger of the two, squeezed into an overburdened, aluminum lawn chair. "We haven't had a bite." Even at age sixteen, I recognized that the fisherman's reply did not correspond with his body language: his posture was rigid, his hands shook, and he began talking a mile a minute. I continued to watch as my father examined the frozen sardines the men were using for bait: resting on a board next to a fly-covered knife, only the heads and tails remained. *Wait a minute!* I thought. *That fisherman just told my father they hadn't had a bite, yet they'd cut up and used two ten-inch sardines for bait.*

My father had been conversing with the two fishermen for another ten minutes or so, when something quite unusual happened: a flopping twelve-inch striped bass emerged from the soft sand at his feet, followed by another, and still another. Reaching into the sand, my father pulled up a metal stringer containing seven more striped bass, all shorter than the legally required sixteen inches. I later asked my father if he had known something was wrong.

"I knew they were up to something when the big guy lied to me," he said.

"How did you know he was lying?" I asked.

"Everybody on the river's been throwing back short stripers all week. These two had used up two whole sardines. How do you do that without getting a bite?"

"Did you suspect they had illegal fish?"

"I figured they had 'em stashed somewhere, but I didn't expect 'em to pop out of the ground."

WARDEN SZODY WALKED TO the water's edge and untied a length of heavy twine that was wrapped around a tree root. At the other end he found several channel catfish, all weighing between six and twelve pounds. "Wow!" said Szody. "You guys have had some luck. What's your secret?"

Without mentioning the massive gobs of red meat they'd used to bait their hooks, the bearded angler finally replied, "I don't know—patience I guess."

"Have you guys been here all night?" asked Szody.

"Yeah, we come in yesterday evenin'," said the bearded fisherman.

"Where are you fellas from?"

"El Centro," said the angler in overalls, lighting a cigarette.

While Warden Szody questioned the two fishermen further, I walked over and lifted the lid on the generous ice chest. Inside, I found the skinned-out hind leg of a large animal. At first I thought it might have belonged to a deer, but the color of the meat wasn't right and dark strands of strange-looking hair were floating in the melted ice. Chunks of meat had been cut away from the shank with the bloody knife I delicately returned to the lid of the ice chest. "Is this what you guys are using for bait?" I shouted, pointing to the ice chest. Neither fisherman answered. "Where'd this meat come from?" Again no response.

I walked over to the fishermen's pickup and saw a lever action 30-30 rifle lodged in the gun rack mounted in the rearview window. Reaching for the rifle, I opened the action and ejected a live round from the chamber. Walking back into camp with rifle in hand, I asked, "Which one of you fellas used this rifle last?"

"The rifle and the pickup belong to me," said the angler clad in overalls. "What difference does it make?"

At that point, Warden Szody and I felt it was time to end the foreplay and ask for fishing licenses and identification.

The fisherman wearing overalls was identified as Llars Wesley Lamb, fifty-eight years old, from El Centro, California. His bearded partner was identified as Miles Henry Biggs, fifty-seven years old, also from El Centro.

"Mr. Lamb, would you please explain what this chunk of meat is and where it came from?" I asked.

"It's horse meat," said Lamb, after some hesitation. "I brought it from home to use for bait."

"It must have been a half-grown foal," I said. "That shank didn't come from a full-grown horse."

I had begun to question Lamb further, when an image of circling vultures popped into my head. The carrion-craving scavengers we had noticed earlier were approximately fifty yards south of the location where Warden Szody had parked his patrol car. Out of earshot from Lamb and Biggs, I shared my thoughts with Warden Szody, who also remembered the vultures. We decided that I would remain with the fishermen while Szody walked back and retrieved his patrol car. While there, he would check out whatever it was that had attracted the vultures.

When Szody reached his patrol car, he again spotted the vultures. Their numbers had actually doubled during the previous hour. Fortunately, there was a well-used wild burro trail through the snake-infested mesquite, salt cedar, and arrowweed thicket. Hoof prints in the crusty, alkaline soil led Szody directly to what we had been looking for—a freshly killed, half-grown wild burro with a bullet hole in its shoulder and one of its hind legs cut away.

Back in the early 1950s, a Nevada woman named Annie Johnson, famously known as Wild Horse Annie, began a two-decades-long campaign to save free-roaming wild horses and burros from being killed and removed from public lands. As a result of her efforts, the United States Congress passed the Wild and Free-Roaming Horses and Burros Act of 1971. Among other things, this act prohibited the killing of wild horses and burros. The California State Legislature followed suit and passed Section 4600 of the California Fish and Game Code, also prohibiting the killing of wild burros.

Many people, myself among them, were concerned about the serious negative impact that wild horses and burros have on the scarce desert waterholes that deer, bighorn sheep, small mammals, and numerous bird species depend upon for survival. I had personally seen desert springs fouled and depleted by these large, nonnative mammals, and I wasn't enthusiastic about a law that would allow them to compete with native wildlife on public lands.

Warden Szody drove his patrol car into the fishermen's camp and filled me in on what he'd found. Someone had shot a young burro with a high-powered rifle. The burro appeared fresh enough to have been killed during the previous twenty-four hours. One of the hind legs had been cut away from the carcass. The approximate size of the other leg matched the shank inside the ice chest. The dead burro was dark brown—the same color as the hair floating in the ice chest.

When confronted with this seemingly overwhelming evidence, the two fishermen stuck to their original story.

"I told you I brought that horse meat from home," insisted Lamb.

"Are you sure you want to stick with that story?" I said.

"You guys are pissin' up a rope," responded Lamb. "You ain't got nothin' on us."

If there had ever been any doubt in Szody's or my mind about whether to charge these two characters with the crime of killing a wild burro, Lamb's response removed it. Lamb and Biggs were behaving as if the whole thing was a joke. They had clearly failed the attitude test. I pulled out my Miranda card and began reading. Still confident that we were bluffing, both men agreed to talk to us.

"Listen carefully," I said, "because this is what's going to happen. Warden Szody will file a formal criminal complaint with the district attorney, charging both of you with unlawful possession of an illegally taken burro. By that, I'm talking about the meat in that ice chest that you both used to bait your hooks. Mr. Lamb, you will also be charged with having a loaded rifle in a vehicle. Speaking of the rifle, it will be seized into evidence and matched with the slug inside the burro. Since there was no exit hole, the slug shouldn't be hard to find."

"All right!" blurted Lamb. "I shot the jackass. No need to bring Miles into this."

Based on Lamb's admission, he was charged with killing the wild burro and having a loaded rifle in the vehicle on a way open to the public. Biggs was charged with possession of unlawfully taken burro meat, since he had used it to bait his hook.

"How did you know there wasn't an exit hole in that donkey?" asked Szody, as we drove back out to the main road.

"Was there?" I asked.

"I didn't see one," Szody replied.

IT WAS ABOUT 11:00 a.m. when Warden Szody and I heard the sheriff's dispatcher calling on the radio.

"Fish and Game five seven one, Deputy LeMaster requests backup at the Ox Bow Lake swimming area. This is a non-emergency."

"Ten-four," responded Szody. "ETA fifteen."

Deputy LeMaster's patrol unit was already parked in the gravel parking area when we arrived. We could see him down by the lake, talking to a group of seemingly angry women and several small children. One of the women was pointing toward a man who was sitting on a towel at the southernmost edge of the beach. I picked up my binoculars. "Don't look now," I said. "That guy doesn't have a stitch on."

DEPUTY LEMASTER LEFT THE women and walked toward the other side of the lake, where the man was still sunbathing. Warden Szody signaled LeMaster that we were close by and would provide backup if needed. "Hey, you need to put some clothes on," shouted LeMaster, as he approached the sunbather. "I also need to see some identification."

"What's the hassle, man?" said the sunbather in a deep, throaty voice. He had reddish, shoulder-length hair tied in a ponytail. Rising to his feet, the sunbather wrapped the towel around his waist.

"That guy makes Calvin look like a dwarf," I commented, walking across the gravel parking area.

"It won't make any difference to Calvin," said Szody. "He's like a little bulldog."

"I need to see some identification," repeated LeMaster, staring up at the towering provocateur.

"Chill out, man. It's in my car."

"Let's go get it," said LeMaster. "I'll follow you over there."

Deputy LeMaster accompanied the sunbather back to an older model green station wagon, packed to the roof with clothes, camping gear, magazines, and assorted junk. A pair of shorts was hanging from the rearview mirror; the young man quickly grabbed the shorts and put them on. He rummaged through his belongings for about five minutes before finally producing a California Driver's License. The license belonged to Dwight William Murphy, thirty-three years old, out of Fontana, California.

"Why am I being harassed?" asked Murphy.

Deputy LeMaster ignored the question, but it obviously agitated him. He walked over to the green station wagon, opened the front door, and began to look inside.

"What are you doing?" shouted Murphy.

"I'm searching for weapons," answered LeMaster.

"What right do you have to search my car?"

Deputy LeMaster opened the back door and continued to rummage through Murphy's junk. When he had finished a cursory search of Murphy's car, Murphy began shouting in the officer's ear again: "What right do you have to search my car? I demand to know!"

It hadn't been that long since Warden Szody and I had been students in Mr. Dillon's search and seizure class at the Riverside Sheriff's Academy. We were particularly interested in how Deputy LeMaster was going to answer Murphy's question. As Murphy continued to shout in the officer's ear, Szody nudged me and whispered, "I think Calvin has had about enough. He's about to arrest this guy for 148 or indecent exposure, maybe both."

Warden Szody and I knew that Deputy LeMaster had reached his boiling point when his chest puffed out and his face turned a bright shade of crimson. Looking straight up at the recalcitrant man, LeMaster spoke in a clear and authoritative voice, giving Murphy the long-awaited answer to his question: "You want to know what right I have to search your car? I'll tell you what right I have to search your car. Screw you! This is Imperial County, scumbag. We do things differently in Imperial County."

"Is that it?" I whispered.

"I think so," said Szody.

Dave and I glanced at each other, both straining to contain ourselves. We hadn't learned anything like that in Mr. Dillon's search and seizure class. Did Calvin know something we didn't?

Apparently Deputy LeMaster's technique had its intended effect: the previously irate sunbather immediately quieted down and began to cooperate. After checking for outstanding warrants, LeMaster ordered Murphy to leave the river and not come back. Murphy must have taken Calvin's words seriously, because that was the last time anyone down along the river ever saw that green station wagon.

Dave and I drove out of the parking lot shaking our heads and roaring with laughter. We didn't stop laughing until we reached Wade Somers's store. Calvin was already inside, enjoying a package of Zingers.

Sometimes the Good Guys Lose

———◆———

ASSIGNING A ROOKIE FISH and Game warden to San Francisco was like throwing him into the Zambezi River during the wildebeest migration. This had to be one of the busiest, most diverse, complicated, and dangerous first assignments in California. Warden Nick Albert wasn't a big man—about five-nine and 165 pounds—but he did come to Fish and Game with two years of invaluable law enforcement experience working for the Seaside Police Department. Seaside was a bedroom community for Fort Ord—one of the U.S. Army's largest training centers.

On any given work day, Warden Albert might have been working waterfowl hunters near Candlestick Park or enforcing sport and commercial fishing regulations along the San Francisco waterfront. His patrol district contained hundreds of markets, pet shops, ivory shops, curio shops, common carriers, and traditional Asian medicine shops for a wildlife protection officer to inspect. Any one of those establishments might have possessed illegal fish or wildlife from anyplace in the world.

"Chinatown was a particularly busy place for me," said Albert. "Not only did some Chinese markets and shops sell illegal wildlife, but we had our hands full with sport fishermen showing up on the back streets and alleys, selling fish directly out of their cars and trucks. I remember arresting two men for selling over a thousand crappie, all of them seined from the backwaters of Clear Lake. The violators were weighing the fish in the bed of their pickup and selling them to a crowd of Chinese residents who had gathered on the street."

When Warden Albert wasn't saving wildlife, he was serving Fish and Game arrest warrants from judicial districts all over California. "San Francisco residents would travel up to the Delta or somewhere in the Central Valley and commit Fish and Game violations," said Albert. "They would be issued a citation with a date to appear in court printed on the bottom. Many of those people forgot about showing up in court the minute they crossed the Bay Bridge back into the city. I had a hundred or more warrants waiting to be served at any given time."

***

ON A WEEKDAY MORNING in late November 1975, Warden Nick Albert was driving in bumper-to-bumper traffic between Daly City and San Francisco when he received an urgent radio call from Region III Fish and Game headquarters.

"Warden Bailey requests an immediate landline at the regional office," said the dispatcher.

"Ten-four," said Albert. "I'll make the call ASAP." In those days wardens didn't have cellphones, so ASAP could mean five minutes or a half hour, depending on how far that warden was from a payphone. Albert happened to be near an off-ramp, so he flipped on his blinker, drove into the first gas station he saw, and dropped a quarter into the slot.

Being new to the job, Warden Albert hadn't met all the Region III wardens. He knew that Warden Harold Bailey worked out of Napa and that he was one of the more senior officers. That was about it.

"This is Warden Albert, responding to a call from Warden Bailey."

"Just a minute," said the dispatcher. "He's here in the office somewhere."

"Nick, where are you?" said Bailey.

"I'm at a payphone in Daly City."

"How soon can you get to the north side of the Bay Bridge?"

"That depends on the traffic. Maybe a half-hour."

"I'm told you're the only one on duty in San Francisco, so here's the situation. I just received a phone call from an informant who absolutely must remain confidential. According to the informant, two men are headed for San Francisco with a large number of ducks right now."

"Where did they kill the ducks?" asked Albert.

"They shot 'em this morning, before daylight, somewhere near Grizzly Island."

"Do you have a license number and description of the car?"

"We don't have a license number, but it's a light green VW Bug. The informant says you can't miss these guys. They're so big they make the car look like a tin can."

"That's just great! I feel better already. Any idea where they're headed?"

"The informant overheard 'em talking about a market in Chinatown. That's all I know."

"What about names?"

"The informant was reluctant to provide names. He's scared to death of these guys. He said the last time they did this, he threatened to turn them in, and they beat the crap out of him. All I could squeeze out of this guy is the driver's last name. It's Farmer."

"That's not much to go on, particularly for a car stop. What about the passenger?"

"Oh yeah, he said he heard Farmer call him Chaz."

Albert and Bailey discussed the possible route that the duck poachers might take to San Francisco. Both agreed they would most likely come through Berkeley on Interstate 80. The poachers' travel time was estimated at less than an hour, so Warden Albert would not have time to secure an undercover vehicle.

"You'll have to follow them the best you can in your patrol car," said Bailey. "Don't get so close that they see you, and don't lose 'em."

"Gee thanks!" said Albert, imagining the task ahead—spotting a green VW Bug among thousands of passing cars, all traveling at seventy miles per hour, was going to be like finding an anchovy in a school of sardines. *Following them through the streets of San Francisco in a marked patrol car without being seen? He's gotta be kidding!*

"If you do make a stop, don't tell them where you got the information," said Bailey.

"Understood," said Albert. "I better get going."

Warden Albert raced eastward on Highway 80, across the Bay Bridge in his 1975 Plymouth Fury patrol car. Like most Fish and Game patrol cars of the day, Albert's was dark green, with Fish and Game emblems on each door and a red spotlight mounted in front of the driver's-side window. Exiting on University Avenue, Albert parked along the westbound lane of the highway, behind a patch of oleander bushes.

Within ten minutes of hiding his patrol car, he saw a green VW Bug with two very large men inside zip by. Warden Albert drove back onto the freeway and was able to follow the suspects across the bridge and into the city. As expected, the suspects took the exit leading into the heart of San Francisco's Chinatown District. Albert skillfully maneuvered through the traffic and was able to stay several cars behind as the VW bug proceeded onto Grant Street. Unfortunately, the farther into the city the duck poachers went, the narrower the streets became. With delivery trucks parked in every loading zone, traffic came to a virtual standstill on several occasions.

Warden Albert had managed to stay two cars behind the suspects until both cars in front of him made sudden right turns and left him completely exposed. As the suspects pulled up in front of a Chinese market, the driver caught a glimpse of Albert's patrol car in his rearview mirror, and off they went, racing back into the moving traffic, barely missing the side of a delivery truck. The passenger turned around and stared back at Albert. Making a sharp right turn, the VW Bug raced two blocks, made a half-second stop at a stop sign, and turned onto Vallejo Street. Albert was thirty yards behind when he turned on his red light. The suspects immediately pulled to the side of the road and stopped.

Unwittingly, the suspects had led Warden Albert to the San Francisco Central Police Station, which was directly across the street. The occupants of the VW Bug could be seen conversing as Warden Albert climbed out of his patrol car, looked back for oncoming traffic, then walked around to the sidewalk and approached from the passenger side. Suddenly both doors flew open. "When those two bruisers stormed out of that little car, I felt like a 165-pound halfback about to be flattened," Albert would say later.

"What right do you have to stop us?" demanded the driver.

"I want your badge number," shouted the passenger.

"It's right here on my chest," said Albert. "Would you please open the trunk?"

"I will not!" shouted the driver. "You have no right to search my car."

"I'm asking for permission to search your car," said Albert.

"I refuse to give it to you," said the driver, his eyes suddenly diverted to three uniformed police officers rapidly approaching from across the street.

"It's Fish and Game," said one of the officers.

Rather than stand and argue with the driver of the car, Warden Albert walked over and met with the City of San Francisco police officers.

"We thought you might need some backup," said the approaching sergeant. The name Wilkens was etched on his name tag.

"I really appreciate it," said Albert. "I received a tip that these guys have a load of illegal ducks in their trunk. They're not being very cooperative at the moment."

"We'd be happy to stand by in case you need us," said the sergeant.

"That would be great," said Albert.

All three city police officers walked over and surrounded the VW Bug, as Warden Albert once again addressed the two poaching suspects.

"Here's the situation," said Warden Albert. "I received information that you have illegal ducks inside your vehicle. I'm going to search your trunk with or without your consent."

The driver stared into Warden Albert's determined eyes. Glancing back at the other officers, he shrugged his shoulders, mumbled a few expletives, and popped open the trunk, located at the front of the car.

Crammed inside the tiny trunk were two large duffle bags, each one stuffed with recently killed wild ducks. Although duck season was open at the time and both suspects had licenses and appropriate duck stamps, they possessed a total of sixty-three wild ducks—most of them mallards and pintails—far exceeding the legal bag and possession limits. All of the ducks were seized into evidence.

The driver was identified as Arthur Neel Farmer, a thirty-two-year-old construction supervisor out of Napa. His thirty-two-year-old partner, Charles Robert Hawkins, also worked in construction and provided a Fairfield address. Farmer and Hawkins were sent on their way with the understanding that charges would be filed and they would be notified when and where to appear in court.

Warden Albert was disappointed he had not been able to catch Farmer and Hawkins in the act of unloading the ducks, thereby avoiding a possible stop and search challenge. Should the duck poachers secure legal counsel, the attorney would undoubtedly demand to know the source of Fish and Game's information. *I'll worry about that later*, thought Albert. *Right now I'm going to contact that Chinese market we passed. If they're buying ducks from these guys, they could be buying from others.*

Albert thanked the San Francisco police officers for their assistance and raced back to the Chinese market. Within seconds of the uniformed Fish and Game officer entering the store, an employee began shouting in a high-pitched voice. Albert didn't understand a word of it, but had a good idea what the shouting was all about. He walked straight to the rear of the market and pushed through a set of swinging doors just in time to hear the door to the walk-in cooler clank shut. Seconds later another employee, this one wearing a green apron, stepped out of the cooler. Panic washed across the employee's face at the sight of Warden Albert; the young clerk's fear was almost palpable.

"I'm here to make a routine fish and wildlife inspection," said Albert. The young man nodded and cracked a slight smile. "Do you understand what I'm saying?" The young man again smiled but did not respond. Since the market regularly bought and sold commercially caught fish, the search fell well within the scope of California Fish and Game Code Section 1006:

> The Department may inspect the following:
> (a) All boats, markets, stores, and other buildings, except dwellings, and all receptacles, except the clothing actually worn by a person at the time of inspection, where birds, mammals, fish, reptiles or amphibia may be stored, placed, or held for sale or storage.

With the door still open, Albert stepped inside the cooler and noticed a large box in the back corner with several aprons and a pair of rubber boots piled on top. While the store clerk watched, he removed the boots and aprons, discovering an assortment of freshly killed wild ducks inside the box.

"Interesting," mumbled Albert. "These must have come from here in the Bay." Instead of the usual mallards and pintails, the box contained a collection of what Warden Albert called "divers": scaup, ring-necks, redheads, and canvasbacks.

Albert glanced over his shoulder and found that the young store employee had vanished. A middle-aged Asian gentleman appeared in the doorway, identifying himself as Mr. Chen Ho, the market owner.

"I would like to see your records for the purchase of these ducks," said Albert.

"I don't know anything about ducks," said the proprietor. "One of my employees must have brought them in."

"What about this fish?" asked Albert, pointing to a nine-pound striped bass.

"I don't know anything about that, either," said Ho.

Warden Albert inspected the remainder of the store for unlawfully possessed fish or wildlife. He found several commercially caught ocean fish, for which Mr. Ho had the required legal documentation. Charges were filed against market owner Chen Ho for being in unlawful possession for sale of seventeen ducks and one striped bass. "Ho didn't receive any jail time," said Albert, "but the fine was quite significant for those days—about $1,000, as I recall. Commercial activities in Chinatown were always a major problem for us. Many cases were made."

SEVERAL MONTHS AFTER FILING charges against Farmer and Hawkins for possession of fifty-three ducks over the legal limit, Warden Albert received a subpoena to appear for a hearing in San Francisco Federal Court. As expected, Farmer's and Hawkins's attorney, paid for by Farmer's wealthy father, had filed a motion to rule the evidence seized in the search as inadmissible.

On the morning of the hearing, Albert received a phone call from Warden Bailey.

"The informant must be protected at all costs," said Bailey. "I promised we wouldn't give him up."

Realizing the predicament that Fish and Game was in, the prosecuting attorney purposely kept Warden Bailey out of the picture. The information provided for the stop and search had come from a "confidential" informant, not an "anonymous" informant. Bailey knew the identity of the informant, but Warden Albert didn't. The plan was to keep it that way.

With Warden Albert on the witness stand, the prosecutor provided the judge with his best argument for what he described as a legal stop and search.

"After all," said the prosecutor, "Fish and Game didn't just pick out a green VW Bug from amongst thousands of passing cars on the highway and decide to randomly stop and search it." Warden Albert looked over at Farmer and Hawkins, both of them seated at the defendant's table, next to their attorney. Albert noticed Farmer doing something quite peculiar: his right hand was clenched in a fist and was continually grinding into the palm of his left hand.

As the hearing progressed, the defense attorney continued his relentless efforts to have Fish and Game divulge its source. "If Fish and Game cannot or will not produce the identity of the informant, the case must be dismissed," he insisted. Unfortunately, the judge agreed and did not feel there was justification for keeping the informant's identity a secret.

The prosecution faced a complicated legal and moral dilemma: if they gave up the informant, he could fall victim to retribution by the defendants. If the prosecutors advised the judge that they couldn't reveal the informant's identity for fear he would be beaten, the defendants would immediately know who the informant was. Much to the disappointment of Warden Albert and the prosecuting attorney, the case was dismissed.

Thirty-nine years later, I asked now-retired Captain Nick Albert for his thoughts. "Hal Bailey had his reasons for protecting his informant," said Albert, "even at the expense of the case. Sometimes the good guys lose."

The A-Frame

———◆———

I T WAS LATE AUGUST or early September of 1975 when I received the call. I
had been on the job about a year and was still learning the ins and outs of
my first patrol district. My boss was James A. Reynolds, the sixty-year-old
supervisor of the Colorado River Captain's Squad. Other members of Captain
Reynolds's band of desert rats were Dave Fry in Needles, Jim Worthington in
Blythe, Dave Szody in Palo Verde, and Burt Pruett in Winterhaven.

"Hello, old son," said Reynolds, calling from his home office in Blythe.
"Inspector Traub says he needs three men from the river to work the deer
opener. I'm supposed to send one of you guys up to Santa Maria and the other
two to Ventura County."

"I'll volunteer!" I said, jumping at any opportunity to escape the sweltering
desert heat for a few days.

"Dave Robinson's Santa Maria district is mostly private land," said
Reynolds. "Last year, all he and Worthington did was respond to trespass
calls. I'd like you to experience what a real deer opener is like, so I'm sending
you and Pruett up to the A-Frame."

"How long has Burt been on the job?" I asked. Warden Pruett and I had
been introduced at one of the squad meetings, but I didn't know much about
him.

"He was a warden up on the North Coast for four or five years before
taking the Winterhaven position," said Reynolds. "You know, that was the
first time in the history of the Department that anyone has ever voluntarily
transferred to a position out here in the desert."

"What is the A-Frame, Jim?"

"Glad you asked. This former commercial pilot built an A-frame cabin out west of the Grapevine, near a place called Lake of the Woods. If I remember correctly, he even has his own air strip. The wardens who work the Ventura deer opener traditionally bunk at the cabin for the weekend. We've been doing that for years. Headquarters will send you directions and all the details. You might want to leave a day early. It takes five or six hours to get there."

Two days before everyone else was expected to arrive at the A-Frame, I hopped in my road-weary Dodge Power Wagon and headed across the desert toward Los Angeles. I remember that trip vividly, because the needle on my patrol truck's temperature gauge shot way over to the right as I climbed the grade between Desert Center and Chiriaco Summit. With the outside temperature hovering around 110 degrees, I had to roll down the windows and turn the heater on full blast to keep the radiator from boiling over.

IT WAS ABOUT FOUR in the afternoon when I passed through Gorman on Interstate 5 and finally came to the Frazier Mountain Park turnoff. I grabbed something to eat at a greasy spoon along the highway and headed west toward Frazier Park and Lake of the Woods. The now famous A-Frame sat at the base of a mountain meadow, near the intersection of Lockwood Valley Road and Cuddy Valley Road. I found a note tacked to the front door:

FISH AND GAME: COME ON IN AND MAKE
YOURSELVES AT HOME.

Photos of airplanes and pilots covered the walls of the cabin. It was a virtual aviation museum. Being the first to arrive, I had my choice of bunks. Single beds, couches, and cots were set up all over the lower living area. Imagining how much snoring, storytelling, and card playing would be going on downstairs, I decided to check out the loft.

"This should be a little quieter," I said. "Only two bunks up here." I unfolded my sleeping bag and threw it down on the bunk next to a large open window. Having been up since the crack of dawn, I removed my gun belt, boots, and uniform shirt, then sat down. I spent a few minutes looking over a U.S. Forest Service map of the area but couldn't stay awake. Enjoying the fresh air, I lay back and closed my eyes, wondering what new and exciting experiences my first deer opener would bring. Every couple of minutes a wind gust would whistle into the room, blowing the nylon curtains over my head, slamming the cord against the wall. Then I went out like a light.

It must have been close to 8:00 p.m. when I awakened to the sound of footsteps on the wooden stairway.

"How ya doin'?" came a voice from the darkness.

"Oh," I said, rubbing my eyes and attempting to focus on a burly, dark-haired figure at the top of the stairs. "Is that you, Burt?"

"None other," replied Warden Pruett, dropping his gear on the adjacent bunk.

"I wasn't sure if you were coming up today or tomorrow."

"How do you like the job so far? Are you getting used to the desert heat?"

"Every day's a new adventure," I said. The long, brutally hot summer had worn me down a bit, but I really was enjoying myself.

"Yeah," said Pruett, "I bet you work at night a lot."

"Yes, I do. And early in the morning."

"That position was vacant for a long time before you came. I think Reynolds sent Colby up there once or twice to fly the colors."

"What about you?" I asked. "Jim told me that you had actually transferred to the Winterhaven position."

"I did," said Pruett. "My wife and I got tired of the fog and rain on the North Coast. I've always been interested in the desert and that Old West area down around Yuma, so we decided to try a change of scenery."

"What kind of activity do you have in Winterhaven?"

"Not a hell of a lot. I have a boat to work the river and the backwaters, but I spend most of my time working the All American Canal at night."

Warden Pruett didn't sound too enthusiastic, so I asked if he planned to stay in Winterhaven.

"Probably not," he replied. "We're about ready to move again."

"Moving is a lot of work, isn't it?"

"Not the way we do it," said Pruett. "The last time we sold all our furniture and moved to Yuma, everything we owned fit into our Bronco and a little trailer."

Warden Pruett and I sat and talked until about 10:00. I had just returned to the loft after brushing my teeth when I glanced out the window and noticed a vehicle driving by on the dirt road in front of the cabin.

"Are they running a spotlight?" I asked. A beam of bright light was darting back and forth in the mountain meadow on the opposite side of the road.

Pruett flipped off the light switch in the loft and we watched from the window as the car continued west.

"They sure as hell are," said Pruett. "Put your boots on. I'll drive."

I hadn't seen anyone work a spotlight since my teenage years in Orland, when I rode on patrol with my father. To say that I was excited was an understatement. We were going to make a spotlighting case before the regional supervisor and the other wardens even arrived. I quickly laced my boots, put on my uniform shirt, grabbed my gun belt, and scampered down the stairs. Pruett's patrol car was a two-wheel-drive sedan—not exactly suited for off-road driving—but he had seniority and wanted to take his car, so I followed his lead and hopped in the passenger seat.

We could barely see the suspect vehicle's taillights as it proceeded southwest on Lockwood Valley Road. Luckily, a half-moon hung in the sky that night. It provided just enough ambient light to keep us from running off the road and into a ditch. Every time the suspects rounded a bend and disappeared from view, Warden Pruett would flip on his sneak light and try to catch up.

Fish and Game Code Section 2005 was much more difficult to enforce in the 1970s. Wardens were required to see the suspected violators shine their spotlight on a deer or other wildlife while in possession of a firearm or weapon capable of killing that animal. The current and much more enforceable version of Section 2005 simply requires that the poaching suspects shine a light into a field where deer or wildlife may be present. Making a spotlighting case was not going to be easy: if we approached too closely, the suspects were likely to see us; if we stayed too far back, we'd have no idea where they were shining their light. Our subjects pretty much had to kill a deer before we could make a clean case.

That night, Burt Pruett and I followed the spotlighters up one mountain trail and down another for over two hours. We lost them several times, only to see their spotlight again on some distant hillside. At one point, we were on one mountain road and they were on another. Warden Pruett decided to take a shortcut down a primitive, grass-covered trail in hopes of reaching the suspects more quickly. With only the half-moon to light our way, we rolled down the trail at a five-mile-per-hour pace.

"Aren't you worried about hitting something?" I asked.

Warden Pruett replied with this astute observation, which I shall never forget: "Driving in the dark is easy as long as you don't have your head up your ass." *BAM!!!* The split second he uttered those words, we crashed into a large rock and severely dented his right front bumper.

Looking over at Pruett, I said, "I'm not going to say anything." It was bad enough that Inspector Traub would be arriving at the A-frame later that day and Warden Pruett would have to explain how the "accident" occurred. I had no intention of mentioning the mishap to anyone but couldn't resist asking one final question: "Burt, when you fill out the accident report for Captain Reynolds, are you going to include the part about having your head up your ass?" Pruett provided a two-word response, which I shall not repeat.

Adding insult to injury, the spotlighting suspects had disappeared over the mountain. It was almost 2:00 a.m., our spotlighters had disappeared, and it had become abundantly clear that we were lost. Having taken so many side roads and switchbacks, neither one of us had any idea where we were.

"Do you have a map of this area?" I asked.

"No," said Pruett. "I forgot to throw one in."

I remembered studying a Forest Service map the previous afternoon at the A-Frame. "My guess is we're somewhere near Mt. Pinos," I said. "On the other hand, we could be down in the Sespe Range, where the condors are. Or we could be near Ojai."

"You're a big help," said Pruett. "Let's turn around and go back to the Forest Service road."

Warden Pruett and I bounced around for an hour or so, trying one dead-end road after another. We finally came to a wooden Forest Service sign that directed us back toward Lake of the Woods. "It would be a lot easier to explain that dent in your fender if we had made a deer case," I said, as we rounded a bend about four miles from the A-Frame. Just then, an older-model, faded-gray Ford Bronco appeared at the side of the unpaved road ahead.

"What do we have here?" I said.

"Looks like somebody either broke down or ran out of gas," said Pruett.

Two men were standing at the front of the Bronco with the hood up. The tall, skinny one, who turned out to be the driver, wore grease-stained blue jeans and a long-sleeved flannel shirt with the sleeves rolled up. His shorter partner had a little more meat on his bones. He wore blue jeans and a gray sweatshirt. Both looked to be in their early twenties and had cigarettes dangling from the sides of their mouths.

I let Warden Pruett do the talking, while I began to look around. Shining my flashlight through the open front passenger window, I noticed a couple cigarette packages but not much else. The backseat was littered with paper cups and hamburger bags. Sticking out from under the passenger seat was a high-powered rifle cartridge box. I couldn't see clearly into the rear compartment, but I noticed a folded green tarp with a shovel and a tool box on top.

When I joined Warden Pruett at the front of the Bronco, he was still talking to the two subjects. The driver was identified as Brett Charles Hastings, out of Newhall. His partner, Harvey William Borges, said his driver's license had been suspended, but he also lived in Newhall.

"These guys say they were just out riding around when their car broke down," said Pruett.

"Strange time to be out for a joy ride," I responded. "I see you rolled your sleeves down. Why'd you do that?"

"I don't know," mumbled Hastings. "I was cold, I guess."

"Would you mind rolling them back up for me?"

Hastings reluctantly rolled up his sleeves. I shined my flashlight up and down his wrists, exposing several blood stains. Some of the stains on Hastings's pants, which I had previously mistaken for grease, also resembled blood.

Warden Pruett and I looked at each other. Both of us were convinced that these were the guys we had been chasing around the woods all night. I guessed that Hastings and Borges had hidden a deer and their spotlighting equipment somewhere nearby in case the game warden happened to come along.

"Did you already check the rear of the vehicle?" asked Pruett.

"No," I said. "Let's have a look."

Hastings opened the rear compartment, where we found a neatly folded green tarp.

"Is that a tick I see crawling on the tarp?" I said.

"Looks like one to me," said Pruett.

Warden Pruett and I unfolded the tarp, finding deer hair and large splotches of fresh blood inside.

"Okay, boys," said Pruett, "where did you hide the deer?"

Neither Hastings nor Borges would answer. I figured they were hiding more than just a deer or they would have been more forthcoming. The blood on the tarp was still moist and the tick had pretty much cooked their goose. Holding out wasn't going to do them any good. Pruett figured that Hastings and Borges had stashed drugs of some kind, probably marijuana. He agreed to watch the two suspects while I took my flashlight and checked out the immediate area.

The first thing I did was make a wide circle in the dirt around the suspects' Bronco; I began looking for footprints or drag marks. If our suspects had dragged a deer, it would be easy to find. If, on the other hand, they had carried it, one set of footprints would be sideways or backwards. It only took a few minutes to find the spot where the suspects had hurriedly dragged a deer across the road and hidden it behind a manzanita bush. Lying next to a dead spike buck were a bloody knife, a spotlight, and a lever-action 30-30 Winchester rifle. Closely examining the rifle, I noticed that it was adorned with fancy engravings.

Warden Pruett and I figured it was the rifle that concerned the two men most. I ran a record check through the Kern County Sheriff's dispatcher to see if it had been reported stolen. Much to our surprise, it hadn't. Hastings finally came clean and said that the rifle belonged to his father. "My dad's gonna kill me if I lose that rifle," said Hastings. "He doesn't even know I have it."

"Your father's rifle belongs to the court now," I said. "It will be up to the judge whether or not he gets it back." The rifle, deer, spotlight, and knife were all seized into evidence. Hastings and Borges were charged with unlawful take and possession of deer during closed season. At this late date, I don't remember what the two deer poachers were fined, but I believe Hastings's father did manage to get his rifle back. The deer was later delivered to the county jail by one of the Ventura area wardens.

Warden Pruett and I managed to catch a couple hours of sleep before the other Fish and Game officers began to arrive at the A-Frame. The first to arrive was Captain Bob Jamison. Captain Jamison and some of his local wardens supplied the food and provisions for the weekend. Everyone chipped in on the food. The department didn't have lieutenants in those days, so the rest of the detail was made up of seven or eight inland wardens from all over Region V and a few marine wardens out of Region VI. The regional enforcement supervisor, Inspector Jack Traub, would arrive later that evening.

My assignment for the weekend was to patrol an area somewhere between Lake of the Woods and the town of Ojai. From 5:00 a.m. until sundown on opening day, I drove that old Dodge Power Wagon up and down just about every dirt road and jeep trail on the area map. Beginning in lower-elevation chaparral, I progressed through riparian thickets, oak woodlands, pinyons and junipers, pine forests, and back to manzanita again. I crossed a dozen streams and came close to getting stuck in more than a few ditches.

The most common violations I discovered during my first deer season opener involved hunters with loaded rifles in their vehicles and hunters who failed to tag their deer. Those cases were fairly routine. The one case that remains vividly etched in my mind took place about 5:00 that Saturday afternoon. The reason I remember this case so well is because it bothered me so much. I take that back. It didn't just bother me—it infuriated me.

I was patrolling through a lower-elevation area of rolling hills and oak woodlands when I heard a shot coming from the canyon ahead. With binoculars in hand, I climbed to the top of the next hill and began scanning the canyon below. Another shotgun blast rang out. I spotted a hunter walking beside a dry streambed. He was wearing light-colored, checkered pants and a striped T-shirt. The man had apparently killed something, because I watched him reach down to pick it up. Quail season was open at the time. It seemed reasonable that the hunter had killed a quail so I didn't think too much about it. Placing the bird into his game bag, the hunter continued walking. A few minutes later, I saw him stop and point his shotgun at the top of a nearby tree. Again he fired, causing a dark gray bird to fall to the ground. "That wasn't a quail," I said to myself. While I pondered what to do next, the hunter disappeared from view.

I ran back to my patrol truck, topped the hill, and headed into the canyon. Following the same dirt road the hunter had walked a few minutes earlier, I spotted a brown, late-model sedan parked under a patch of mature oak trees. The car began to back up as I approached, so I pulled in behind it.

"Hello," I said, climbing from my pickup. "How are you today?"

"We are doing well," said the driver, in a thick Eastern European accent. "How are you, officer?"

"Fine, thanks," I said, ducking the cloud of cigarette smoke billowing from the driver's-side window. Everyone in the car was smoking.

"Have you fellas been out hunting?"

The two younger men inside the car stared back at me with blank looks on their faces. I wasn't sure if they even understood my question. The driver, an older man in his fifties, finally responded that they hadn't killed anything and only he had been hunting.

I immediately recognized the younger man sitting in the front passenger seat as the hunter who had just shot and killed the gray bird. He was still wearing his checkered pants and striped T-shirt. A shotgun rested in the seat between him and the driver. Glancing downward through the driver's-side window, I spotted a second shotgun lodged between the driver and the door. As if that wasn't enough to make the hair stand up on the back of my neck, the beady-eyed character staring at me from the backseat had a rifle lying across his lap. He wore dark green army fatigues and a black bandana across his forehead.

"I'd like to ask the driver to please turn off the engine and step out of the car."

"Yes, officer. Whatever you say," said the driver.

The driver was identified as fifty-two-year-old Vito Petrovic. Short, stout, and bald on top, Petrovic seemed nervous and overly talkative. "Both shotguns belong to me," he insisted. "Boys are not hunting. I have license and deer tag."

After instructing the two younger men to remain seated in the car, I checked to see if either of the shotguns was loaded. The pump-action, 12 gauge Model 870 contained a loaded round in the chamber. I unloaded the gun and laid it on the hood of my pickup. The other shotgun, which I had seen the younger Petrovic use to kill two birds, was a double-barreled 20 gauge. It contained a live round in each chamber. I unloaded it and laid it on the hood of my pickup. The rifle in the backseat was a World War II-era, .30 caliber M-1 carbine, with a peep sight. It, too, had a live round in the chamber. Again, I unloaded the rifle and laid it on the hood of my pickup.

While the two younger men remained seated in the car, I asked for everyone's identification, hunting licenses, and any deer tags they might possess. Vito Petrovic produced a California Driver's License, a valid California Hunting License, and a valid deer tag. Twenty-three-year-old Adrian Petrovic, who turned out to be Vito's nephew, handed me a Green Card. Twenty-four-year-old Teo Kovac also produced a Green Card. Neither Adrian nor Teo were able to produce any other form of identification.

"Before we go any further, could I get you to pop the trunk?" I said to Vito Petrovic. I knew there were at least two birds unaccounted for. The elder Petrovic just stood there, his expression blank, while the younger Petrovic began to exit the car. "Please stay in the car," I said in a firm voice. Vito Petrovic said something to his nephew in a language I didn't understand. Apparently he repeated what I had said, because Adrian climbed back in the car. "Thank you," I said. "Now please open the trunk."

Vito Petrovic popped open his trunk, after which I asked him to hand me the car keys. When I looked inside, it took all of the professionalism I could muster not to turn around and slap the cuffs on the miscreant standing next to me. The entire trunk was filled with dead song birds: mockingbirds, thrashers, robins, meadowlarks, towhees, and a single male Bullock's oriole. I'll never forget the sight of that beautiful multi-colored bird lying there on top of the pile. Petrovic added insult to injury by telling me about a delicious Eastern European dish made from songbirds.

"Birds like this are delicacy in old country," said Petrovic.

I immediately checked to make sure the two younger men were still sitting inside the vehicle. "In this country we appreciate our songbirds and don't eat them," I responded. "All of these birds are protected by federal and state law."

I charged everyone in the car with joint possession of twenty-seven unlawfully taken nongame birds, all protected under the federal Migratory Bird Treaty Act. In addition to the bird violations, Vito Petrovic was charged with unlawful possession of two loaded shotguns and a loaded rifle in a vehicle on a way open to the public. Adrian Petrovic was charged with hunting without a license. All of the birds and the weapons were seized into evidence.

I'm sorry to say that I don't remember, thirty-nine years later, the final disposition of this case. I do recall recommending a maximum fine, jail time, and forfeiture of weapons. I'm happy that we appreciate and protect our songbirds here in America but was disheartened to learn that other countries were still killing, selling, and eating them by the millions. Illegal songbird trafficking remains big business in European countries like Bulgaria, Romania, Serbia, and Montenegro. Some species are in serious danger of being completely wiped out.

It was just getting dark when I rolled up to the A-Frame. Everyone else was there, enjoying a barbeque dinner provided by the host captain's squad. When I walked in the door, one of my younger warden friends asked how I had done. Without mentioning all the loaded gun and deer tag cases I had made, I began telling him about the great songbird investigation I had just completed. One of the veteran wardens overheard our conversation and made a wisecrack about "dicky bird cases."

"How many cases did you make today, Doug?" asked my friend.

"Uh, I scratched a couple loaded gun citations," responded Doug, a beer in his hand.

"That's what I figured," said my friend.

Some of the older wardens shared Doug's archaic view that we should only concern ourselves with game species. I felt strongly that it was our job to protect all of California's natural resources. That included nongame birds, nongame fish, reptiles, amphibians, marine mammals, invertebrates, and even plants. It also meant protecting our lakes, streams, and ocean waters from degradation and pollution. Times were changing, and dinosaurs like Doug would have to change with them. Along with the hunters and fishermen, more people were interested in bird watching, wildlife viewing, wildlife photography, and other wildlife-related outdoor activities.

After grabbing something to eat, I took a quick shower and spent the rest of the evening listening to stories. The best storyteller of all was Inspector Jack Traub. People used to say that Jack had missed his calling and could have been a successful standup comedian. He remembered every joke and funny story he had ever heard and had the rare ability to tell them as well as any professional. Among the funny stories Jack told that night was one about my father's longtime friend Gil Berg and my supervisor at the time, Captain Jim Reynolds. I had known Gil Berg since his days in Gridley, when he was my father's neighboring warden. Gil had transferred to Santa Barbara during the 1960s and ended up working under Captain Reynolds for two or three years. A dedicated warden, Berg was also known as one of the department's funniest characters.

Jack's story went something like this:

There was this foulmouthed, middle-aged English woman named Irene Finch. Ms. Finch didn't think California's fishing regulations applied to her. Warden Gil Berg had already arrested her twice for fishing violations when he found himself having to arrest her a third time. On this occasion, Finch's offense was taking clams out of season and taking undersized clams. During the arrest, Finch called Warden Berg every four-letter word in the book.

The case resulted in a court trial, with Warden Berg's supervisor, Captain Jim Reynolds, in attendance. During the trial, the Santa Barbara Court judge asked Warden Berg to explain the arrest sequence. Not wanting to utter four-letter words in open court, Berg simply stated that Irene Finch had become very foulmouthed during his dealings with her.

"I want you to tell me exactly what she said," demanded the judge.

"Well, Your Honor," said Berg, "she told me to stick the clams up my ass."

"That's a damn lie, that's a damn lie!" shouted Finch, from the defendant's table.

"What did you say?" asked the judge, after admonishing Finch not to interrupt.

"I told him to stick the clams up his ass sideways," Your Honor.

"Guilty!" said the judge, slamming his gavel down on the bench. "That will be five days in the county jail."

"Your Honor," said Finch. "May I apologize to the officer and shake his hand?"

"That seems reasonable," said the judge. "Go ahead."

Finch shook Warden Berg's hand. "I'm sorry," she said, "but you're still a no good son of a bitch." Having said that, Finch gave Berg a hard shove. She was led from the court in handcuffs.

Thirty-nine years later, I asked ninety-year-old Gil Berg if the story Traub told that night was true. "Every word of it," Berg replied. "I thought Captain Reynolds was going to fall out of his seat laughing. After the trial was over, he told me it was the funniest thing he'd ever seen." Berg went on to say that Irene Finch was married to a 300-pound professional wrestler. "The nicest guy you'd ever want to meet," said Berg.

Everyone was exhausted so the lights went out in the A-Frame around 10:00. Burt Pruett and I were glad we had secured bunks in the loft. With eighteen snoring game wardens down below, the walls would soon be shaking.

"Hey, Burt," I said, as I climbed into my sleeping bag, "was the inspector mad about the big dent in your fender?"

Before Pruett could reply, Inspector Traub ended the day by stepping out on the front porch of the A-Frame and entertaining us all with his famous Tarzan yell.

"Does that answer your question?" said Burt. "He told me to get it fixed and be sure to turn in an accident report."

The Lobster Tale

———— ◆ ————

I HAVE FEW REGRETS ABOUT my years working for the California Department of Fish and Game. One that has always plagued me, however, is a missed opportunity to work marine patrol. What better chance to protect the ocean I love than to be a marine warden patrolling Southern California's Channel Islands, Monterey's National Marine Sanctuary, or the magnificent Farallones off the coast of San Francisco? No one values the ocean's myriad of wonderful creatures more than I, yet my career path always led inland. Opportunities for me have long since come and gone, but I still vicariously enjoy hearing the fascinating stories of former marine wardens I had the pleasure of knowing and working with over the years.

One such story coincidentally took place twenty years, to the month, after my 1959 boyhood trip to the Channel Islands.

***

"HERE THEY COME!" SAID Larry Hester. He was lying on his stomach, hidden behind a San Clemente Island toyon bush. With sweat dripping down his forehead into his eyes, the thirty-year-old marine warden labored to focus his binoculars on the rapidly approaching lobster boat.

"Boy, does that feel good!" responded rookie Fish and Game Warden Gary Clark, referring to the cool ocean breeze that climbed the ridge from below and swept across the bone-dry plateau. Clark had been on the job a little more than a year and relied on Hester to enlighten him about the known violators who operated off the Orange and Los Angeles County coasts.

"This looks like Butler's boat on the way in now," said Hester. "Yep, that's the *Sticky Wicket* all right."

"The *Sticky Wicket*?"

"Interesting name for a lobster boat, huh? I see Ray Jenkins at the helm. Have you run into him yet?"

"No, I don't think I've had the pleasure."

"If you ever have to deal with Jenkins, be very careful. You never know what that crazy son of a bitch is gonna do."

"Who owns the old scow in the cove? It looks like some kind of converted tugboat. There must be a hundred traps stacked on that deck."

"That's the *Rabble-Rouser*. It belongs to Hank Deats. His deckhand is Russ Cassidy. They're two of the biggest outlaws in Southern California. The regional manager told me he pinched Deats for the first time back in 1946."

"You mean Bob Kaneen pinched him?"

"Yeah, believe it or not. Bob started out as a warden just like us."

"What did he pinch him for?"

"Deats had a boatload of short lobsters," said Hester, brushing a crawling tick from his right wrist. "These damn bloodsuckers are all over the islands!"

"Are we talking about ticks or lobster poachers?"

"Both," said Hester, chuckling.

Word had reached the Long Beach Fish and Game office, through a reliable informant of Larry Hester's, that commercial lobsterman Jack Butler and his deckhand, Ray Jenkins, had been secretly transporting short lobsters to the mainland and selling them on the black market. Their reported partners in crime were well-known outlaws Henry "Hank" Deats and Russell Cassidy. According to the informant, Deats and Cassidy had found a massive lobster nest near a pinnacle somewhere in the southern Channel Islands.

"I heard there were thousands of them," said the informant. "The greedy bastards are afraid someone else will find their glory hole so they're cashin' in while the gettin's good. The undersized bugs—they're just rippin' the tails off and throwin' the bodies overboard. Some of the seafood restaurants around here are buying the tails. They just cut out the meat and chop it into little pieces for cioppino and lobster bisque—you know—stuff like that. That way it's impossible to tell if the lobsters were legal-sized or not."

The informant didn't know which of the southern islands the outlaws were working out of, so an extensive stakeout detail became necessary. For two consecutive days in mid-October 1979, as many as twenty California Fish and Game wardens were staked out in strategic locations along the Southern California coast and on three of the Channel Islands: Sam Clemente, Catalina, and Santa Barbara.

San Clemente Island was a U.S. Navy base and target range, strictly off-limits to civilians. Arrangements had been made for as many as six wardens to come ashore on the island and be transported to various surveillance sites by naval personnel. A Jeep and a seaman driver were assigned to Hester and Clark for the duration of the surveillance. All the wardens had to do was radio the naval station and the seaman would return to pick them up. For the time being, Hester and Clark were busy watching every action that was taking place in a protected cove on the northeast end of the island.

Still hidden from view, Warden Hester removed a Department of Fish and Game portable radio from its canvas carrying case and attempted to contact Leo Singer, the Fish and Game Marine Region's warden pilot. Singer was flying somewhere between Catalina and San Clemente Islands at the time.

"Eight two six, sixty-one fourteen, on direct," said Hester.

"Eight two six, go ahead," said Singer.

"Our suspects have entered a cove near the northeast side of San Clemente Island."

"Ten-four, we're about five away."

The plan was for Singer and his accompanying warden spotter to keep Butler's boat in sight as it crossed the channel back to the mainland. By flying at a higher altitude, the Fish and Game plane avoided detection by the lobstermen below. The Southern California coastline, from San Diego to Ventura, was dotted with any number of harbors and other places where boats could come ashore and unload contraband, so constant surveillance was essential. When the lobstermen did come ashore, Singer would radio their location to nearby officers on the ground.

"They just tied Butler's boat to the *Rabble-Rouser*," whispered Clark, still watching with binoculars from behind the toyon bush. "Cassidy just dumped a big garbage can full of lobsters out on the deck."

"Which deck?" asked Hester, still fiddling with the antiquated portable radio.

"Deats's boat," said Clark. "I can see 'em flopping around. Now they're ripping the tails off and throwing the bodies overboard. Butler's bringing over a big ice chest from his boat. My God! Did they trap every lobster in the ocean? There's hundreds of them."

"Sixty-one fourteen, eight two six," said Warden-Pilot Singer over the radio.

"Sixty-one fourteen, go ahead."

"We have the subjects in sight and will stand by."

"Ten-four."

While the motor on Butler's boat idled, Wardens Hester and Clark watched the four commercial lobster fishermen continue to rip the tails off undersized lobsters. Every time a tail went into the ice chest, a carcass was tossed overboard. When the ice chest was full, Butler and Jenkins carried it back to their boat. Deats and Cassidy brought out another garbage can that appeared to be full of something. They loaded the garbage can and two full gunny sacks onto Butler's boat.

"I hear Jenkins revving the motor," said Hester. "They must be getting ready to shove off. Deats is handing Butler a piece of paper. That must be the lobster tally."

"Eight two six, sixty-one fourteen, on direct."

"Eight two six, go ahead."

"Our subjects are leaving," said Hester.

"Ten-four, we'll take it from here," responded Singer.

Wardens Hester and Clark watched Butler's boat cruise out of the cove, accelerate, and head in the direction of the mainland. When the boat was clearly out of sight, the wardens redirected their attention to the *Rabble-Rouser*. Deats and Cassidy would be kept under surveillance for as long as possible, but would not be contacted immediately, for fear of them alerting Butler and Jenkins by radio.

About 4:00 p.m., Butler's boat approached San Pedro and the Los Angeles Harbor. "Two two six to any Fish and Game ground unit in the San Pedro area," said Singer from the air.

"Sixty-two forty-two, go ahead," responded Warden Bob Prosser.

"Sixty-two forty-two, our subjects are nearing Terminal Island. Stand by."

"Ten-four."

Dressed in civilian clothes, Warden Bob Prosser and Lieutenant Rod Shackelford were sitting in an unmarked car near the Los Angeles Harbor boat docks. They waited for approximately five minutes before Warden Pilot Singer again transmitted.

"Sixty-two forty-two, eight two six."

"Sixty-two forty-two, go ahead."

"Sixty-two forty-two, our subjects appear to be docking immediately adjacent to the Star Kist cannery. We're running low on fuel. Ten ninety-eight, ten-nineteen." The first number meant "assignment completed," the second, "returning to base."

"Ten-four. We're minutes away and will take it from here. Thanks."

"Eight two six."

Bob Prosser was the kind of warden referred to by veteran Fish and Game officers as a "hard charger." Since coming on the job a few years earlier, he had made a name for himself in and around the Los Angeles and Long Beach area docks for being conscientious, hardworking, and completely dedicated to protecting California's marine resources. In his early thirties, the freckle-faced, six-foot-two-inch dynamo showed no fear in taking on large-scale commercial violators if the situation warranted it.

One of Warden Prosser's more daunting duties was measuring boatloads of mackerel, Spanish mackerel, and anchovies that came into the docks for processing. During the late 1970s, it was illegal for commercial fishermen to take or possess sardines. One hundred percent of a load could be made up of Spanish mackerel, but no more than fifteen percent could be composed of Pacific mackerel or anchovies. To make matters even more complicated, no more than fifteen percent of the anchovies could be less than five inches long. After measuring the required number of samples, wardens sometimes found it necessary to seize entire loads of illegal fish. It demanded a great deal of courage and determination to take the necessary legal action, given the angry reactions Fish and Game officers sometimes received from commercial fishermen. One fisherman had actually turned a wash-down hose on Warden Prosser as Prosser was attempting to make an inspection. The man was arrested and booked for assault on a peace officer.

Rod Shackelford had spent a little too much time at the dinner table, but the veteran warden had a reputation for being rock-solid steady, with a good head on his shoulders. When the department created field supervisor (lieutenant) positions, Shackelford became one of the first to earn his bars.

Prosser and Shackelford were familiar with the layout of the harbor where Butler and Jenkins had come ashore. The two wardens positioned themselves to watch as the suspects unloaded their cargo of illegal lobsters. Butler and Jenkins carried two gunny sacks, a forty-gallon garbage can, and a one-hundred quart ice chest onto the dock.

"Let's go," said Shackelford, throwing his binoculars back in the car and locking the passenger door. Both officers began a fast walk down the wooden ramp to the docks and made their way through a maze of walkways, incredibly expensive yachts, and commercial fishing boats.

"There they are," whispered, Prosser, extending his right arm to stop Shackelford's forward momentum. Butler and Jenkins were still unloading gear from their boat and placing it on a wooden cart. Thirty-year-old Jack Butler had inherited the *Sticky Wicket* from his alcoholic father four years earlier. Having also inherited his father's thirst for booze and lack of respect for the law, Butler had resorted to smuggling illegal lobsters to keep his languishing lobster business afloat. Fellow high school dropout Ray Jenkins was a big man with a hair-trigger temper. At one time or another, Jenkins had fought with or been fired by just about every boat operator on the docks.

From fifty yards up the walkway, Prosser and Shackelford slowed their pace to a casual walk and approached the two suspects. Posing as a couple of civilians strolling down the dock, they hoped to get close enough to prevent Butler and Jenkins from panicking and tossing evidence into the bay. Unfortunately, the wardens' plan didn't turn out as well as they had hoped.

Civilian clothes or no civilian clothes, some law enforcement officers just look like cops. Prosser and Shackelford might just as well have hung signs around their necks, reading: WE'RE GAME WARDENS.

As soon as Butler and Jenkins looked up and saw the wardens approaching, Jenkins picked up the ice chest full of lobster tails and threw it into the bay. Thinking quickly on his feet, Warden Prosser said, "You dropped something. Do you need any help getting it out of the water?" Neither Butler nor Jenkins said a word. Prosser and Shackelford continued walking past the two lobster poachers.

"Who are those guys?" asked Butler.

"I thought they were game wardens," said Jenkins, a puzzled look on his face.

"You idiot. You just tossed a ton of money into the bay," said Butler.

Prosser and Shackelford continued walking, Prosser trying desperately to keep from laughing. They strolled around a building and back up an adjacent ramp to the top of the dock. While Butler and Jenkins were busy attempting to retrieve their ill-gotten lobster tails, Prosser and Shackelford returned to the scene of the crime, identified themselves as California Fish and Game wardens, and placed both men under arrest.

According to California law, there was no limit on the number of lobsters a licensed commercial lobster fisherman could take or possess, as long as the required placard was displayed on the boat and lobster season was open. A size limit for each lobster did exist, however, which was strictly enforced. Lobsters also had to remain intact until prepared for consumption. A total of 675 illegal lobster tails were seized into evidence from the two gunny sacks and the garbage can on board the *Sticky Wicket*. That's not counting two hundred additional lobster tails that had fallen out of the ice chest and lay scattered at the bottom of the bay.

The day after Butler and Jenkins were arrested, Fish and Game Lieutenant Mike Wade put on his diving gear and was also able to recover a few of the tails from the sunken ice chest. Not wanting these remaining hundred or so lobster tails to go to waste, Warden Prosser contacted the Terminal Island Fire Department. "Would you guys like to do us a favor and help make sure that no one gets in trouble for possessing short lobster tails?" said Prosser. "Maybe you could conduct a training exercise, recover the remaining lobster tails, and dispose of them somehow." The lobster tails were gone by the end of the day and it was rumored that the boys in blue enjoyed a gourmet meal that night.

Warden Prosser filed formal criminal complaints against John Michael "Jack" Butler and Raymond DeWayne Jenkins for unlawful possession of 675 undersized lobster tails. Both men were ordered to appear in Catalina Island Court, under the jurisdiction of Los Angeles County.

On the day of the court trial, Warden Bob Prosser, Judge Burdett Andrews, and Los Angeles County Deputy District Attorney Lawrence Patterson rode the same ferry twenty-six miles across the channel to Avalon Harbor. All three men were standing on the steps of the courthouse when Jack Butler and Ray Jenkins approached.

"Good morning," said Warden Prosser.

"Hi," mumbled Butler, reluctantly.

"Screw you!" said Jenkins.

Warden Prosser did not respond to Jenkins's outlandish remark. A bespectacled Judge Andrews, clad in civilian clothes, happened to be standing on the step just above Warden Prosser. Astounded by the defendant's offensive display, he gave Jenkins a stern stare. Jenkins stopped directly in front of Andrews, looked him in the eye, and said, "What are you looking at, four eyes?" Judge Andrews remained calm and cool in the face of Jenkins's verbal assault. Silently, Andrews followed Butler and Jenkins into the courtroom, walked into his chambers, and closed the door.

Butler and Jenkins took their seats at the defendant's table, next to their attorney. Warden Prosser and Deputy District Attorney Patterson took their seats at the adjoining prosecutor's table.

"All stand," said the uniformed bailiff, as the judge entered the room, clad in his black robe. "The Catalina Justice Court for the County of Los Angeles will now come to order. Judge Burdett R. Andrews presiding."

"Be seated," said the judge, as he sat down behind the hundred-year-old, antique hardwood bench and scanned the courtroom below.

Warden Prosser glanced over at the defendant's table and saw Ray Jenkins sitting at the far end with his head down and both hands covering his face. Jenkins had obviously recognized the judge as the same person he had just verbally assaulted. Whatever Butler's and Jenkins's spurious defense might have been, they were in panic mode now. Butler began whispering in their attorney's ear.

"Your Honor," said the diminutive, bespectacled attorney, fresh out of law school.

"Yes, Mr. Breindel, what is it?"

"Your Honor, my I have a few minutes to confer with my clients?"

"I'll give you five minutes," said the judge. "We have a full docket today."

Breindel and his two clients went into a conference room at the rear of the court and closed the door. A few minutes later, Butler and Jenkins returned to the table and Breindel walked over and whispered to the deputy district attorney.

"Your Honor," said Breindel, "may I have a few extra minutes to speak with Mr. Patterson?" Suspecting that the two attorneys were likely to come up with a plea bargain, the judge agreed. After a short conversation in the conference room, Deputy District Attorney Patterson approached Warden Prosser and discussed a possible plea bargain: Breindel's offer was for each of his clients to pay a fine of $500 and be placed on six months' summary probation.

Warden Prosser shook his head in disbelief. He walked back to the conference room with Patterson and explained the seriousness of the crime to the young, inexperienced deputy district attorney. Prosser wrote down on a legal tablet the minimum fine and sentence that he and the Department of Fish and Game were prepared to accept: a $3,000 fine (for each defendant) and loss of commercial fishing privileges for two years.

"If they don't like that, let's go to trial," said Prosser. "Jenkins can take his chances with the judge he just threatened."

"Okay," said Patterson, appearing timid and unsure of himself. "I'll see what Mr. Breindel says."

After another ten minutes of negotiations with Breindel, Paterson came back to Warden Prosser with the defense attorney's counter offer.

"Mr. Breindel has apparently convinced his clients not to go to trial if we drop the fine to $2,000 each and only take their commercial fishing privileges away for one year."

"That's like a slap on the wrist!" said Prosser, trying to keep his voice down. "Who knows how long these guys have been doing this? If I had my way, they'd lose their permit for life."

Warden Prosser continued making his case to the deputy DA at the back of the courtroom, until the judge tapped his gavel.

"Mr. Patterson, my patience is wearing thin," said the judge. "Have you and the defense come to an agreement or should we proceed to trial?"

Much to Warden Prosser's disappointment, Patterson accepted the plea bargain and agreed to Breindel's terms. Butler and Jenkins were fined $2,000 each, and their lobster-fishing privileges were suspended for one year.

During sentencing, Judge Andrews admonished Jenkins for his offensive behavior in front of the courthouse. "Had you conducted yourself like that inside my courtroom," the judge said, "you would be spending the next six months wearing an orange vest and picking up garbage along the highway."

As for Deats and Cassidy, their boat was boarded and searched by Fish and Game officers late on the same day that Butler and Jenkins had been arrested. Deats and Cassidy suffered the same fate as their compadres: they were arrested and charged with take and possession of undersized lobsters. I wasn't able to find out what punishment they received for their actions.

Warden Bob Prosser went on to a distinguished and highly productive career, retiring in 2001.

Black Market Abs

---◆---

NOT SO LONG AGO, five species of abalone were commonly taken in California waters by sport and commercial divers: pink (*Haliotis corrugata*), green (*Haliotis fulgens*), red (*Haliotis rufescens*), black (*Haliotis cracherodii*), and white (*Haliotis sorenseni*). Annual commercial harvests from the Channel Islands and coastal waters south of San Francisco were in the millions until numbers began to decline significantly in the 1970s. With commercial take allowed to continue, the entire fishery collapsed and was finally shut down in 1997. Sadly, the white abalone was added to the federal Endangered Species List in 2005; the black abalone followed in 2011.

Why did California's once-abundant abalone fishery collapse? The reasons include withering disease, diminished food supply, competition from sea urchins, loss of habitat, predation, pollution, changing ocean temperatures, ocean acidification, and reproductive issues. Successful reproduction depends on males and females of the same species being close enough to each other so the males can effectively fertilize the spawn released into the water by females. That can't happen when populations have been decimated and densities are reduced to the point where males and females are few and far between.

I believe the two primary reasons for California's abalone catastrophe are commercial harvesting, which was allowed to continue far too long, and illegal harvesting (poaching), which has been occurring for decades and is still going on today.

San Clemente Island was the setting for a 1979 incident that shows how badly California's abalone fishery has been exploited. The southernmost of California's Channel Islands, San Clemente, with its incredibly productive marine ecosystem, was home to several abalone species. The most common were the pinks, with a legal size limit of 6.25 inches; followed by greens, with a legal size limit of 7 inches; and whites, with a legal size limit of 6.25 inches. By the late seventies, white abalone had been harvested to the point of virtual nonexistence. This species became the first marine invertebrate to be added to the federal Endangered Species List.

***

IT WAS APPROACHING 4:00 a.m. on a Saturday in early October 1979. Forty-two-year-old Kenji Takada pulled into a vacant parking spot at the Long Beach Harbor and began the short walk down the ramp to his boat slip. With overhead lamps lighting the way, Takada continued down the long wooden dock, pushing a wooden wheelbarrow filled with food supplies and empty mesh bags. Commercial fishing boats along the walkway were buzzing with activity, their crews busily preparing for the day's trip out to sea. A few acquaintances waved or said good morning as Takada walked by. He waved back but had no time to stop and talk. There was only one thing on Takada's mind that morning—filling his pockets with money when he returned to the mainland.

Instead of selling the day's catch to a licensed wholesaler and receiving the required receipt (pink ticket), Takada had made other arrangements. That evening he would drive to Garden Grove and meet with a businessman from Orange County's rapidly growing black market for abalone and other marine species. It didn't matter to this unscrupulous operator if Takada's product was undersized or on the verge of extinction. He was paying top dollar for all the abalone he could get his hands on, no questions asked.

Takada's dive boat was a twenty-six-foot Radon called the *Jiro*. It was blue and faded white, with a low freeboard forward cabin and a davit crane in the rear. In addition to the crane, the spacious rear deck contained Takada's hookah equipment and dive gear: a 7mm wetsuit with hood; a weight belt; a compressor; two one-hundred-foot air hoses, a half inch in diameter; a regulator; fins; snorkel; facemask; and an abalone iron for prying reluctant mollusks off the rocks. The hoses were neatly rolled and ready for the next dive. Also on the deck were several wooden boxes for sorting and stacking abalone, three five-gallon plastic buckets, and two large Coleman ice chests.

With a cup of coffee in one hand and the wheel in the other, Takada slowly cruised through the bustling harbor. When he had passed the five-mile-per-hour buoy, he pushed the throttle forward, brought the *Jiro* up on plane, and began the sixty-mile, two-and-a-half hour voyage to the back side of San Clemente Island.

The ocean on that slightly overcast morning in October was almost glassy. It was relatively easy to traverse the channel during the early morning hours, but often rough and a bit risky in the afternoon when the offshore winds picked up. With few swells to contend with, Takada's speedy Radon skimmed across the water at thirty knots, as if it were crossing a mountain lake.

About twenty miles out and in view of Catalina's Avalon Harbor, Takada veered south. The backside of Catalina Island was still open to commercial abalone diving, but pinks and greens had been picked over so much by commercial divers that finding a load of product had become almost impossible. Besides, Takada knew that the possibility of being contacted by Fish and Game was far less likely off the coastline of distant San Clemente Island.

It was approaching 8:00 a.m. when Takada reached San Clemente Island and made his way south along the eastern shoreline. He was pleased by the ocean conditions, which remained calm and free of whitecaps. Passing popular fishing spots like Purse Seine Rock, Fish Rock, and Pyramid Head, Takada's speedy Radon powered around the south end of the island and came to an abrupt stop near a rocky outcropping. Wasting no time, the diver cut the engine and dropped anchor.

Seldom had Takada seen waters on the west side of the island so clear and calm. Looking down from the rear deck, he could see fifty feet below, all the way to the rocky, algae-strewn bottom. Most of the good spots for legal-sized pink, green, and white abalone had already been harvested. Undersized pinks and greens were still fairly plentiful in normally rough and inaccessible locations like this one. Whites, which were found in deeper waters, had become so scarce that commercial divers were no longer expected to report them.

Takada hastily prepared his hookah equipment for the first dive. He turned on his air compressor and attached a length of coiled air hose to a clip on his weight belt. Adjusting his facemask and putting the regulator in his mouth, he stepped over the side and descended toward the rocks below. With the rubber strap of his abalone iron wrapped around his left arm and a large mesh bag in his right hand, Takada immediately began searching the rocks, crevices, and underhangs for abalone. There was really no need for a measuring gauge. On this day anything bigger than his fist would be fair game.

Takada's plan was to begin in the deeper water and progress into shallower depths as the day went on. With the exception of two whites, all of the abalone found at a depth of fifty feet or greater that day were pinks. Pink abalone had wavy, corrugated shells, which made them easy to identify. White abalone shells were thinner and more oval in shape. All of the pinks and whites that Takada harvested during this trip to San Clemente Island were in the five-to-six-inch range—none of them legal sized. When Takada had filled his mesh bag with three dozen abalone, he attached a hook to the bag and hoisted it to the boat with the davit crane.

Takada continued to work his way through the kelp beds and into shallower waters, stopping periodically for safety intervals. Reaching a depth of twenty feet, he began finding green abalone, easily identified by ribs along the lower edge of the shell and additional pore holes. Leopard sharks and halibut bolted from the ocean floor as the purposeful diver scurried from rock to rock. Brilliantly colored orange garibaldi darted in and out of holes, while kelp bass and sheephead lingered in the giant kelp beds above. At one point, Takada's collecting frenzy almost cost him a hand: he reached into a dark underhang to pry an abalone loose and was warned off by a four-foot moray.

By 2:30, Takada had filled four mesh bags with a total of ten dozen abalones, all of them undersized and illegal to take or possess. The afternoon wind was kicking up and the *Jiro* began bobbing like a cork in the increasingly turbulent waters. Still wearing his stiflingly hot wetsuit, Takada quickly grasped the seriousness of his situation. The reason his chosen dive spot hadn't been picked clean by other divers was becoming more evident by the minute.

A twelve-foot wave swept under the *Jiro*, lifting it skyward and breaking the anchor's hold on the ocean bottom. As the *Jiro* lunged sideways in the powerful surf, it came within yards of an exposed rock formation. Takada started the engine and quickly hoisted the anchor. Another wave rolled under the *Jiro*, enveloped the nearby rocks, and continued shoreward. Foam splashed over the bow and up against the windshield, as Takada accelerated out of his precarious position and into deeper waters.

Normally Kenji Takada might have secured the day's plunder inside a hold space under the rear deck, but he was in a hurry now and a little shaken up by the sudden change of ocean conditions. The four abalone-laden mesh bags remained exposed on the rear deck, right where the nervous outlaw had left them.

With swells continuing to build, the trip back to the mainland turned out to be a lot rougher than Takada had anticipated. Cruising at less than twenty knots, he began thinking about the distant possibility of being contacted by Fish and Game. *Am I getting seasick after all these years?* Takada wondered as he ascended a fifteen-foot swell then descended into the wave's trough. *Or is it worry that's causing my stomach to churn?* This scenario repeated itself all the way across the channel.

In my entire career, I never met a serious poacher who admitted to pangs of conscience. I believe Takada and dozens of opportunists like him would sell the last abalone on Earth if the price were right. It was the fear of being caught that caused the knot in his belly, nothing more.

The *Jiro* reached San Pedro at 5:45 p.m., according to the clock in Fish and Game Lieutenant Mike Wade's patrol car. As Takada slowly meandered through the crowded harbor, he had no way of knowing that he was being watched. Thirty-two-year-old Michael Thomas Wade was familiar with every vantage point overlooking the Long Beach/L.A. Harbor; at any given time he might have a pair of binoculars or a spotting scope focused on one of the commercial operators. After working the Southern California docks for three years as a warden, Wade had a pretty good idea which operators played by the rules and which ones didn't.

Those who knew and respected Mike Wade described him as six feet and two hundred pounds of unwavering dedication to California's marine resources. It was that same dedication to duty that had earned Wade the U.S. Navy's Meritorious Service Medal twelve years earlier. Mike Wade and his U.S. Marine infantry unit were on patrol in the jungles of Vietnam when they were ambushed by Viet Cong. While exposed to enemy fire, Wade rescued a wounded Marine and carried him back to his squad's secure position. He then ran back to retrieve the wounded soldier's weapon to keep it from falling into enemy hands.

A wooden box on top of the *Jiro*'s cabin displayed Kenji Takada's abalone permit number, with the large letter "A," for abalone, followed by three numerical digits. Lieutenant Wade had contacted Takada enough times to recognize the cagey outlaw and his boat, even without the numbers. Although Takada had never been arrested for fish or abalone violations, Wade had been receiving uncorroborated information about his illegal activities for years. Takada's reported modus operandi was to take as many abalone as possible in a day, then separate the legal-sized ones from the shorts. He would reportedly sell the legal ones legitimately to licensed wholesale fish buyers and peddle the shorts to Southern California's growing Asian community for cash.

"That's odd," said Wade, watching from his car window with a 60-power spotting scope. "Kenji's not headed for his usual docking area." Wade continued to dog the *Jiro* as it slowly motored through the massive Los Angeles Harbor complex. Finally losing sight of the boat, the tenacious wildlife officer parked his patrol unit a short distance from where he anticipated Takada would tie up and ventured into the docking area on foot.

The docks in this section of the harbor were built to stand fifteen to twenty feet high so the larger boats could tie up. Wade cautiously walked to the end of a pier and looked down. Much to his surprise, Takada was directly below, tying his boat to one of the pier pilings. The sharp-eyed lieutenant immediately spotted four mesh bags filled with abalone, lying in open sight on the deck.

"Kenji, how's it going?" shouted Wade. Takada looked up at the uniformed officer with an expression of complete terror on his face. As Wade described it later, Takada was so surprised he almost fell off the bow into the water. Takada ran to the wheel, shoved the boat into reverse, and began backing away from the pier. "State Fish and Game!" shouted Wade. "Don't touch those abalone or you'll be in real trouble!"

His boat now twenty yards from the pier, Takada completely ignored Lieutenant Wade's warning and began pushing the bags of abalone over the side. "Leave that bag on the deck!" shouted Wade.

Takada again ignored the angry command and tossed the last bag overboard.

"I'm ordering you to pull your boat over to the dock immediately," shouted Wade.

With the desperate outlaw's illegal abalones now at the bottom of the bay, Takada heeded Lieutenant Wade's last order and returned to the dock. "Turn around and put your hands behind your back," commanded Wade, jumping on board. The short and stocky Takada was instructed to sit inside the cabin so there was no chance of him falling overboard while wearing handcuffs. Wade began searching the boat for more abalone, but came up empty. When questioned about the four mesh bags he had tossed into the harbor, Takada refused to answer. "He wouldn't even admit to throwing the abalone overboard," Wade would say later, "after I had just watched him do it."

Lieutenant Wade seized Takada's commercial fishing license and abalone permit. Releasing Takada, Wade advised him that he could do no more diving until the investigation was completed and the case was resolved.

Lieutenant Wade went back to his patrol vehicle and called for a Department of Fish and Game dive team. Because it was growing darker and visibility in the polluted bay was less than two feet, it was decided that the underwater search would begin the following morning. Not willing to provide the devious abalone diver with an opportunity to return to the scene of the crime and remove evidence, Lieutenant Wade stood guard on the site all night.

The next morning, visibility in the bay was even poorer than Wade had anticipated. An ingenious method was devised for searching the murky bottom. By using a twenty-five-foot length of rope, two divers were able to swim in a circular pattern until they found the four mesh bags full of abalone. The bags contained ten dozen undersized abalone. With the exception of two whites, they were all greens and pinks.

Lieutenant Wade filed a criminal complaint against Kenji Takada, charging him with unlawful possession of 120 undersized abalones and failure to show on demand. Takada was convicted and ordered to pay a substantial fine. After the conviction, Wade appeared before the California Fish and Game Commission and requested that Takada's abalone permit be revoked. The request was granted, effectively putting the longtime violator out of business.

Takada would later tell Lieutenant Wade that he had given up diving completely. "I was always so nervous, it was ruining my health," said Takada. "The money was just too good to resist and everyone was doing it to some degree."

Retired Patrol Captain Mike Wade and I discussed this case thirty-five years after Kenji Takada's court conviction. During our conversation, Wade reinforced a lesson I had learned myself, many years before: "No matter how straight they seem to be," he said, "you are the game warden and they will always play you."

"Is this kind of thing still going on today?" I asked.

Wade chuckled, as if my question was naïve. "People have no idea how serious this problem is," he said. "I guarantee you we could poach fifty abalone, put them in the trunk of a car, drive them to San Francisco, pull into any alley in Chinatown, and sell them for twenty-five dollars apiece. Of course we wouldn't do that, but there's that much demand out there."

The Kneeland Prairie Deer Investigation

———◆———

L ANDON CULPEPPER DID NOT like the government. His family had owned one of the largest cattle ranches in Humboldt County for three generations, and as far as the old man was concerned, no one was going to tell him what he could do on his own property. That included the Department of Fish and Game—*especially* the Department of Fish and Game.

Ten years earlier, when Culpepper was in his mid-sixties, he had tried to divert water from a small steelhead spawning stream flowing through one of his pastures. Fish and Game found out about it and told him he needed a stream alteration permit. Conditions of the permit would prevent damage to the stream and ensure that sufficient water remained to support salmon and steelhead. Culpepper reluctantly complied, but never let the local wardens forget it. For years after that, he wouldn't speak to a game warden or even wave when one of the officers drove by his ranch.

ONE COLD DECEMBER NIGHT in 1979, the state telephone rang at the Eureka residence of Fish and Game Warden Jon Dunn. Awakened from a sound sleep, Dunn glanced over at the clock. It was twelve minutes after midnight. He climbed out of a warm bed and stumbled down the hallway toward his office. "I'm coming," he said, as the phone rang for the sixth time. "Hold your horses."

Bleary eyed and still half asleep, Dunn answered the phone. "Fish and Game," he mumbled. "Warden Dunn."

"This is Landon Culpepper. I got three guys trapped up here on the place and you better come get 'em! They shot a deer."

"Wait a minute, Mr. Culpepper. Let me find something to write with. Okay, somebody shot a deer on your place?"

"Yeah, they shot a deer just past the house. I chased 'em down and took their car keys. I think they killed that big buck that's been hangin' around up here."

"As soon as I get dressed, I'll be right up."

"I'll be waiting at the house."

Thirty-two-year-old Jon Dunn was hired by the Department of Fish and Game in 1973, following two military tours of Vietnam and three years of study at Humboldt State University. His first assignment was the San Francisco Bay Area, where he worked for three years. When a warden's position opened up on the North Coast in 1976, Dunn put in for a transfer and happily returned to his old stomping grounds.

Warden Dunn had spoken to Landon Culpepper only once or twice since taking over the Eureka warden's district, but he was well aware of the grumpy old codger's animosity towards Fish and Game. Dunn figured the matter had to be pretty serious for Culpepper to call in the middle of the night; he threw on his uniform, jumped in his pickup, and raced twenty miles up the twisting mountain road to Culpepper's ranch. The farther up the mountain Dunn drove in his four-wheel-drive patrol truck, the more slippery the road became. Melting snow dripped across the pavement and immediately turned to deadly black ice.

"I better slow down or I won't make it at all," said Dunn, talking to himself. "I think the ranch house is up around this next bend, but it's so damn dark I can't see anything. You'd think that cantankerous old grouch would leave some kind of outside light on for me."

As Warden Dunn pulled into Culpepper's front yard, a pack of barking dogs ran out to meet him. Culpepper must have seen the headlights, because he finally turned a light on.

"Come on in," shouted Culpepper. "The dogs won't hurt ya."

Warden Dunn stepped down from the cab of the truck and immediately felt a stabbing pain on the back of his left calf. He had forgotten about Culpepper's squirrelly border collie. The dog didn't bark like the others but liked to bite when people weren't looking. This time he had come at the unsuspecting warden from underneath the truck and was still hanging onto his pant leg. Warden Dunn shook the dog loose and headed for the porch, only to have the sneaky little mutt bite him again as he climbed the steps. Fortunately, the dog missed the leg this time and sunk his teeth into the back of Warden Dunn's boot.

"Now, now, mustn't bite the game warden," said Culpepper.

The six-foot-three-inch warden again dislodged the dog and stared down at the top of the old man's hairless dome. Without a hint of apology for what his dog had done, Culpepper invited Dunn into the house.

Walking into the 1880s-era ranch house kitchen was like stepping back in time. The original wood plank floor creaked and groaned under Dunn's 210-pound frame.

"What a night," said Dunn, noticing his own breath as he spoke. It was practically as cold inside the house as it was outside.

"Have a seat," said Culpepper, as he wadded up a section of newspaper, grabbed a handful of kindling, and attempted to light a fire in his antique Majestic cook stove.

There were no chairs in Culpepper's kitchen, only a pair of benches and the handmade wooden table that his grandfather had built many years before.

"I heard a shot from a .22 rifle just past the house," said Culpepper, lifting the stove lid and depositing a section of split cedar. "So I jumped in my pickup and caught up with three men dragging a deer out of the creek bed."

"What time was this?" asked Dunn.

"It was about 11:30 when I pulled up in my truck. They dropped the deer, jumped in their car, and took off."

"Did you get a good look at the car?"

"It was one o' them little foreign jobs."

"What color was it?"

"I don't know—kinda greenish-yella, I guess. What the hell difference does it make? They ain't goin' nowhere without their keys."

"Good point," said Dunn, an uncomfortable grin on his face.

"Anyway, I was right on their tail when they made the mistake of turning down a road that ended at one o' my locked gates. I blocked 'em in and walked up to the driver's winda with a .38 in my hand. I told the driver to hand over the car keys. He argued at first, but I told him they wasn't goin' nowhere until the game warden got there. I took their keys and came back here to call you." The old man handed Warden Dunn the keys to the suspected poachers' car. "I'm goin' ta bed," said Culpepper. "Be careful goin' back to your truck so you don't get bit again."

When Dunn reached the bottom porch step, the same black-and-white cow dog slunk out from beneath the porch and crouched, poised for a third attack. Dunn was prepared this time, with a broom he had found at the top of the stairs. "Come at me once more and you'll get this broom handle in the chops," said Dunn, turning and facing his attacker. Having lost the element of surprise, the dog cowered and ran back under the porch.

Warden Dunn was familiar with the dead-end road that Culpepper had described, so he drove directly to that location. Sure enough, he found three half-frozen men, all in their early twenties, huddled inside a beige-colored

Toyota Corolla. After securing the three subjects and finding no weapons, Warden Dunn led them, one at a time, up to the cab of his heated pickup for identification and questioning.

The driver and owner of the Corolla was a scrawny little weasel with greasy blond hair and a missing front tooth named Trevor DeWayne Gatlin. Obviously the leader of the group, Gatlin didn't stop talking from the time he entered the Fish and Game pickup until he walked back to his car. "I want you to arrest that crazy old man for pointing a gun at us and taking our car keys," he demanded. The only truthful statement Gatlin made was that he lived in Blue Lake.

The front-seat passenger was identified as Tyler Paul Butts. Butts was of such proportions he could barely fit into the cab of the pickup. In spite of the freezing weather, he wore gray shorts, an orange T-shirt, and a baseball cap turned around backward. A bit slow on the uptake and unable to think on his feet, Butts simply repeated what Gatlin had coached him to say.

When Warden Dunn had finished interviewing Gatlin and Butts, he found the third man shivering in the backseat of Gatlin's car. Richard Samuel Gleason was quite thin, about five-feet-ten inches tall, and wore wire-rimmed glasses. Warden Dunn had the feeling that Gleason didn't fit in with the other two and if anyone was going to crack and tell the truth, it would be he. For the time being, however, all three deer poaching suspects provided the same story. They had visited friends in another town and decided to take the long way home through the mountains. When they pulled down a side road for a pit stop, this crazy old man threatened them with a gun and took their keys.

"We don't have a gun and we haven't shot anything!" shouted Gatlin in Warden Dunn's ear. "We're cold and we want to go home." Warden Dunn didn't believe a word they said, but without a gun and a deer, he didn't have enough evidence to make an arrest. By the time he finished interviewing the three suspects, it was 2:30 in the morning, spitting snow, and the road into the canyon was getting slicker all the time. To make matters worse, not one of the deer poaching suspects was wearing so much as a light jacket. They were all freezing to death, and Dunn was afraid they'd catch pneumonia or get frostbite. Without Culpepper there to show Dunn where the deer was located, they could be on the mountain until daylight. Warden Dunn felt his only reasonable option was to allow the suspects to go home and tell them he would be in contact the next day. He had good identification on all three men and knew they wouldn't be hard to find in the tiny lumber community of Blue Lake.

Gatlin's two-wheel-drive Corolla was slipping and sliding all the way up and out of the canyon, but Dunn saw the taillights finally reach the top of the hill and disappear. He decided to drive back to the creek near Culpepper's house and search for the deer. Shining his flashlight into the creek bed, Dunn spotted the largest black-tailed buck he had ever seen in Humboldt County. It was a classic four-point—far too large for one person to load into the pickup—so he decided to come back with help the next morning.

Warden Dunn made it home just before daylight. After thawing out and getting something to eat, he telephoned Warden Dana Finney to ask if he would help retrieve the deer and look for the hidden weapon. Finney agreed, and both officers were back on the mountain by 10:00 that morning.

Fortunately, Dunn and Finney were able to find a small bullet hole in the side of the deer. Turning the deer over, they were unable to locate an exit hole, giving Warden Dunn hope that he could eventually produce the slug for analysis. The slug wouldn't do them any good, however, unless they could find the proverbial murder weapon.

Finding the rifle was clearly not going to be easy. Dunn and Finney spent several hours following the route along which the suspects had been chased by Culpepper. They looked in bushes, under trees, over road banks, and inside a fallen-down barn. The weapon used to kill the gigantic buck was nowhere to be found. What Dunn and Finney did find, however, was a handheld spotlight and a second freshly killed deer. The second deer was a yearling doe. This time the bullet had gone completely through the body and out the other side. "My God," remarked Dunn. "Who knows how many deer those derelicts might have killed if Culpepper hadn't waylaid them?"

Warden Dunn took the buck to a friend's processing plant. The friend was an avid hunter and had helped Dunn find slugs in other unlawfully killed deer. By following the trajectory of the bullet from the entry point, they were able to recover a .22 caliber slug. The slug was intact and contained nine grooves. A California Department of Justice ballistics expert suggested to Dunn that he should be looking for a Marlin Micro-Groove .22 caliber rifle. Should they be lucky enough to find the rifle, there was a good chance the ballistics expert would be able to match it with the bullet.

Warden Dunn again contacted the three suspects. They all stuck to their original story, but Gleason appeared to be weakening. "I've got to find that rifle," Dunn said to himself, leaving Blue Lake and heading up the mountain toward Culpepper's ranch. Dunn continued searching for the rifle from the point where the chase began to where it had ended—a distance of over three miles. When it became too dark to search any more, he drove back to Eureka.

The following day, Warden Dunn was working in the Eureka Fish and Game office when the telephone rang in the warden's squad room.

"Warden Dunn."

"There's an angry woman on the phone," said the office receptionist. "She says three friends borrowed her rifle to go pig hunting and got caught by the game warden. Would you like to take this call?"

"Absolutely!"

"Okay, hang up and I'll put her through."

"This is Warden Dunn. May I help you?"

"I want my gun back!"

"Who am I speaking with?"

"My name is Molly Pabich. These three idiots I know borrowed my .22 rifle and I want it back."

"Miss Pabich, I would like nothing better than to get your gun back for you. Would you mind if I come out and talk to you in person?"

"Sure, if it will get my gun back."

Molly Pabich was a twenty-five-year-old student at Humboldt State University, majoring in wildlife management. Tall and slender, with dishwater blond hair tied in a ponytail, she spoke with a Tennessee accent. "Replace the lumberjack boots and the faded blue jeans with high heels and a nice dress, and she could have easily passed for a model," said Dunn. "Molly was intelligent, absolutely fearless, and cussed like a sailor."

According to Pabich, her roommate's brother and his two friends had been partying at her apartment when they decided to go hunting about midnight. "They talked me into loaning them my .22 rifle," said Pabich. "Trevor, one of the morons, promised they'd have it back to me the next day."

"What model is your rifle?" asked Dunn.

"It's a Marlin semiautomatic," said Pabich. "I told those sonsabitches if I didn't get my gun back, I was going to turn their asses in and testify against them."

"Did they tell you where they hid the rifle?"

"Yeah, Trevor said he threw it into the blackberry bushes next to a creek and a rotting old barn."

"Have they gone back up there to get the rifle?"

"No. They're scared of that crazy old man."

Pabich agreed to ride up to the ranch with Warden Dunn and retrieve the rifle. As it turned out, the rifle was face down in the blackberry brambles, ten yards from where the dead buck was found. On the way back, Dunn asked Pabich if she was still willing to testify against the three deer poachers. "Absolutely!" she said, without the slightest hesitation. "They told me they were going pig hunting. I learned in one of my wildlife management classes how damaging those damn pigs are. I didn't know those guys were gonna poach a deer."

"From the looks of it, they killed two deer," said Dunn.

"That does it!" said Pabich. "You can count on me to testify."

"Do you mind if I ask you one more question?" said Dunn.

"I know what you're going to ask," replied Pabich. "How did I get mixed up with those miscreants in the first place?"

"You guessed it," said Dunn, laughing.

"Dickie Gleason is my roommate's brother. Betty and I had a few classmates over after a big exam the other night. Dickie and his two idiot friends showed up unexpectedly. In addition to taking my rifle, they drank most of our beer. I probably had one too many myself, or I wouldn't have let 'em take my rifle."

After dropping Pabich off at her apartment, Warden Dunn immediately drove to the Department of Justice Ballistics Lab and logged in the rifle. He requested that the lab run the rifle for any possible fingerprints and attempt to match it with the slug he had delivered several days earlier.

While waiting for results from the lab, Dunn again contacted each of the suspects individually. He advised them that he now had the rifle, the bullet from the deer they had killed, and a reliable witness statement from Molly Pabich. Gatlin and Butts refused to admit anything and stuck to their original story. Gleason didn't come clean, but seemed willing to give up the shooter if a deal could be made. Dunn advised him that he couldn't make any promises but believed the district attorney would look favorably upon his cooperation.

The next day, Warden Dunn received a preliminary phone call from the Department of Justice Lab. No usable fingerprints had been found, but the bullet Dunn had pulled out of the giant buck matched up perfectly with the Marlin .22 rifle he had found in the blackberry brambles. With Molly Pabich as a witness and Gleason giving up the shooter, Warden Dunn was ready to tie a bow around his case and present it to the district attorney. Unfortunately, things never seem to be quite that simple for wildlife officers; there's usually a rat in the woodpile. In this case, there were two rats—Gatlin and Butts.

Molly Pabich telephoned Warden Dunn, shouting obscenities into the receiver. "Those rotten sonsabitches broke out all of the windows in my pickup and my camper shell."

Dunn raced to the scene. On the way, he radioed Eureka Police Department and requested that an officer respond to Pabich's apartment to take a vandalism report. When uniformed Eureka Police Officer Dale Street arrived, Dunn filled him in on the circumstances of the investigation.

"I have a pretty good idea who did this," said Dunn, as the two officers stood next to the severely damaged truck in the apartment complex parking lot. "I'll let you know when I have enough to make the case." Unbeknownst to Dunn and Street, Molly Pabich had left the scene and gone inside her apartment.

Enraged by what her acquaintances had done to her truck, Pabich frantically searched the phone book for Trevor Gatlin's number. Gatlin wasn't listed, but she did find a phone number and address for Tyler Butts. When Butts answered the phone, he was showered with a barrage of expletives from the furious Pabich.

"You and that little son of a bitch Trevor destroyed my truck," shouted Pabich, her voice cracking. "I'm going to make sure you bastards go to jail for killing those deer."

"You better not testify against us," responded Butts, "or next time we'll burn the rest of your truck with you in it."

Pabich stormed out of her apartment with a baseball bat in hand and tried to climb into her truck. Warden Dunn and Officer Street were forced to restrain the furious young lady in order to find out what had transpired inside her apartment.

"They threatened to kill me!" screamed Pabich, tears streaming down her cheeks. Warden Dunn quickly realized that his misdemeanor closed season deer investigation had elevated to a case of felony threatening a witness. The battered truck was all the evidence he needed to prove the sincerity of the threat.

"Molly, if you do something foolish, it will just make things worse," said Dunn. "You need to calm down."

"They don't scare me," said Pabich, handing the bat to Warden Dunn.

"I believe that," said Dunn. "Now stand back and let us do our job."

Walking toward the rear of Pabich's pickup and examining the tailgate, Warden Dunn noticed fresh blood in the shattered glass and on the ground. He envisioned a possible scenario: One of the suspects had stood by the driver's side of the tailgate and swung a baseball bat, or possibly an ax handle, at the back window of the camper shell. When the glass shattered, it cut his left forearm badly enough for a significant amount of blood to spill. "With this amount of blood," said Dunn, "I'm guessing that someone needed stitches."

Warden Dunn carefully gathered the blood-spattered glass, marked it with an evidence tag, and delivered it to the Department of Justice Laboratory for analysis. Leaving the lab, he drove out to Blue Lake. Sure enough, Butts was wearing a professionally applied bandage on his left forearm.

"How did you hurt your arm?" asked Dunn.

Butts thought for a second before answering. "I fell on a rock while fishing last weekend and had to go to the emergency room at the hospital for stitches."

"Oh," said Dunn, "where did this happen?"

Butts wasn't quick enough to see where Warden Dunn was headed with his line of questioning and dug a deeper hole for himself with each answer. "Down by Shelter Cove."

"What hospital did you go to?"

"That one on Harrison Avenue—Saint John's or somethin' like that."

"St. Joseph's?"

"Yeah, that's it."

"You drove all the way back to Eureka to get stitches?"

"Yeah."

"What time of day was it?"

"I don't know… about noon."

"Who'd you go fishing with?"

About that time, Trevor Gatlin came roaring up in his Corolla, shouting out the window at Butts not to answer any questions. "That's all right," said Dunn, as he climbed into his patrol truck. "I'll be seeing you boys again soon." As Dunn drove away, Butts and Gatlin stood at the curb with puzzled looks on their faces.

Just about every district attorney's office had at least one deputy DA who enjoyed working with Fish and Game on wildlife-related cases. The Eureka office was no exception. Warden Dunn's go-to prosecutor was a young, energetic deputy, three years out of law school, named Lisa Parker.

"Lisa, are you busy?" asked Dunn, standing in the office doorway.

"Of course I'm busy, John, but I've always got time for you guys. Come in and sit down. What do you have for me?"

Warden Dunn handed Parker a preliminary report he had typed up before coming to her office. It contained a chronological history of what had transpired so far. While Parker read the report, Dunn sat across the desk, watching the expressions on the young deputy DA's face. The more Parker read, the more interested she became, particularly when she came to the part about Molly Pabich's pickup being destroyed and the verbal threat to her life.

"Can we count on this Molly to testify?" asked Parker.

"How about I arrange for her to come in and talk to you?" Dunn said.

"I'm in court tomorrow morning. See if you can get her to come in tomorrow afternoon about three. I should be free then."

"Thanks, Lisa. I'll see you tomorrow."

After meeting with Molly Pabich the following afternoon, Lisa Parker wasn't just willing to take on the case, she was committed to putting the suspects behind bars. Although Warden Dunn normally wrote his own search warrants and affidavits, writing them for hospital records could be a little tricky, so Parker offered to do most of the work. As expected, the records clearly proved that Butts had been lying about falling on a rock during his supposed fishing trip.

Butts had shown up at the hospital ER the same evening that Pabich's truck had been vandalized—not over the weekend, as he had told Warden Dunn. There was one additional detail in the hospital records that Dunn hadn't anticipated: tiny fragments of glass were pulled from the wound; these clearly hadn't come from a rock.

Deputy District Attorney Parker advised Warden Dunn to immediately prepare a search warrant requiring Tyler Butts to submit to a blood test. The results would be compared with the blood samples at the DOJ lab. Since Butts had not cooperated up to that point, Dunn also secured a warrant for his arrest.

It took Warden Dunn several days to finally locate Butts, make the arrest, and take him in handcuffs to the Eureka laboratory. The lab drew blood from Butts and forwarded it directly to the Department of Justice Lab. Butts's blood type matched that found on the broken glass recovered from Pabich's truck window. This wasn't conclusive proof that Butts had bashed in Pabich's window, but it contributed to the significant amount of circumstantial evidence Warden Dunn was collecting.

Before writing the final arrest report and filing criminal complaints against all three suspects, Warden Dunn and Deputy District Attorney Parker decided to interview Richard Gleason one more time. Dunn still felt that if anyone cracked and told the truth, it would be Gleason. A meeting was arranged with Gleason and his attorney. No promises were made, but it was explained to Gleason that if he had not been involved in the vandalism or threatening the witness, now was the time to tell the truth and agree to testify against Gatlin and Butts.

"I knew I shouldn't have gone with 'em," said Gleason, "but those guys talked me into it. I wanted to tell you the truth before, but I was afraid."

"What really happened?" asked Dunn.

"We were driving through the hills with Tyler shining the light out the window. Trevor said, 'There's one,' and hit the brakes. I thought he was talking about a pig, then I saw this little doe staring back at the spotlight. Trevor reached over and held the light while Tyler shot it. Both of them started laughing and we just left it there. They didn't even get out of the car."

"Then what happened?"

"We went a couple miles farther, when this huge buck crossed the road in front of us. Trevor shined the spotlight out the window and the deer stopped by the creek and looked back at us. Next thing I know, Tyler sticks the rifle out the window and kills it, too. Trevor was all excited about keeping this one, because it had a big set of antlers."

"Is that when you were contacted by the rancher?"

"Yeah. Tyler and Trevor were dragging the deer up out of the creek bed when the old man pulled up in his truck."

"Where were you?"

"I was hiding in the backseat. I told 'em I didn't want any part of killing that deer."

"Did you see where they hid the rifle?"

"No, one of 'em must have thrown it in the bushes when they saw the old man's truck coming."

"So what about breaking all the windows in Molly's truck?"

"That was Trevor and Tyler. I wasn't there, but they were laughing about it when they came by my house to tell me to keep my mouth shut."

The wheels of justice turn slowly and this case was no exception. During the months that followed, Molly Pabich transferred from Humboldt State University to the University of Alaska in Fairbanks. Preliminary hearings were held regarding the felony charges. Warden Dunn was allowed to testify in Pabich's place. Pabich, herself, would be required to testify at the actual trials. Tyler Butts's trial was in March of 1980. The district attorney's office sent Molly Pabich plane tickets and a subpoena to appear in court as a witness.

Butts was represented by a Eureka ambulance chaser named Anthony Bertram. Bertram had a reputation for pulling dirty tricks, making outrageous accusations, objecting to everything, and wasting the court's valuable time. He began by contesting Warden Dunn's testimony and the evidence he had collected. That didn't work. He tried to discredit Gleason's testimony, claiming the prosecution had promised rewards. This tactic didn't work either. Then he set his sights on Landon Culpepper.

"Isn't it true that the game warden instructed you to stop the car and seize the keys?" said Bertram.

"Mister, I barely speak to the game warden and sure as hell don't do anything he tells me to," responded Culpepper.

When it came time to cross-examine Molly Pabich, Bertram showed no mercy. He tried every dirty trick in the book to get her riled and make her appear mentally unstable. Pabich managed to hold her temper about having her rifle borrowed and not returned. She barely held it together when Bertram questioned her about the truck being vandalized.

"You're known for losing your temper and shouting obscenities at people, aren't you, Miss Pabich?" asked Bertram. "Couldn't any number of other people have broken your truck windows?"

"No, it was those two right over there," said Pabich, pointing at Butts, at the defendant's table, then Gatlin, sitting in the front row behind him.

"How can you be sure?"

"Because that son of a bitch right there told me they did it," screamed Pabich, with tears in her eyes. She stood up and pointed across the room at Tyler Butts. "He said if I testified against them, the next time they would burn my truck with me in it! And I could hear Trevor in the background, telling him what to say."

The judge tapped his desk with the gavel and immediately called a recess, giving the prosecution time to calm their witness. Warden Dunn and Deputy DA Parker led Molly Pabich into a small room down the hall. Parker reminded Pabich that one of the requirements of proving the crime was showing that she felt threatened or intimidated by what Butts had said. If Pabich indicated that she wasn't afraid, the judge might get the wrong impression.

Back in court, Bertram continued to badger Molly Pabich. He needled her incessantly, trying to push the right button that would send Pabich into another tirade and prove to the judge that she wasn't frightened or intimidated by Butts and Gatlin. This time Molly was able to hold her fiery temper and wear the defense attorney down. The judge ruled that Pabich had every right to fear for her life and found Butts guilty on all counts.

A few days after Butts was found guilty in court, Gatlin and Gleason pleaded no contest and were also sentenced. Butts and Gatlin were both convicted of felony threatening a witness, for which they served thirty days in Humboldt County Jail. They were convicted of one count of taking deer during closed season and each was required to pay a fine of $1,150. Conditions of formal probation included loss of hunting privileges for three years and warrantless search. As convicted felons, Butts and Gatlin were no longer allowed to possess firearms. Although Molly Pabich had already flown back to Alaska, Butts and Gatlin were ordered not to have any contact whatsoever with her or Richard Gleason.

Richard Gleason was placed on summary probation for three years, during which time he was not allowed to hunt or be in the company of anyone who was hunting.

CHANGING
TIMES

1980–1990

Stakeout at Battle Creek

———— ◆ ————

I'M SOMETIMES ASKED IF I had any favorite places to work during my twenty-one years supervising the warden force in western Shasta County. Lower Battle Creek immediately comes to mind—from the mouth, where Battle Creek flows into the Sacramento River, to the barrier weir at Coleman National Fish Hatchery.

Every fall, from mid-September to early November, this three-mile stretch of Battle Creek would come alive with fall-run Chinook salmon. Right behind the salmon were the poachers—some by day and some by night—with fist-sized snag hooks, dip nets, spears, gaffs, and pitchforks. Many's the year we had to practically stand guard on this extraordinary stream and its anadromous visitors.

I often parked my patrol truck and hiked the trails and footpaths running the length of lower Battle Creek, many of them created by decades of illegal activity. Quietly passing through this riparian paradise, I was in constant awe of the giant native sycamores and majestic valley oaks that grew along the shoreline. Every break in the vegetation offered a window to Battle Creek itself—its reflective surface decorated with brilliant fall colors, its gravel bottom excavated with salmon redds laden with fish eggs, its waters alive with the sights and sounds of salmon splashing their way upstream.

Although I was involved in countless salmon-related investigations on lower Battle Creek, two nights in late October 1986 will remain fixed in my mind forever.

It all started early one morning with a phone call from the Coleman National Fish Hatchery. Warden Merton Hatcher, a tall gray-haired veteran who had worked Battle Creek and the surrounding area for many years, answered the phone in the squad room at the Redding Fish and Game office.

"Fish and Game. Warden Hatcher."

"Mert, this is Jack, down at Coleman Hatchery."

"Hey, Jack, how's it going?"

"Somebody snuck into the hatchery late last night. From the looks of all the eggs scattered around, they took several salmon."

"Where exactly did you find the eggs, Jack?"

"All over the rocks and up the bank, at the southwest side of the barrier weir."

"Thanks for the call, Jack. We'll be right out."

I happened to be in the squad room when Warden Hatcher took the call, so he and I responded and began examining the evidence. As the hatchery employee had described, bright red salmon eggs were scattered in the rocks and up the bank, immediately south of the hatchery's entry pond and egg-collecting station.

"These guys couldn't have been too smart," I said. "They left a trail for us to follow."

"A trail?" said Hatcher.

"Yeah, look at this." I began walking from the hatchery's southwest boundary, following fish eggs as I went.

"Maybe it was a bear," joked one of the hatchery employees.

"Bears don't wear tennis shoes," I replied. "Looks like we have at least two culprits. See, there's a couple eggs over there, a few more here, and six or seven up ahead. You can even see impressions in the dirt where they dragged a bag or a fish across the ground."

"Did you see that big, hook-nosed buck near the ladder?" asked Hatcher. "He must weigh fifty or sixty pounds."

"That was about the biggest live salmon I've ever seen," I said.

"We've seen several that size this fall," said the hatchery employee.

"I think they're after the roe," said Hatcher. "They probably took the hens and left the males." "Hens"—gravid female salmon—entering the hatchery could carry as many as 8,000 eggs, depending on the size of the fish. Warden Hatcher believed that the poachers were transporting the egg-laden Chinook hens somewhere, ripping out the egg skeins, and illegally selling them. Fresh salmon roe, a favorite steelhead bait, was in big demand with bait dealers and fishermen.

Warden Hatcher and I followed a diminishing trail of fish eggs west for two or three hundred yards, along the north bank of Battle Creek, then turned right and walked another hundred and fifty yards to a locked metal gate at Coleman Fish Hatchery Road. Just inside the gate was an overgrown blackberry bramble with some of its lower branches smashed down. Among the leaves and thorny branches were more scattered fish eggs. It appeared that several large salmon had been sequestered there while the poachers waited for their getaway vehicle to arrive.

With most of the Coleman Hatchery employees living in government housing on the hatchery grounds, Hatcher and I figured the poachers were slipping in after midnight, when everyone was asleep. We decided to pull an all-night stakeout, beginning that same evening.

Warden Hatcher dropped me off at the metal gate about 11:00 p.m. Equipped with a flashlight, a handheld radio, binoculars, and a warm coat, I quickly climbed the steep hillside north of Coleman Fish Hatchery Road. Hatcher continued toward the fish hatchery, where he would hide his patrol vehicle and wait for any signs of activity.

Plodding up the hillside through the poison oak, buckbrush, blue oaks, and dry grass, I reached a clearing fifty yards above the valley floor. From my lofty lookout, I could see the streetlights at Coleman National Fish Hatchery, a half mile to the east. Directly below me were the road, the metal gate, and a well-worn trail leading across an open field to Battle Creek—all of which were barely visible under a waning gibbous moon.

With my flashlight turned off and my size-eleven Hi-Tech boots braced against a half-buried lava rock, I leaned back against the steep hillside and stared into the darkness for the next six hours. During that time, I saw no cars and detected no poaching activity. The only noises I heard all night came from two great horned owls hooting back and forth at each other from the massive, old-growth sycamores growing along the stream bank.

The sun was just coming up when I spotted something prancing across the open field in my direction. "What do we have here?" I said to myself, focusing my binoculars on the subject. "That better not be a house cat out there stalking my quail. Nope! I'd recognize those pointy ears and that bushy tail anywhere." Just as I was commenting about how beautiful the little canine looked in his shiny new winter coat, he suddenly stopped.

Directly in the fox's path, not five yards away, stood two rooster pheasants. "This is interesting!" I said. The fox stood erect, in a nonthreatening posture, staring directly at the two seemingly unfazed birds. The pheasants leaned forward, extended their necks, and stared back at the fox. I couldn't believe my eyes when the fox completely ignored the birds and continued on his way. Instead of flying or running away, both pheasants jumped aside then began following the fox. Every time the fox slowed and looked back, the cagey birds would stop and hyperextend their necks. When the fox crossed the road and began climbing the hillside, the pheasants followed closely behind. Finally, the fox disappeared into a patch of buckbrush, and the pheasants, one by one, flew over the road and back into the adjacent field. The lesson to be learned

from this event is *you never know what you're going to see if you remain still
and let nature come to you.*

MINUTES AFTER THE PHEASANTS had flown away, Warden Hatcher radioed
me and asked if I was ready to go home and get some sleep. "I don't know," I
replied. "I'm having so much fun up here, I might stay a while longer."

"Ten-nine," said Hatcher, questioning my unusual response.

"Come pick me up," I said, laughing. "I'll be waiting at the road."

After sleeping the rest of the day, I telephoned Warden Hatcher and
suggested that we try the same stakeout again that night. I volunteered
to watch from the hillside again. The plan was to let the salmon poachers
conduct their illicit business and make their way back to the metal gate. When
the getaway car arrived and the illegal fish had been placed inside, we would
spring the trap and arrest the entire gang.

Much like the night before, it was approaching 11:00 when Warden
Hatcher dropped me off at the metal gate. I traversed the steep hillside, but
instead of climbing to my original lookout position, I found a clearing about
twenty-five yards above the road and directly in line with the gate. The use
of my flashlight was absolutely essential to prevent my tripping over rocks or
crashing into a patch of poison oak. Although the nights were getting colder,
midday temperatures remained in the high seventies, so the remote possibility
of stepping on a rattlesnake was always in the back of my mind.

Events of the first two hours were virtually identical to those of the
previous evening. It was just after 1:00 a.m. when I heard a car approaching.

"Eleven thirteen, eleven ten, on direct," I said over the radio.

"Eleven thirteen, go ahead," replied Warden Hatcher.

"Be advised, I hear a car heading this way from Gover Road."

"Ten-four, I'll stand by."

A minute or two later, I saw headlights approaching from around the
bend. A small, compact car came to a sudden stop ten feet past the gate. The
passenger door opened and a dome light came on. I heard laughing, as the
first occupant climbed out of the passenger seat. He was quite large—so large
that the car sprang upward as he exited. A smaller man emerged from the
backseat.

"Tell Brad to pick us up at three," said the larger man, leaning in through
the passenger-side door.

The voice sounded vaguely familiar, but I couldn't place where I'd heard
it before.

"Okay, I will," came a female voice.

The car backed up, turned around, and left in the same direction from
whence it had come.

I heard the metal gate squeak and moan under the strain of someone's weight, followed by laughter and muffled voices. Minutes later, a narrow beam of light appeared in the field across the road. It shined for a second or two then went dim. A bottle whistled through the still night air, followed by the sound of breaking glass and more laughter.

"Eleven thirteen, eleven ten, be advised, our subjects are walking across the field in the direction of Battle Creek. They may be intoxicated."

"Ten-four," said Hatcher.

It took the suspects twenty or thirty minutes to reach the Coleman Fish Hatchery and make their way up to the Battle Creek barrier weir. That night, the fish were stacked against the weir like cordwood, searching for a way upstream. Warden Hatcher watched, from forty yards away, as the silhouettes of two men appeared at the top of the stream bank.

"I saw some kind of long pole before they dropped out of sight," whispered Hatcher over the radio.

"Is it a spear?" I asked.

"It probably is. I can't tell from here."

"Can you hear them?"

"No, the water falling over the weir is so loud I can't hear anything."

"Let 'em do their thing. We'll catch 'em back at the gate, when their driver comes to pick 'em up. I heard 'em mention three o'clock."

"Ten-four."

"By the way, how long was that pole?"

"Maybe seven or eight feet."

"It wouldn't have fit in the little car I saw. They must have it stashed out there somewhere."

"Ten-four."

An hour went by before Warden Hatcher contacted me again. "Eleven ten, eleven thirteen, on direct."

"Go ahead."

"One of the suspects just topped the stream bank, carrying that long pole. He's headed downstream with it."

"Ten-four."

"Now there's another man up on the stream bank."

"Do they have fish?"

"I can't tell. All I can see are their silhouettes. That one guy's as big as a house. Wait a minute ... the little guy just came back without the spear. Now the big guy is picking something up."

"Can you see what it is?"

"He's dragging it along the ground. It's probably a gunny sack full of fish.

The little guy dropped out of sight, then came back dragging another bag. I think they're leaving."

"Ten-four. Get back to your truck. It's two thirty-five now. I'll call you when it's time to come in."

"Ten-four."

Like clockwork, I heard the sound of a vehicle approaching at exactly 3:00 a.m.

A truck rounded the corner, pulled to the right, and lit up the gate with its headlights. I could see just enough of the getaway vehicle to identify it as an old delivery truck—the kind used to deliver bread or packages. The headlights immediately went off, and the driver ran around to the back. Flinging open the rear doors, he began shouting to the others.

I heard large objects flopping to the ground, then the familiar squeaking and groaning of the metal gate as someone climbed over.

"Eleven thirteen, start slowly heading this way. I'll tell you when to step on it."

"Ten-four."

When the rear doors of the delivery truck were finally closed and our salmon poachers were inside, I again radioed Warden Hatcher.

"Eleven thirteen, they're leaving. Come on in!"

Ten seconds later, Warden Hatcher's patrol truck, with the red spotlight turned on and in the forward position, blocked the suspects' path as they attempted to back away from the gate. I was in such a hurry attempting to reach the crime scene, I slipped in the wet grass, fell backward, and slid halfway down the hillside.

"Department of Fish and Game," shouted Hatcher. "Driver, turn off your motor and put your hands on the steering wheel where I can see them." The driver's door was still open and the driver was in full view as Warden Hatcher approached.

I came around from the passenger side, just as one of the suspects was about to step out through the open door. "That's far enough," I said, shining my flashlight in his eyes. "Where's the other guy?"

"What other guy?" responded a short, slender young man wearing water-soaked Levis, muddy tennis shoes, and a tattered sweatshirt.

"That guy right there," I said, shining my flashlight into the back corner of the delivery truck.

"Hello, Dennis," I said. "I see you're up to your old tricks again."

"This is embarrassing," said the gargantuan outlaw, sitting on a five-gallon bucket and panting heavily.

"I'll let you catch your breath before I ask you why you're out here poaching our salmon at three o'clock in the morning," I said.

COINCIDENTALLY, I HAD BEEN engaged in another stakeout the first time Dennis Adamo and I had crossed paths. It was a clear afternoon in early February, two years earlier. Having received previous reports of closed season duck shooting on a pond south of the Redding Airport, I was hiding nearby, listening for shots.

From the driver's seat of my patrol truck, I noticed some suspicious activity at the east side of an isolated, run-down house, a half mile from my location. I picked up my spotting scope and focused it on two men, one of average height and weight, the other of enormous proportions. "They look like they're skinning some kind of animal," I said to myself. "Probably a sheep or a goat." For the next fifteen minutes, I watched from a distance as my subjects went about their business. I couldn't imagine anyone being so brazen as to butcher a closed-season deer out in the open during broad daylight. Just in case, I decided to drive over and investigate.

Approaching from the west, I drove around the corner of the house and came to a stop directly in front of two men, both up to their elbows in dried blood, each holding a skinning knife. The animal turned out to be a yearling doe, and one of the violators I arrested that day was Dennis Adamo.

After being released from the county jail on his own recognizance, Adamo failed to appear in court at the designated date and time. A warrant was issued for his arrest, and he was taken into custody a month later after running a stop sign somewhere near Fairfield. The only option I had for bringing Adamo before a Shasta County magistrate was transporting him to Redding myself. All the way up Interstate 5, I listened to the story of Dennis Adamo's life.

"I can tell you things that you wouldn't believe," said Adamo, regaling me with stories about his former life as a commercial fisherman and habitual duck poacher.

"What made you become a poacher?" I asked.

"Believe it or not, I always wanted to be a game warden," said Adamo, "but I couldn't pass the test."

"That's too bad," I said. "We could have saved a lot of wildlife."

"Yeah. I would have made a great game warden."

"You may have, but I was talking about all the wildlife you killed."

"Good point," said Adamo, smiling. "I'm through with that now. It used to be exciting, but my heart can't take it anymore. Maybe I'll sell all my guns and take up golf."

"What do you do for a living?"

"I was a bus mechanic until I got laid off."

"How'd you end up in the Redding area?"

"My drinkin' buddies and I used to rent a houseboat on Shasta Lake every summer. We'd fish all day and party all night .... Wait a minute! I knew I recognized you from somewhere. You and another guy busted us for having too many bass."

"We've boarded a lot of houseboats on Shasta Lake. I'm sorry I didn't remember you."

"That's probably because I've gained sixty or seventy pounds since then."

"That could be it."

"Hey, man, what's going to happen to me?"

"That'll be up to the judge and whether or not you plead guilty."

"You caught us red-handed, what good would it do to plead not guilty? I would have paid the fine like my buddy, but I was between jobs at the time."

Adamo pleaded guilty and received a thirty day jail sentence. He was released after ten days, due to overcrowding in the jail, and didn't show up again until that memorable night in October of 1986.

"IT'S BEEN A WHILE," said Adamo, still hyperventilating.

"Apparently not long enough," I said. "I thought you weren't going do this kind of thing anymore."

"What can I say, man? You're too smart for me."

"Well, you know the routine by now." All three subjects were identified, checked for weapons, and instructed to sit down in front of the gate while Warden Hatcher searched the delivery truck.

"I was right," said Hatcher, shouting from inside the truck. "They were carrying gunny sacks full of fish. It looks like they're all hens, too."

"Don't tell me you guys have been selling fish eggs," I said.

No one responded, but the look on Adamo's face pretty much confirmed my suspicions.

Hatcher dragged two gunny sacks out through the rear doors of the delivery truck and dropped them on the ground in front of the gate. They contained a total of seven female salmon.

Dennis Anthony Adamo, thirty-one-year-old Ralph Edward Spooner, and twenty-four-year-old Shane Allen Poole all claimed to work for a wood products company south of Anderson. Spooner, the delivery truck operator, was a tall, red-headed character who didn't seem to understand the seriousness of his violation.

"Hey, man," he said, "I was just giving these dudes a ride back to town. I didn't know they were poaching salmon."

"What did you think they were doing out here at three in the morning?" asked Warden Hatcher.

"I don't know," said Spooner, giggling and showing off for his friends, "catching frogs?"

Poole, the youngest of the group, displayed an equally uncooperative attitude. When asked where he'd hidden the long pole with the spear on the end, he responded, "I don't know what you're talking about."

"Here are your options," I said. "You can cooperate, in which case we'll take down some information and send you on your way. A complaint will be filed with the district attorney, charging all of you with possession of seven unlawfully taken salmon. You'll receive a notice to appear in court. If you fail to appear in court, a warrant will be issued and we'll come down to your job site and arrest you. Or, we can have your truck towed right now and spend the next three hours booking you into the county jail. Mr. Adamo remembers what that's like. Which will it be?"

"Tell 'em where the spear is," said Adamo.

"Mr. Poole, how about you and I walk back and get the spear?" I said.

"I'll babysit these guys until you get back," said Hatcher.

In the end, Adamo, Spooner, and Poole each paid fines of $650, plus the penalty assessment. I never saw Dennis Adamo again. Spooner showed up at the Anderson River Park softball complex a few years later and jokingly reminded me of our first encounter. I asked if he was behaving himself.

"I have a good job now and I got married," he said.

"Do you still have that old delivery truck?" I asked.

"No, the engine blew up right after you busted us. I thought it was cool when I bought that piece of junk, but it was nothin' but trouble."

"Well, good luck in your game."

"Thanks, man. You too."

Undercover Joe

———— ◆ ————

"**H**ow are you boys doing?" said Sandberg, as he sauntered into the squad room. It was a sunny April afternoon in 1986. Warden Dave Szody and I were killing time at the Redding Regional Fish and Game Office before heading up to Shasta Lake for an evening's boat patrol.

"Well, look who's here," I said. "It's the phantom of Fish and Wildlife."

Forty-one-year-old Joe Sandberg had been working undercover for the U.S. Fish and Wildlife Service since 1979, when he decided to leave the Oregon State Police and spend the rest of his enforcement career saving wildlife in a covert capacity. As a U.S. Fish and Wildlife special agent, Sandberg did most of his work in Northern California and Southern Oregon, but the skillful investigator had also been given undercover assignments in Alaska, Nevada, and Arizona.

Standard summer attire for this six-foot-one-inch, 200-pound master of deception was a pair of sandals, Bermuda shorts, and a loose-fitting, inconspicuous T-shirt. On this particular day, Joe had dressed up a bit and was wearing a red, green, and white Hawaiian shirt adorned with palm trees and hula dancers. Agent Sandberg sported a bushy, unkempt mustache and wore his dishwater blond hair halfway down the back of his neck.

"What have you been up to, Joe?" I asked.

"The usual crap," Joe replied. "I'd rather be out bustin' poachers with you guys. Ya know, Steve, you and Dave are my favorite state game wardens."

"Aw, shucks, Joe," I said. "I bet you tell that to all the state game wardens." The good-natured banter would continue for several more minutes until Joe got around to telling us the purpose of his visit.

"So what are you guys up to?" said Sandberg.

"We're about to go up and spend the evening working Shasta Lake," said Szody.

"Would you mind dropping me off down the street from a pawn shop here in Redding? I need to check out a guy who works there, and I don't want anyone to see my truck. I'll only be in there a couple minutes."

"Sure, Joe," I said. "No problem."

Warden Szody and I dropped Agent Sandberg off about two blocks west of the pawn shop. As Sandberg strolled east along the sidewalk, I looked over at Warden Szody and said, "Watch this." Initially walking tall and erect, Sandberg quickly morphed into one of his alter egos, with rounded shoulders and a slight limp in his left leg. "Any minute now, he'll mess up his hair."

"There he goes!" said Szody, laughing.

"Keep watching," I said. "Just before he reaches Market Street, he'll really get into his act and start that sashaying bit he does."

"Wow!" said Szody, as both of us laughed out loud. "He's good!"

***

U.S. FISH AND WILDLIFE Special Agent Joe Sandberg always had two or three covert operations going on at the same time. He usually worked solo, but if the case involved non-migratory species like deer or bear, he would sometimes ask a California Fish and Game warden for assistance. One of Sandberg's ruses was posing as Leon French, a shady freelance jewelry salesman specializing in necklaces, bracelets, Native American handicrafts, and other trinkets and doodads.

Late in October 1985, Agent Sandberg was returning from an undercover salmon and steelhead assignment on California's North Coast when he decided to stop at a gun shop in the Trinity County town of Weaverville. While in the shop, he met a middle-aged gentleman named Virgil Darsey and struck up a conversation.

"I make traditional handcrafted jewelry," said Sandberg, "and usually throw in a bear claw or two to make it look authentic. Do you know any bear hunters around these parts who might have bear claws to sell?" Sandberg opened a leather case from the cab of his undercover pickup and displayed a few gold jewelry items to Darsey.

"Yeah, I might know somebody," said Darsey. "Do you have a business card or something?"

Agent Sandberg handed Darsey a business card with the name Leon French and an undercover phone number printed on the front. "If you know anybody, have him give me a call," said Sandberg. "I'll make him a good deal."

Four months later, on the afternoon of February 25, 1986, the undercover phone rang at Agent Sandberg's Sacramento Valley residence. Sandberg's wife was home at the time and answered.

"Hello."

"Hello, is Leon in?"

"No. May I take a message?"

"This is Jesse Deaver, from up in Trinity County. Uh, Virgil Darsey is a mutual friend and he gave me Leon's number."

"Leon should be back tonight. Do you want me to have him call you?"

"Do you know Virgil?"

"No. I assume Leon does. What's your number, please?"

"Just tell him I'll call him back tomorrow night."

"Okay, I'll give him the message. Thanks for calling."

The undercover phone rang again the following evening at 8:15. This time Agent Sandberg answered.

"Hello."

"Hello, Leon?"

"Yeah."

"This is Jesse Deaver, from up in Trinity County."

"Oh, yeah. My wife said you called last night. Sorry I missed you."

"I guess you know Virgil Darsey from up here? He gave me your number and said I should call you. I tried your number two or three times earlier, but no one answered."

"I'm not here much—out trying to make a buck. You know how that is."

"What do you do?"

"Oh, I do some gold panning and this and that. Got a couple houses here in Sacramento that I manage. The wife works part-time. We do a lot a little things to get by."

"Virgil says you make jewelry."

"Yeah, I do. I dabble in that." Sandberg had mastered the art of avoiding the real subject until he was sure the suspect trusted him. By appearing cautious about his supposed dealings in animal parts, it made his cover more credible and generally put the suspect at ease. "I wanted to do some dredging up on the Trinity, but most of the good spots are already staked out."

"Yeah, they are," said Deaver.

"I was talking to Virgil a few months ago and he said he might know some people who have bear claws for me."

"Yeah, I'm probably the only one who would."

"Uh-huh."

"Virgil told me you were also interested in some big teeth."

"Has he been talking to my dentist?"

"What?

"I was just kidding," said Sandberg, realizing that his joke had been wasted on Deaver. "Yeah, I can use some nice canines."

"Well, I've got a few saved up. You probably know it's illegal for me to sell those things."

"I sure do," responded Sandberg. "I'm just a businessman, not a cop."

Deaver and Agent Sandberg continued to discuss bear teeth for the next five minutes, with Deaver claiming to have twenty-five or so on hand. "I got maybe ten or twelve galls," said Deaver, without any prompting from Sandberg. Under California law, it's a felony to sell bear parts. The possession of more than one bear gallbladder is considered prima facie evidence that the items are possessed for sale. Not wanting to spook Deaver, Sandberg didn't' comment on the gallbladders and instead focused on the bear claws.

"I can take my bear claws over ta Reno and get ten bucks apiece for 'em any day of the week," bragged Deaver.

"You must be kidding," said Sandberg. "I wouldn't pay more than two or three dollars for a bear claw unless it's a really nice one."

Again, the seasoned undercover officer downplayed his interest in purchasing bear parts. Sounding more relaxed, Deaver began talking about his bear guide business.

"I charge four hundred dollars for a small bear and six hundred for a big one," said Deaver. "I even guide mountain lion hunts over in Nevada."

The conversation finally ended with Agent Sandberg telling Deaver he would enjoy meeting him sometime in the future. It was obvious to the undercover agent that Jesse Deaver had telephoned him to find out how much he'd pay for bear claws. It remained to be seen whether Sandberg and Deaver would eventually do business.

On the first of April, Agent Sandberg telephoned Jesse Deaver.

"I'm going to be up in Trinity County this Sunday," said Sandberg. "I was wondering if we could get together."

"That would be great," said Deaver, "but I'm gonna be runnin' a turkey shoot. You're welcome to come up and join us."

"I think I would enjoy that. Do you mind if I bring a friend along?"

"Don't mind at all. Be sure to bring your shotguns."

Deaver had no way of knowing that Sandberg's friend was Warden Ed Nagel. Nagel worked with the California Department of Fish and Game's Special Operations Unit and was usually the first state undercover officer Sandberg called when he needed assistance. In his early thirties at the time, he was lean, muscular, and two or three inches shorter than Sandberg. The two officers worked well together, and after a few investigations, Ed Nagel had become Agent Sandberg's trusted sidekick.

"What time will you be here?" asked Deaver.

"Probably about noon," said Sandberg. "How will I recognize you?"

"Just ask for Jesse the bear hunter," said Deaver. "I'll be either running one of the shoots or at the barbeque cookin'."

Agent Sandberg and Warden Nagel arrived at the turkey shoot Sunday afternoon, April 6, at approximately 12:40. Sandberg came dressed in his usual casual attire: shorts, running shoes, and a white T-shirt with the logo of a famous Baja California nightclub on the front and back. Warden Nagel, on the other hand, could have easily been mistaken for the square dance caller at a Western hoedown, sporting cowboy boots, pressed Levis, and a long-sleeved Western shirt with button-down pockets. Sitting atop Nagel's well-groomed head was an odd-looking navy-blue baseball cap with an unusually thick bill.

Both men had climbed from Sandberg's pickup and strolled halfway across the unpaved parking area when Agent Sandberg suddenly stopped.

"Ed, come with me," said Sandberg. He led Warden Nagel back through several rows of full-sized pickups, each one outfitted with a gun rack mounted in the rear window.

"Joe, what are we doing?" asked Nagel.

When the two wildlife officers reached the passenger door of Sandberg's truck, Sandberg turned to Nagel and said, "Where did you get that ridiculous baseball cap?"

"Buddy had them made up for everyone on the SOU team," said Nagel. "The bill is thick like this because there's a little tape recorder hidden inside." Nagel removed the cap and showed Sandberg how it worked.

"Ed, between that piece of shit cap and the Roy Rogers outfit you're wearing, it won't be ten minutes before somebody pegs us as game wardens." Sandberg opened the passenger-side door, reached behind the front seat, and handed Nagel a faded blue and gray sweatshirt. He took the thick-billed cap from Nagel's head, threw it behind the seat, and replaced it with a San Francisco Giants baseball cap that someone had sat on a few times. Grinning from ear to ear, Sandberg slapped Nagel on the back. "Am I gonna to have to dress you every time we work together?"

Shotguns were blasting away in rapid succession as Sandberg and Nagel walked into the shooting area. Anyone who wasn't shooting was sitting in a lawn chair with a beer in one hand and a paper plate piled with beans, garlic bread, and chunks of dark-colored meat in the other.

"Come on," said Sandberg, "I'll buy you lunch."

Warden Nagel followed Sandberg over to a canopy and several picnic tables where lunch was being sold for $3.50 a plate—beer and soda extra. As they walked through the food line, Sandberg reached into an ice-filled chest and pulled out a beer. "Joe," whispered Nagel, "we can't drink on duty!"

Sandberg didn't respond or even acknowledge his partner's comment. With food and drink in hand, both men sat down.

"How ya doin'?" said Sandberg to an elderly gentleman wearing a plaid shirt and suspenders, sitting at the opposite end of the picnic table. "Say, do you know Jesse Deaver?"

"Sure do," said the old man, scooping the last spoonful of beans off his plate. "He's over there cookin' that bear meat you're eatin'."

Sandberg and Nagel glanced over at Deaver, who was standing at the barbeque grill wearing a blood-spattered full-length apron. Deaver was about Sandberg's size, but ten years older, with short, graying hair.

"Where do ya sign up for the turkey shoot?" asked Sandberg.

"Them beans is good, ain't they?" answered the old man.

"Yeah, they sure are," said Sandberg. "I was asking you where we sign up for the turkey shoot."

"Oh! Over there," said the elderly gentleman, pointing to a nearby table. "Sorry, I had my hearin' aid turned off with all the shootin' goin' on."

"Whaddya get if ya win?"

"They got all kinds a prizes: canned hams, frozen turkeys, sides a bacon."

"Wow!" said Sandberg, loud enough for everyone within ten feet to hear. "I think I'll see if I can win a ham."

Warden Nagel, popeyed, stared across the table at Sandberg. "What are you gonna do with a canned ham?" he said, as Sandberg left the table and grabbed two more beers out of the ice chest.

"Do you want one?" asked Sandberg. Nagel shook his head. Sandberg paid for the beers and walked toward the barbeque grill.

"Jesse," said Sandberg. "I'm Leon French. That was the best bear meat I've ever eaten. You look like you could use a cold one."

"Thanks," said Deaver. "How long have you been here?"

"We just got here. I brought my gold-panning buddy along. That's him over there at the table."

"Did ya bring your shotgun?"

"You bet I did. I'm anxious to win one a those hams. How about we get together and talk when you're finished cooking?"

"Sounds good," said Deaver. "I'm lookin' forward ta seein' that gold jewelry of yours."

"See you in a little while," said Sandberg, walking toward the parking lot to retrieve his shotgun.

For the next hour or so, Agent Sandberg showed off his skeet-shooting skills while Warden Nagel kept an eye on Deaver from the sidelines. As Sandberg walked back from the range, Nagel quietly confronted him.

"Joe, I need to talk to you."

"Here, honey, I won you a ham," said Sandberg. "I'm gonna get another beer. Do you want one?"

"No, that's what I want to talk to you about." Sandberg kept walking toward the refreshment stand. He walked back to the table with a beer in his hand and popped it open. "Joe, we can't drink on duty!"

"Ed, let me explain how I work. First of all, you need to stop calling me Joe. While we're here at the turkey shoot, my name is Leon. I know you're concerned about me drinking beer, but it's all an act. I take a sip or two out of each can and leave it sitting on the table. If we don't act like we're enjoying ourselves, we'll look suspicious."

"I see you won a ham," shouted Deaver, walking up and interrupting the conversation. I saw you shooting over there. You're a damn good shot."

"I was lucky," said Sandberg. "Jesse, I'd like you to meet my gold-panning buddy, Ed Miller."

Deaver and Warden Nagel shook hands. "Speakin' of gold," said Deaver, "I wouldn't mind takin' a look at that jewelry, if you got it handy."

"Sure," said Sandberg. "It's in my pickup."

Sandberg and Nagel led Deaver out to the parking lot where Sandberg's undercover pickup was located. Agent Sandberg pulled a leather case from behind the seat and opened it on the tailgate for Deaver's inspection. Deaver seemed interested in a few of the items—one gold necklace in particular.

"I like to add a few bear claws to these gold necklaces and bracelets," said Sandberg.

"I collected a couple coffee cans full a bear claws," said Deaver, "but my kids got into 'em and gave 'em all away."

"That's too bad," said Sandberg. "Didn't you tell me on the phone that you had a few bear galls?"

"Yeah, I do," said Deaver. "What do you pay for those?"

"That depends on their condition and how big they are," said Sandberg. "I usually pay between thirty and fifty dollars apiece."

"You guys ain't game wardens, are ya?"

"Hell no," said Sandberg. "Like I told you on the phone, I'm just a businessman."

"That's good," said Deaver, " 'cuz I sold a bunch a galls to another guy who took 'em up to Washington and got himself arrested. I think I got about twenty-eight of 'em saved up now."

"Well," said Sandberg, "we're here and you're here."

"I was gonna sell 'em to a guy in Redding, but I tell you what ..." said Deaver, pausing to think. "The galls are at my brother's house in Weaverville, so call me tonight about eight o'clock."

Sandberg and Nagel hung around the trap shoot for a couple more hours, long enough for Sandberg to win another ham, a frozen turkey, and a side of bacon. Nagel tried his hand with Sandberg's shotgun and ended up winning a ham himself. The officers were about to leave when an attractive middle-aged woman approached Sandberg.

"Isn't your name John?" she said. "You're a park ranger from up in The Dalles, Oregon."

"I'm afraid you're mistaking me for someone else," said Sandberg. "My name is Leon."

"You even sound like him," said the woman.

Sandberg smiled back at the woman and began walking toward the parking area. Warden Nagel had witnessed the close call and followed from a distance. Both men wisely decided to leave the trap shoot and head for their motel in Weaverville.

"What was that all about?" asked Nagel.

"Before I worked for U.S. Fish and Wildlife, I was a state game warden in The Dalles, Oregon. That woman didn't remember my real name, but she came way too close for comfort."

"It's a small world, isn't it?"

"I'll say! She even recognized my voice."

"That's scary."

"This job's gonna give me an ulcer yet, Ed."

Agent Sandberg didn't want to appear anxious, so he waited until 8:40 p.m. to telephone Deaver from a pay telephone. Deaver said the bear galls were still at his brother's house and he would pick Sandberg (French) and Nagel (Miller) up at 7:30 the next morning.

It was about 7:20 on the morning of April 7, 1986, when Jesse Deaver knocked at Sandberg's and Nagel's motel room door. Deaver walked into the room carrying a tanned bear hide and a bear claw necklace.

"This necklace ain't for sale," said Deaver. I just brought it to show ya. And this is what the bear hides look like when they're tanned." Deaver began describing his bear guide business, bragging about his unusually high success rate. "A bear hunt will cost between three hundred and five hundred, depending on the size of the bear," said Deaver.

Sandberg and Nagel rode with Deaver to a house on the east end of Weaverville. During the ride, Deaver again asked, "You guys ain't any type of law enforcement, are ya?"

"Hell no," said Sandberg. "I could be selling to your neighbor and you wouldn't know it. That's the way I work."

"That's good," said Deaver. "I won't tell anybody either."

It was not uncommon for houndsmen who dealt in bear parts to hide their contraband somewhere other than their own homes. Gallbladders might be kept at a friend's residence or safely sequestered in a brother's or even an elderly mother's freezer.

When Deaver pulled into his brother's driveway, no one appeared to be home. Sandberg and Nagel watched Deaver open the cupboard door on the left side of the carport and remove a key. He proceeded to the opposite side of the carport and unlocked a chest freezer. Agent Sandberg and Warden Nagel watched closely as Deaver lifted the freezer lid and exposed his copious collection of bear gallbladders, each one individually enclosed in a plastic baggie.

All three men carried the frozen gallbladders over to a place on the carport floor, where Agent Sandberg began categorizing them. He offered Deaver figures of thirty, forty, and fifty dollars each, depending on the size. With eleven larger galls and fifteen smaller ones, Deaver agreed to a payment of $860 in cash plus the gold necklace that had captured his interest. The agreed-upon worth of the necklace was $150, making the total amount of the transaction $1,010. Two small gallbladders were later discovered inside one of the baggies, bringing the final tally of unlawfully sold bear galls to twenty-eight.

The first transaction with Jesse Deaver ended on April 7, 1986, with Deaver dropping Sandberg and Nagel off back at their motel. Deaver picked out the necklace he wanted and went on his way. Sandberg, known to Deaver as Leon French, promised Deaver he would call again as bear season approached.

On May 4, 1986, Agent Sandberg telephoned Deaver to schedule a guided bear hunt during the upcoming fall bear season. During the conversation, Deaver invited Sandberg to attend another trap shoot, to be held on June 7 at the same shooting range. Sandberg said he would attend and pay the deposit for the fall bear hunt at that time. Before hanging up, Sandberg said, "If you got any more goodies, save 'em for us."

"Yes, I will," said Deaver.

****

ON MAY 19, 1986, U.S. Fish and Wildlife Special Agent Joe Sandberg received an undercover assignment from U.S Fish and Wildlife Regional Law Enforcement Coordinator David Martens. Martens's office was located in Colorado. A Denver, Colorado man named Jung-Hwa Yu, alias Johnny Yu, was reportedly buying and selling bear gallbladders from out-of-state sources. Yu was described by Martens as twenty-nine, five-feet-five inches tall, 130 pounds, with black hair and brown eyes.

Agents had developed a case against a Washington man for selling bear gallbladders and transporting them across state lines. The violator, Daniel Paul Leach, had agreed to cooperate with a sting operation targeting Yu, in return for possible leniency at the time of Leach's sentencing. No promises were made.

"Joe, our agents out here have been collecting information on this Johnny Yu for a while now, but haven't been able to find a way into his business without spooking him," said Martens. "You're one of the best covert operators we have, so I'd like you to telephone this guy and see if you can find a crack in his armor."

"Did you say Johnny U?" asked Sandberg.

"Yeah, I know what you're thinking."

"I'm working two or three other investigations right now," said Sandberg, "but I'll give it a try."

"These chiseling bastards know it's illegal to sell bear parts in California and Washington," said Martens, "so they're smuggling them into states like Colorado where it's legal. Once the bear galls are in the legal states, there's no way for us to tell where the stuff came from."

"I know," said Sandberg. "That's why it's so frustrating for those of us in the field."

"Feel free to tell this Yu character that you learned about him through a mutual friend," instructed Martens. "Danny Leach has agreed to work with us and corroborate your story. Background information on Yu and Leach is in the packet I'm sending you."

"Okay, Dave, "I'll do my best."

"When you record your conversation with this guy, make sure you emphasize that the bear parts will be coming from California. We'll hammer him for Lacey Act violations."

"Will do. Thanks, Dave."

On May 27, 1986, Agent Sandberg dialed Jung-Hwa Yu's Denver phone number. A woman answered and told Sandberg that Yu wasn't home. Agent Sandberg identified himself as Mike Mahoney, a businessman from California, and left a phone number. On May 29, at approximately 5:15 p.m., Agent Sandberg's undercover phone rang.

"Hello," said Sandberg.

"May I talk to Mike?"

"Speaking."

"This is Jung-Hwa Yu."

"Oh, yeah, thanks for calling me back. Say, we have a mutual friend in Danny Leach."

"And, uh … Danny introduced you to me?"

"Yeah, he said you were a good guy to deal with."

"Oh, okay."

"And I'm an avid hunter. I do a lot of bear hunting out here in Northern California."

"Oh, you can hunting very much in California State?"

"Yeah, and I have a lot of bear galls."

"I see."

"Danny thought you might be interested in buying them."

"Are you friend with Danny?"

"Yeah, he told me that you're a person I can trust."

"Hah! Sure you can do it. Don't worry about my side."

"You're not a cop, are you?"

"No," said Yu, laughing. "Here in United States only four years, you know."

"Well I'm just a bear hunter in California and I have a lot of galls."

"Uh, yeah, but, in California that not right to sell hunting game, right?"

"Right. It's illegal, but Danny said you wouldn't tell anyone."

"How many galls you can provide?"

"I can provide as many as you can handle," said Sandberg.

"Uh, what size?"

"I've got fourteen big ones right now," said Sandberg, "the size of softballs."

"I buy all fourteen," said Yu. "Forty dollars each."

Always the professional and not wanting to appear too anxious, Sandberg countered with a suggested price of sixty dollars each.

"I pay fifty dollars each," said Yu. "Total seven hundred dollars."

"It's a deal," said Sandberg. "I'll send them to Denver, C.O.D." Yu seemed excited and provided Sandberg with a shipping address.

"Okay I call you Mike?" asked Yu.

"Sure, what should I call you? Uh, I mean—"

"You can call me Johnny."

"Okay, Johnny. I'll be in touch. Bye."

One of the challenges for officers involved in any undercover bear parts sale was coming up with bear parts. Most of the gallbladders used in this investigation were collected from road kill and depredation bears by California Fish and Game wardens. A few were evidence gallbladders from previously adjudicated California cases. Unfortunately, only eight bear gallbladders were available at the time of Agent Sandberg's initial dealings with Jung-Hwa Yu.

On May 29, at approximately 8:30 p.m., Agent Sandberg telephoned Yu and advised him that he could only come up with eight galls. Yu offered to buy the eight gallbladders for $400. Sandberg agreed and shipped the frozen gallbladders in a cooler filled with dry ice. On June 3, federal agents watched Yu pick up the cooler at the Denver International Airport and pay the $400 C.O.D. charge. Yu telephoned Agent Sandberg that evening, telling him that he had received the eight gallbladders and was possibly interested in buying more. He said he would prefer that the gallbladders be in a dried condition because he planned to take them to South Korea.

South Korea is believed to be the world's number one consumer of bear bile. By the early 1980s, Asia's wild bear populations—sun bear, sloth bear, Asiatic black bear, brown bear, and giant panda—had all suffered severely or been essentially wiped out in the wild due to habitat loss and the trade in bear parts. South Korea and other Asian countries like China, Vietnam, and Laos began farming bears to provide bear bile and its much-sought-after main ingredient, ursodeoxycholic acid. Thousands of Asian bears were kept in small cages and subjected to excruciating pain while bile was extracted through instruments implanted, often permanently, in their bodies. Although unpopular, this incredibly cruel practice still goes on today.

The ultimate goal of this investigation was to lure Yu to California to take part in a guided bear hunt or to obtain additional bear gallbladders. He would then be arrested and charged with California felonies as well as federal Lacey Act violations. Although Yu had given Sandberg the impression that he was naïve and relatively new to the black market animal parts business, he turned out to be an experienced international black marketeer, shrewdly calculating every move before exposing himself to any possibility of being arrested. Much to Agent Sandberg's chagrin, he discovered that Yu was regularly traveling to Los Angeles and back on business without informing Sandberg about his excursions. During a June telephone conversation, Yu revealed to Sandberg that he had just returned from Los Angeles to Denver the previous day.

"I thought you were going to call me and let me know so I could sell you more galls," said Sandberg.

"Oh," said Yu. "I forgot about it. I just went down to L.A. Airport and pick up something there. You know, I have another company, other than the galls."

Agent Sandberg could only imagine what else Yu was buying and selling. Again, he tried to entice Yu into coming to California. "When bear season opens, I'll be able to get you all the galls you want," said Sandberg over the phone. Yu sounded interested for a while, then asked about a possible guided bear hunt. During the next fifteen or twenty minutes of conversation, it became clear to Agent Sandberg that Yu was stringing him along and had no intention of taking the hook at that time.

***

ON JUNE 7, 1986, Agent Sandberg and his sidekick, California Fish and Game Warden Ed Nagel, arrived at the Weaverville trap shoot about noon. Support for Sandberg and Nagel was provided by two undercover U.S. Fish and Wildlife agents, already present and mingling with the crowd. The two supporting agents noticed Jesse Deaver cutting up meat and adding it to the chili that was being sold at the trap shoot. People were overheard saying that the meat was bear and that Deaver had freezers full of it. "Who's the mountain man talking to Deaver?" asked Sandberg, referring to a middle-aged, bearded gentleman decked out in faded Levis, an animal skin frock, knee-high moccasins, coonskin cap, and a bear claw necklace.

"I've never seen him before," replied Nagel. "That's not someone I'd forget." Nagel chuckled and slapped Sandberg on the shoulder as the two officers made their way through the crowd.

"How ya doin'?" said Deaver, watching Sandberg and Nagel approach. "This here's my huntin' buddy, Herb Frizzell."

"I like your necklace," said Nagel.

"I got between four hundred and five hundred o' these bear fingers," said Frizzell, his voice loud enough for the two supporting agents to hear. "But they ain't for sale. You can get in big trouble for sellin' them things." By "fingers," he meant claws.

Deaver spoke up, appearing more confident than he had during his previous meeting with Sandberg and Nagel. "Are you guys interested in bear skulls?"

"I might be," said Sandberg, "if they're clean and in good condition."

Deaver explained how he'd hung the skulls from a tree and let the "bugs" work on them. "They ain't quite ready yet," said Deaver. "They're still smellin' a little rank."

"Maybe next time we see ya," said Sandberg.

Before leaving the turkey shoot, the two supporting agents collected a sample of the chili for future analysis.

Agent Sandberg would meet with Jesse Deaver again on August 3 and buy five bear skulls for $100. During the transaction, Deaver offered to take Sandberg and Nagel on a guided mountain lion hunt in Nevada for $1,500 each. Deaver did not possess a guide's license for the state of Nevada at that time. Plans were made to contact Deaver at a later date.

***

IT WAS LATE JULY, 1986, when Agent Sandberg again heard from Johnny Yu. Yu expressed an almost desperate need to come up with ten bear gallbladders for one of his customers. Sandberg said he would see what he could do and asked Yu if he would be coming out to California any time soon.

"Uh, not yet," said Yu. "I went to California twice already this year. I have not scheduled to go there."

"Hopefully next time you're out in California, you'll give me a call and let me know where you are so I can meet you and sell you some galls," said Sandberg. "Meanwhile, I'll see what I can come up with. It's the wrong time of year right now."

Agent Sandberg would eventually come up with five bear gallbladders, which Yu purchased for $270. The Jung-Hwa Yu investigation could have ended after the first bear gall bladder sale, but as is the case with most wildlife-related undercover investigations, the ultimate goal is to see where the trail leads and arrest others involved. Yu had hinted that he was buying galls from others besides Sandberg and some of his clients were unhappy with the product they were receiving.

"From now on, my clients want chunk of bear fur with gall," said Yu, "to show they not come from pig."

BY EARLY 1987, AGENT Sandberg had exhausted California Fish and Game's limited supply of bear gallbladders and become involved in several other investigations—one in particular involved the sale of eagles and eagle feathers. It was decided that Sandberg would introduce Yu to one of his supposed hunting friends in Virginia. That friend was undercover U.S. Fish and Wildlife Special Agent John Merchant. Merchant, who conducted his covert activities under the name Jay Dalrymple, convinced Yu that he belonged to a hunting club in Virginia and could provide as many as forty bear gallbladders a year.

"Just between you and me," said Merchant, "it's against the law to sell bear galls in Virginia, so I'd advise you not to mention where the galls came from."

"Yes," said Yu. "I understand, full."

Yu agreed to buy ten bear gallbladders from Agent Merchant for $450. The gallbladders were shipped by way of Continental Airlines and picked up by Yu. Merchant received a check for $450 the following week.

The Lacey Act, passed into law in 1900, became the first federal law protecting wildlife. The provisions of this law were designed to deal with enforcement issues such as the one described in the Jung-Hwa Yu Investigation. Under the Lacey Act, it is unlawful to import, sell, acquire, or purchase fish (or parts thereof), wildlife (or parts thereof), or plants that were taken, possessed, or sold in violation of any state or foreign country's laws. During the time of this investigation, it was illegal to buy or sell bear parts in California (California Fish and Game Code Section 4758) and in Virginia (Virginia Code Sections 29.1-521 (10) and 29.1-536). That was all federal officers needed to arrest and convict Jung-Hwa Yu in 1988 for the unlawful purchase of twenty-three bear gall bladders. Shortly after completing his thirteen-month jail term, Yu returned to South Korea and was not seen in the United States again.

***

JESSE MERLE DEAVER'S DAY in court also came in 1988. He was charged with the unlawful sale of twenty-eight bear gallbladders and five bear skulls. After some plea bargaining, Deaver pleaded no contest to one felony count of selling twenty-eight bear gallbladders. He was fined a total of $2,550 and ordered to pay restitution to the Department of Fish and Game in the amount of $1,130. Conditions of formal probation included warrantless search and loss of hunting privileges for three years.

Eagle Feathers

———— ◆ ————

B ALD AND GOLDEN EAGLES are protected by a number of federal and state laws, one of them being the federal Bald and Golden Eagle Protection Act of 1940. Put simply, this act prohibits the take, possession, sale, purchase, trade, import, or export of bald or golden eagles, or parts thereof, without a permit issued by the Secretary of the Interior. Under such a permit, Native Americans have been allowed to possess eagles or eagle parts for religious purposes. A system was set up to provide qualifying individuals with dead eagles and eagle parts through the National Eagle Repository, a federal storehouse for eagles that have died or been killed. This provision in the act was intended to allow Native Americans to practice centuries-old religious and ceremonial traditions without going out and killing eagles themselves. Unfortunately, it also opened a loophole for abuse by certain opportunists who cared more about filling their pockets with money than practicing the ways of their ancestors.

One April afternoon in 1985, U.S. Fish and Wildlife Special Agent Joe Sandberg, working in a covert capacity, ventured into a Chico, California arts and crafts fair. There he met an attractive, thirty-eight-year-old Native American woman named Ramona Ward. With flowing, coal-black hair, and dressed in a fringed buckskin dress and moccasins, Ward was the quintessential Indian princess. Sandberg struck up a lengthy conversation with Ward, impressing her with his extensive knowledge of Native American handicrafts. The business card he handed her indicated that he was Leon French, a freelance jewelry salesman specializing in necklaces, bracelets, and handmade Native American items. Ward said she and her husband lived in the northeastern corner of California, in a beautiful place called Surprise

Valley. She provided Sandberg with a phone number and invited him to drop by if he were ever in the area.

As Agent Sandberg was about to walk away, Ward pulled something from inside a leather handbag. The wildlife agent immediately recognized it as a secondary wing feather from a golden eagle.

"I don't want you to go away empty-handed," said Ward, flashing a flirtatious smile. "You can have this for ten bucks."

"Well, thank you!" said Sandberg, smiling back. She handed Sandberg the feather. He placed a folded ten dollar bill in the palm of her hand. "I hope to see you again," he said.

"That would be nice," said Ward, distracted by another customer.

ONE MONTH AFTER THE Chico crafts fair, Agent Sandberg telephoned Ramona Ward. "Hello, Ramona?"

"Yes. Who's this?"

"This is Leon French. Remember me from the Chico Crafts Fair last month?"

"Uh—"

"You sold me a feather and invited me to drop by if I was ever in the area."

"I sold you a feather?"

"You gave me a beautiful smile and pulled the feather out of your leather bag as I was leaving. You said you didn't want me to go away empty-handed."

"Oh, yeah!" said Ward. "I remember you now. How are you, Leon?"

"I'm doing great, Ramona. Say, I have to be in Alturas on Saturday, so I thought I might drive over the mountain for a visit the next morning, if you're going to be around."

Ward glanced over at her husband, who was sitting on the couch with a cigarette hanging out of his mouth, watching Western reruns on TV. "Sure. We'll be home all day," said Ward.

"Would ten be all right?" asked Sandberg.

"That'll be fine," said Ward, providing Sandberg with directions. "See you then."

Few law enforcement officers possessed the skills or the instincts to pull off an awkward telephone conversation like the one Agent Sandberg had with Ramona Ward. She either didn't remember selling him the eagle feather, or she initially suspected that the man who called himself Leon French was an undercover wildlife officer. Either way, Sandberg's deft handling of the call kept the door open for future dealings with Ward. Other officers used to say that Joe Sandberg could sell ice to an Eskimo. His nonthreatening demeanor and smooth, uninhibited delivery worked almost every time. "They don't teach it at the academy," Joe would say. "You either have it or you don't."

A cool, stiff breeze was blowing across the valley that Sunday morning in early May. Climbing out of his light-blue van, Sandberg was dressed in his typical undercover attire—Bermuda shorts, sandals, and a comfortable white T-shirt. Two mixed-breed dogs climbed down from a weather-beaten wooden deck and ran out to greet him. One of them began jumping up on the unfamiliar visitor.

"Butch, get down," shouted Ramona, stepping from the front door of a gray-and-white, double-wide mobile home. "They won't bite, but they might lick you to death."

"It's still kinda cool up here," said Sandberg, reaching across the seat for a light jacket.

"Come on inside. How about a cup of coffee?"

Ramona's husband, about forty years old with a 1960s-era flattop haircut and a pencil-thin mustache, was sitting on the couch, smoking cigarettes and watching TV. Light-complected with dishwater blond hair, he did not appear to be Native American. Ramona introduced him as Wayne.

"Nice to meet you, Wayne," said Sandberg, smiling.

"How ya doin?" mumbled Wayne, not bothering to stand up.

"What do you do, Wayne?" asked Sandberg, trying to be friendly and strike up a conversation. Wayne didn't answer.

"Wayne," said Ramona, "Mr. French asked you a question."

"Huh?" said Wayne, his eyes still glued to the TV.

"Wayne always watches this program on Sunday mornings," said Ramona. "He runs a saw shop in Cedarville."

Looking around the living room, Sandberg noticed several handmade Native American items, most of them adorned with raptor feathers. After a brief conversation, he asked Ramona if she had any beadwork or baskets for sale. Ramona brought out a large case filled with beadwork; none of the items inside contained eagle feathers. Having bought and sold everything from eagle feathers to scrimshaw, Sandberg had a knack for knowing when it was safe to ask compromising questions.

"Do you happen to have any eagle feathers for sale?" asked Sandberg.

"I don't have any on hand right now," said Ward, seemingly undaunted by the question, "but I do buy and sell eagle feathers. I guess you know I'm not supposed to sell them, even to other Indians, so I usually remove the feathers from my traditional dance fans then give the feathers to the buyer after the sale."

"That's pretty clever," said Sandberg.

"I might be able to help you out with eagle feathers," said Ward, hinting at a reliable source and mentioning a white owl carcass that she was saving for beadwork. Based on Ward's description, Sandberg figured she was talking about a snowy owl. Snowy owls were rarely seen in California and protected under state and federal law.

"I'm interested in buying eagle feathers," said Sandberg, "but it's illegal, so we have to be careful."

Ramona nodded in agreement, while Wayne continued to sit at the coffee table, staring at the mountain of cigarette butts he had created. Sandberg couldn't help wondering what a nice-looking, seemingly intelligent woman like Ramona was doing with a loser like Wayne. *Keep your mind on business*, thought Joe. *Can't get caught up in that.* No transactions occurred that day. Agent Sandberg left with the understanding that he would return when Ramona had more merchandise.

A YEAR AND A HALF went by, and Agent Sandberg had not heard from Ramona Ward. In February of 1987, he and California Fish and Game Warden Ed Nagel, both working in an undercover capacity, contacted Ward at her residence in Surprise Valley. Confident that Sandberg and Nagel were not law enforcement officers, Ward began telling them about her numerous eagle feather sales to Native Americans. Once again, she described how she had cleverly evaded the letter of the law by selling the handcrafted items and giving away the associated feathers.

According to Ward, most of her feathers had come from eagles that died from eating poison-laced ground squirrels. She said she sometimes received feathers from a nearby Native American named Bob Shirley. "Bob also sells deer hides and antlers, if you guys are interested," said Ward. "I'll give him a call and tell him you're coming over."

Bob Shirley's single-wide mobile home sat in the middle of a one-acre patch of bare ground surrounded by two sheds, a chicken coop, three junk cars, scattered beer bottles, and a herd of Nubian goats. Sandberg and Nagel couldn't help noticing one of the goats standing on top of a rusted-out Hudson sedan. The dilapidated old car was up on blocks and had long since lost its wheels. "My uncle used to have a car just like that," said Sandberg.

"Come on in," said Shirley. "Any friend of Ramona's is a friend of mine." Unlike the reserved, soft-spoken Native American men Sandberg had dealt with over the years, Bob Shirley had a gregarious, almost fun-loving personality. Tall and big-boned, with weathered chestnut skin that spoke of years in the sun, forty-year-old Shirley wore his hair in a ponytail bound with multicolored beads.

"Ramona told us that you might be able to help us out with some eagle feathers," said Sandberg, scanning a living room filled with handcrafted dance fans.

"They just busted a couple guys I know over in Nevada for selling eagle feathers," said Shirley.

"Really?" responded Sandberg.

"I've shot eagles with my .22 rifle," bragged Shirley, "but they're hard to kill, and it's better to use somethin' a little more powerful. I just sold a batch of feathers to one of my relatives."

"I could use whole eagles for taxidermy work," said Sandberg. "It sounds like you can get your hands on eagles any time you want."

"Most of the time," said Shirley. "In the last two years, I've picked up seven dead eagles that died from eatin' poisoned ground squirrels. I know where I can get six whole eagles if you're really interested in buying them."

Shirley seemed so excited and eager to do business, Agent Sandberg was worried that he would go out and shoot eagles just to fill the order.

"I'm interested," said Sandberg, "but we need 'em in good condition, not all shot up. Just get me the poisoned ones that are already dead."

"How 'bout deer hides? I got plenty of deer hides and antlers out in the shed," said Shirley, giving Sandberg and Nagel the impression that he desperately needed the money.

"I'm not really in the market for deer hides," said Warden Nagel, "but I'll take a look at what you've got." Nagel offered Shirley twenty dollars for a set of four-point velvet antlers he was inspecting.

"I shot that four-pointer you're holdin' in the headlights before the season opened," bragged Shirley.

"We've gotta be goin'," said Sandberg, "but if you have any eagle feathers you want to sell today, we'll take 'em off your hands." Agent Sandberg purchased thirty-eight golden eagle feathers from Shirley, for a total of $50.

"I've got your number. I'll call you guys next time I have whole eagles or feathers to sell," said Shirley.

"Okay, Bob," said Sandberg, pulling away. "Nice meeting you."

AGENT SANDBERG MADE A follow-up phone call to Bob Shirley on June 16, asking about the six golden eagles that Shirley had mentioned in February. Shirley said he knew the man who still had them and would arrange the sale. As was the case with most of the flakey outlaws that Agent Sandberg dealt with, Shirley did not follow through on his promise. Agent Sandberg didn't hear from him again until late August, when the undercover phone rang at Sandberg's residence.

"Hello," said Sandberg.

"Leon, this is Bob Shirley."

"Hi, Bob. How ya been?"

"We moved to Reno for a while."

"You did? Did you quit hunting?"

"No, hell no! I'll keep hunting the rest of my life, guy. There ain't nothin' gonna stop me from doin' that."

"Say, did you find out anything about those birds?"

"Yeah, that's why I called. He's still got 'em in his freezer and he's comin' for a visit at the end of this week. I'll call you when he gets here."

"Okay. I'd like to buy all six of 'em, if I could."

"I think he told me he had eight there at his house. He picked up two more. Not sure if he shot 'em or got poisoned ones from some rancher."

"Hey, I'll take all eight!"

"He said he wanted to keep two of 'em for some project he's working on."

"Then I'll take six. Do you know if they're golden or bald?"

"I never bothered to ask."

"That's all right. I'll pay him a fair price, and for helping to arrange the sale, I'll give you a token of my appreciation."

Little did Shirley know that Sandberg's token of appreciation would have been a set of handcuffs and an unpaid vacation in the federal penitentiary. Unfortunately, Shirley's man failed to show up as planned, and Agent Sandberg didn't hear from Bob Shirley again until Sandberg's phone rang on September 7.

"Say, you having any luck with those birds?" asked Sandberg.

"I haven't seen that guy since we last talked on the phone. He said he would get in contact with me but he never has. I know he has the birds, Leon. I'm not bullshitting you."

"I understand," said Sandberg.

"Say, Leon. How'd you like to go on a guided deer hunt up in Surprise Valley? We got some monster bucks up there."

"That sounds great," said Sandberg, "but I don't have a deer tag for that area."

"Myself, I don't even get tags any more," said Shirley. "It's too much trouble now, getting drawn and all that crap. I just go without a tag."

"Hey, same here, buddy," said Sandberg, laughing.

"Besides, said Shirley, "the season's closed right now so I wouldn't think a guy would need one."

"You've got a point, Bob," said Sandberg, still laughing. "I'll see you soon."

Agent Sandberg arrived at Bob Shirley's mobile home in Reno on September 16, 1987, in preparation for a prearranged guided deer hunt. While smoking a marijuana cigarette, Shirley told Sandberg about the $4,300 he had made the previous year from his pot grow. Both men climbed into Shirley's black four-wheel-drive pickup and headed up Highway 395, bound for Alturas.

It was 7:43 p.m. when Shirley and Sandberg drove through Alturas and began searching for deer on Fandango Pass Road. Shirley removed a handheld spotlight from behind his bench seat and shoved the cord into his cigarette lighter receptacle. As he rambled through fields of sagebrush and irrigated alfalfa, Shirley shined the spotlight out through the driver's-side window. One alfalfa field was abundant with feeding deer—many of them bucks—but Sandberg refused to shoot, claiming he would only kill a trophy animal. It was around midnight when they drove to Shirley's trailer in Surprise Valley.

After only four hours of sleep, Sandberg resumed the hunt at 5:00 the next morning. Again, several bucks were seen but no shots were fired. The sun was just coming up when Bob Shirley turned off Highway 299 onto Surprise Valley Road. As exhausted and sleep-deprived as Agent Sandberg was, he couldn't help noticing the incredible beauty of this special place—irrigated pastures occupied by hundreds of feeding deer. Dozens of farm ponds dotted the landscape, each one teeming with waterfowl. Everywhere he looked, Sandberg saw pheasants—more than he had ever seen in one place. It was an outdoorsman's Shangri-la, every foot of it fenced and posted with signs reading: NO HUNTING OR TRESPASSING.

"Ever seen anything like this?" asked Shirley.

"I guess that's why they call it Surprise Valley," said Sandberg.

Cruising northward toward the Oregon border, Shirley pointed to a two-story ranch house. "That guy's got a drawer full of eagle feathers," he said. "There's another guy, up on the reservation, who's got eleven eagles in his freezer right now. I'm sure he'd sell six or eight of 'em."

The guided hunt ended with no animals killed and no business transactions made. Shirley said he would contact Sandberg again when he had eagles or other animals to sell.

AGENT SANDBERG HADN'T HEARD from Bob Shirley for two months when he received a late-night phone call in early November. "Leon, I finally got ahold of that fella."

"Oh, which one is that?"

"The one I discussed with you the last time we talked."

"You mean the one with those eight for sale?"

"Yep. He's got three left."

"Do you know what kind they are?"

"One's golden, I know that. I don't know what the other two are. I think there's two golden and one bald."

"Are they in good shape?"

"Oh, yeah. He just got 'em two weeks ago. I been coyote huntin' with this guy and selling pelts."

"I could use a couple pelts. How much does he want for 'em?"

"Fifty apiece. We got three nice ones right now."

"Okay, I'll take all three. How about the birds?"

"Well, I know he wants tops for them, 'cuz they're in good shape. You can hardly see any holes or anything to that effect."

"How about I meet you guys in Susanville?"

"Yeah, we could probably do that. You would probably come up through Red Bluff, wouldn't you?"

"Yeah."

"Well, I'll talk to this guy and call you back in twenty minutes."

Agent Sandberg accepted a collect call from Bob Shirley at 9:10 that same evening. Sandberg agreed to meet Shirley and his buddy on Tuesday at 6:00 p.m. They would meet at the A&W parking lot in Susanville.

"I'll be drivin' my blue van," said Sandberg. "Are the birds frozen?"

"Yeah, they are," said Shirley. "You might want to bring a couple big coolers."

"What's the guy's name?"

"Huh?" said Shirley.

"The guy who's going to be with you. What's his name—his first name?" asked Sandberg.

"Uh, George. His name is George."

"Is he cool?"

"Oh yeah, you damn right."

"Okay, I'll see you guys Tuesday at 6:00, at the A&W in Susanville."

Agent Sandberg hung up the phone and began mulling over the conversation he had just had with Bob Shirley. It was becoming clear to the veteran investigator that the man with the eagles, the one Shirley could never quite pin down, was actually Shirley's outlaw partner. George ... or whatever his real name was, had stayed out of the picture up to this point. He was probably being extra cautious in case Shirley stepped in it and sold to an undercover game warden. Sandberg knew he was dealing with some unscrupulous individuals who would probably do anything or kill anything for a fast buck.

"Are you all right?" asked Sandberg's wife.

"Yeah, I'm okay," replied Joe, flopping onto the couch and resting his sore feet on the coffee table. "I love my job, but dealing with these lying scumbags is wearing me down. Do we have any ice cream?"

"You're not helpless—get it for yourself. And get your feet off the coffee table."

ON NOVEMBER 10, 1987, at 5:40 p.m., Agent Sandberg followed Highway

36 down the steep mountainside into Susanville. Once known for logging, mining, and its close proximity to Eagle Lake, Susanville had become better known as a prison town during the past few decades, with the construction of a medium-security correctional institution in 1963.

Driving down Main Street, Sandberg spotted the A&W sign up ahead and mentally prepared himself for any and all possibilities. If things go as planned, I'll make an eagle purchase, in which case I'll eventually file federal felony charges against Bob Shirley and his partner. Accustomed to dealing with flakes and liars, the veteran undercover officer was also prepared for a more likely scenario: The outlaws wouldn't show up at all. *Shirley will call later to apologize, telling me his buddy George couldn't make it.*

"Whaddya know? There's Shirley's truck," mumbled Sandberg, as he pulled into the A&W parking lot.

"Bad news," said Shirley, running up to Sandberg's driver's-side window. *Here it comes*, thought Sandberg. *All this way for nothing.* "We only have one eagle," said Shirley.

"Oh!" responded Sandberg, an astonished look on his face. "Where would you like me to park?"

"We're out in the open here," said Shirley. "I think it would be safer behind Denny's, down the street."

"Okay, I'll follow you," said Sandberg. "Where's George?"

"Uh—"

"Your friend," said Sandberg.

"Oh, he's across the street at the liquor store, buying cigarettes," said Shirley, turning and walking away. "Just follow us."

Sandberg noticed a greasy-looking character, sporting a week-old beard and long stringy hair, crossing the street toward Shirley's pickup. He was carrying a brown paper bag containing what Sandberg surmised was a bottle of hooch. "That must be George," mumbled Sandberg.

Parked at the rear of the Denny's Restaurant parking lot, Bob Shirley removed a large cooler from his pickup and placed it inside the open side door of Sandberg's van. He and his partner climbed inside, where Sandberg was waiting.

"Leon, this is my trapping buddy, Blake Kitchen," said Shirley, thoughtlessly revealing his partner's real name.

"Glad to meet ya," said Sandberg, not questioning the name discrepancy. Sandberg's eyes were immediately drawn to the gruesome display of tattoos on Kitchen's neck and forearms. Shirley's forty-plus-year-old Caucasian partner stood about five-nine in his triple-heeled lumberjack boots and might have weighed 160 pounds, soaking wet.

"What's up, man?" said Kitchen, lighting a cigarette and blowing smoke all over the inside of Sandberg's van. "You want one?"

"No, I'm trying to quit," said Sandberg, not wanting to offend. Kitchen's beady eyes nervously scanned the inside of the van. "Are you looking for something?" asked Sandberg. Without answering, Kitchen lifted the lid on Shirley's cooler, exposing three coyote pelts.

"Bob said you were interested in these dog pelts."

"I might be," said Sandberg. "How much do you want for 'em?"

"Fifty apiece."

"Do you live here in Susanville?" asked Sandberg, purposely changing the subject.

"No," snapped Kitchen.

"Used to," quipped Shirley, snickering under his breath.

"I guess you want to see this," said Kitchen, reaching into the bottom of the cooler and handing Sandberg a dead golden eagle.

Sandberg began examining the eagle, running his fingers down the breastbone. "It's been shot with a .22," said Shirley. "Blake took a shot at another one yesterday, but missed."

"What happened to the other seven?" asked Sandberg.

"They're up in Klamath Falls," said Shirley, offering no further explanation.

"Bob mentioned that you were a trapper," said Sandberg, hoping to strike up a friendly conversation and defuse some of the tension. "Have you ever accidentally trapped an eagle?"

"I catch 'em all the time. Hawks and owls too," said Kitchen, sounding cocky. "They can't resist those big chunks of jackrabbit meat I bait the traps with. I sell 'em to the Indians up in Oregon."

"What do you guys want for this one?"

Before Blake could answer, Shirley blurted, "Four hundred twenty-five dollars."

"I can't pay that much," said Sandberg. "How about two fifty?"

After a few minutes of negotiating, Shirley agreed to $300 for the eagle and $130 for the three coyote pelts. Kitchen didn't say anything, apparently letting Shirley handle the business end of their arrangement. Sandberg asked the two outlaws not to shoot any more eagles, claiming the bullet holes were difficult for taxidermists to deal with. "Just get me the poisoned ones," said Sandberg.

"Poisoned ones are hard to get because they fly off and die," said Shirley. "The ranchers usually start putting out that shit in April or May, to kill the ground squirrels."

Sandberg found it ironic and counterproductive that some ranchers would poison hawks, eagles, coyotes, and other predators that preyed upon the very rodents they were trying to rid their lands of. After paying Shirley and Kitchen, Sandberg emphasized the illegality of their transaction and cautioned the two outlaws not to discuss it with anyone. Shirley promised to call Sandberg the next time he had eagles to sell.

Two weeks after the initial eagle transaction with Shirley and Kitchen, Bob Shirley called again.

"Bring plenty of money!" said Shirley. "We got three birds this time."

On November 24, 1987, Sandberg would again drive to the Denny's parking lot in Susanville. After drinking coffee in the restaurant, he followed Bob Shirley and Blake Kitchen out to Shirley's pickup. Kitchen grabbed a large cooler from the pickup bed, and all three men once again climbed through the side door of Sandberg's van. Kitchen opened the cooler, revealing three mature golden eagles, all wrapped in individual white plastic garbage bags.

"Were these poisoned or did you kill 'em yourselves?" asked Sandberg, who had not noticed the pencil-sized hole in the breast area of each bird.

"I shot all three out the window at 200 yards," bragged Kitchen. "With my heavy-barreled .22-250, they never knew what hit 'em."

"I told you guys I didn't want you to shoot any more eagles," said Sandberg. "It blows 'em up too much."

"I tried shooting a couple with my little .22 rifle, at fifty yards," said Kitchen, "but I couldn't kill 'em."

Agent Sandberg was tempted to scrap the undercover detail, call in his backup, and slap the cuffs on "those two hardheaded idiots," but there were still bigger fish to fry, so the investigation continued.

"I only want birds that have been poisoned, trapped, or are already in the freezer," said Sandberg, looking each of them in the eye—first Shirley, then Kitchen. Shirley seemed to understand, but Sandberg's stern instructions had clearly gone right over Kitchen's head. All he knew was killing, and the easiest way to kill eagles was with a bullet through the chest.

"If you don't buy 'em, we can always sell 'em to the Indians," replied Kitchen.

Bob Shirley suggested they end their transaction. "We want nine hundred for the three eagles," he said. "The big female is worth four hundred, and I know I can get that from a taxidermist in Klamath Falls."

Agent Sandberg persuaded Shirley and Kitchen to accept $875 for the three birds. Once again, he admonished the two outlaws not to shoot any more eagles. Shirley climbed out of the van, telling Sandberg he had to get back home by 4:00 p.m. because he was taking some B.I.A. guy from Willows, California, on a deer hunt that night.

ON FEBRUARY 11, 1988, Agent Sandberg met with Bob Shirley at the Coral Tavern, in Lakeview, Oregon.

"We got trouble," said Shirley. "Blake Kitchen has been shootin' off his mouth about sellin' eagles to you. Me and him ain't speakin' and I'd advise you not to deal with him anymore."

"That's not good," said Sandberg. "We better cool it for a while."

Agent Sandberg and his supervisors decided it was time to file federal criminal complaints against Bob Shirley and Blake Kitchen. Unfortunately, they had both disappeared shortly after Sandberg's February 11, 1988 meeting with Shirley. One year later, on February 13, 1989, Bob Shirley was arrested on a federal warrant in Southern Oregon. After being advised of his rights by federal agents, Shirley said he wanted to talk.

"The eagles that we sold to Leon, or whatever his real name is, were all shot and killed by Blake Kitchen," said Shirley. "All of the money went to Blake and I didn't receive a penny."

"Go on," said the interviewing agent.

"I didn't get any poisoned eagles from ranchers. They all came from Kitchen. He's been in the eagle-sellin' business for a long time," said Shirley.

"What about the man with the drawer full of eagle feathers that you told the other agent about?" asked the interviewing agent.

"If I told your agent I knew someone with a drawer full of eagle feathers, it had to be Blake Kitchen."

"Where is Blake Kitchen now?"

"The last I heard, Blake was living in a trailer near Fallon, Nevada."

"Anything else?" asked the agent.

"I know a lot of people who are involved in sellin' eagles and other wildlife," said Shirley. "More than you'll ever know."

Robert Eldon Shirley pleaded guilty in federal court to one felony count of selling three golden eagles. Three other felony charges were dismissed. Shirley was sentenced to nine months in federal prison and placed on one year of supervised probation.

Blake Richard Kitchen was eventually located in Nevada and arrested. He pleaded guilty to one felony count of selling three golden eagles and spent thirteen months in federal prison.

Special Agent Joe Sandberg retired from the U.S. Fish and Wildlife Service in 2002. During his long and productive career, he had made over 800 wildlife-related cases, sending between eighty and one hundred individuals to jail or prison for trafficking in wildlife or wildlife parts. With an incredible ability to read people—along with that easygoing, non-threatening personality—no one was better suited for the job.

Mollusk Madness

———◆———

"THE CHIEF IS ON the phone," said the receptionist at the California Department of Fish and Game's Region Five Long Beach office. "He says he has something important to talk to you about."

"What now?" replied Degraffenreid, burned out by the continual flow of paperwork into his office and a phone that never stopped ringing.

Patrol Captain Ed Degraffenreid had come a long way since his military tour of Vietnam. Big enough to play linebacker for the Rams, he'd decided to take advantage of his physical attributes and go into law enforcement. "I cashed in my veteran's points and the GI Bill at the same time," said Degraffenreid. "While working in the Custody Division for the L.A. County Sheriff's Department, I picked up a bachelor's degree at Pepperdine University."

After two additional years on patrol, Degraffenreid decided he'd rather arrest poachers than respond to domestic dispute calls and bar fights. He became a warden for the California Department of Fish and Game in 1976. Beginning his Fish and Game career in East Los Angeles, Warden Degraffenreid spent four more years in the land of overcrowded freeways, shopping malls, and cement-lined ditches before transferring to the wilds of Lassen County in 1980. Five years later he was offered a promotion and found himself right back where he'd started—planning his work day around Southern California's five o'clock rush-hour traffic.

"Ed," said the chief, "I'd like you to come to work for me."

"Oh no!" said Degraffenreid. "You want me to move to Sacramento?"

"No, Ed. You can live in Southern California or wherever you want. I want you to help supervise the Special Operations Unit."

The California Department of Fish and Game's Special Operations Unit, better known as SOU, had been set up to address resource-related problems that could not easily be solved by uniformed enforcement officers. Under the direction of the chief of patrol, the unit was created to investigate the illegal commercialization of fish and wildlife and to do so in a covert capacity.

"What exactly would I be doing?" asked Degraffenreid.

"You would be heading up a major covert investigation into the multimillion-dollar abalone industry."

According to Degraffenreid, the chief of patrol was receiving pressure from what he called the "legal abalone industry" to do something about the "illegal abalone industry." Outlaw abalone divers were reportedly entering areas closed to the commercial take of abalone, north of San Francisco, and harvesting large numbers of the valuable mollusks. Although a major investigation such as this was badly needed and a long time coming, it was widely believed, among enforcement officers, that the so-called "legal abalone industry" was more concerned about unfair competition than the diminishing condition of California's abalone resource.

When Captain Degraffenreid accepted the chief's offer, he didn't know that the entire California coast was a quagmire of illegal activity, much of it aimed at cashing in on an abalone resource already on the verge of collapse. He didn't know that he and his officers would be away from home for weeks at a time, sleeping in cars and subsisting on fast food and coffee. He didn't know about the weeklong stakeouts on cold, windswept ocean cliffs, waiting for the outlaws to show up. Above all, he didn't know this would turn out to be the most exciting and worthwhile assignment of his career and that he'd enjoy every minute of it.

***

FISH AND GAME PATROL Captain Mike Wade was in charge of all the uniformed wildlife protection activities in Sonoma and Mendocino Counties. As Wade describes it, "Ed Degraffenreid's people would stake out the bad guys, working undercover, then hand it over to the uniformed officers when it was time for a bust."

One afternoon in 1988, while all the commercial abalone poaching was going on, Wade and Degraffenreid teamed up for a recon mission to familiarize Degraffenreid with likely dive locations. They took Wade's undercover vehicle, a light-blue S10 Chevy Blazer, with wetsuits and dive equipment piled high in the back.

"Where we going?" asked Degraffenreid.

"I know a secret dive spot up by Sea Ranch where there's still lots of abs," said Wade.

Sea Ranch is a rocky stretch of mostly private coastline, approximately a hundred miles north of San Francisco. Known for its headlands, secluded beaches, and fabulously beautiful seascapes, it remained one of the few spots on the Sonoma and Mendocino Coasts that hadn't yet been exploited by abalone poachers—or so they thought.

Wade and Degraffenreid arrived at Sea Ranch and parked on a bluff near a grove of Monterey cypress trees. Both wearing civilian clothing, they walked to the edge of the cliff and looked two hundred feet down to the ocean below. As the fog began to lift, beams of morning sunlight poked through and turned the ocean's dull-gray surface to purple, green, and brilliant shades of blue.

"It's fairly calm," said Wade. "I see a little swell, but not much."

"What do you think the visibility is?" asked Degraffenreid.

"Maybe five feet at the most. The water here looks clearer than it really is. All that bull kelp keeps it pretty dark near the bottom. There's also a lot of particulate in the water."

"Do you think those cars over there are divers?" asked Degraffenreid, looking at a second unpaved parking area a half mile to the south.

"They probably are," replied Wade. "Let's wear our wetsuits to make it look like we're going in."

It took about twenty minutes for the two wildlife protection officers to remove their street clothes and put on their wetsuits. "It's been a while," said Degraffenreid. "I hope this damn thing fits."

"I know what you mean," said Wade. "Every time I put mine on, it seems a little tighter." Six feet tall and rock solid, Wade had stayed in good shape since his early years in Southern California. "Just let the top half of your wetsuit hang loose. You won't get so hot that way."

"Okay, Mike," said Degraffenreid, straining to pull the bottom half of his wetsuit over his legs. "I'm gettin' there."

"Ed, why don't you head south along the bluff and I'll go north? There's a little hidden cove I want to check out. I'll catch up with you in a little while."

As Degraffenreid walked south along the bluff, he noticed two thirty-plus-year-old men climbing a footpath from the beach. Dressed in wetsuits, they carried typical abalone diving gear: fins, masks, abalone irons, and nylon mesh collection bags. Degraffenreid noticed that the collection bags hanging from the divers' waists were wet and considerably stretched out, but mysteriously empty. Reaching the top of the bluff, the smaller of the two abalone divers rushed past Degraffenreid, causing the wildlife officer to step from the narrow footpath into a patch of blackberry vines.

"Where's the fire?" said Degraffenreid, glancing over his shoulder.

The diver looked back for a brief moment but continued at a fast walk toward the parking area.

"Your buddy's in a big hurry," commented Degraffenreid.

"Huh?" mumbled the much larger diver, squeezed into a skintight, black wetsuit and bearing a striking resemblance to a well-fed elephant seal.

"I said, 'Your buddy's in a hurry,' " repeated Degraffenreid, smiling. "He almost pushed me into those blackberries."

"Oh, sorry, man," said the diver. "I couldn't hear with this hood on."

He unlatched his cumbersome, thirty-pound weight belt and dropped it to the ground.

"Are you all right?" asked Degraffenreid, noticing that the grossly overweight diver was still panting heavily from his long trudge up the steep hillside.

Without answering, the diver peeled a neoprene diving hood from his puffy-faced dome, exposing a thick crop of matted, dark brown hair. "What?" he said.

"I just asked if you were all right."

"Yeah, I'm all right."

"Did you guys do any good?"

"Huh?" said the diver, obviously preoccupied and watching for the return of his dive buddy.

"Did you get any abalones?"

"Oh, we always get our abs here."

"How many'd you get?"

Instead of answering Degraffenreid's question, the diver stepped within an arm's length of Degraffenreid and stared directly into the six-foot-four-inch wildlife officer's eyes. "Why, are you a game warden?"

Degraffenreid was temporarily caught off guard and found it curious that a man he had just encountered would ask that question. *Do I look that much like a game warden?* "Uh, me and my buddy are in the construction business," replied Degraffenreid. "Things are slow right now and we're tired of eatin' hamburger, so we decided to come up here and see if we could get ourselves a couple abs."

"I know how that is, man. We ain't worked the docks for six months."

"My name's Ed. What's yours?" asked Degraffenreid, offering his hand.

"Tony," said the diver, later identified as Anthony Donald Franze.

"Well, Tony, I see your dive buddy's coming back. He looks like he's still in a hurry."

"Hey, I saw a Fish and Game truck go by while I was at the car," said the smaller diver, quickly approaching from twenty yards away.

"Paul, this is Ed," said Franze. Paul was later identified as Paul Gerald Cellini.

"We don't want to get caught with all those abs," said Cellini, nervously scanning the distant highway and failing to acknowledge Degraffenreid. "The fine is huge!"

Degraffenreid could see Captain Wade approaching.

"Are you sure it was a Fish and Game truck?" asked Franze.

"It was a dark green pickup with a Fish and Game emblem on the door. A big yellow lab was sitting in the passenger seat. Yeah, I'm sure."

"Oh, shit," said Franze. "Hey, man, do you want some abs?"

Degraffenreid was surprised to find Franze looking straight at him.

"Me?" said Degraffenreid.

"Yeah, you," said Franze.

Cellini gave Franze a questioning look.

"Don't worry. He's cool," said Franze.

"Sure!" said Degraffenreid. "But let me ask my buddy. That's him coming. He may have his heart set on getting wet." Franze and Cellini stood watching as Degraffenreid walked up the path to meet Captain Wade. "Mike," shouted Degraffenreid, "diving is gonna to be easy today." Wade had a confused look on his face. "Go along with me on this," whispered Degraffenreid, reaching his partner.

"What's going on?" Wade whispered back.

"We won't need our wetsuits," said Degraffenreid, loud enough for the two divers to hear.

"Abs without getting wet," replied Wade, finally catching on. "Sounds good to me."

Degraffenreid waited while Captain Wade ran back to the car to retrieve their collection bags. Degraffenreid and Wade then walked back across the sandy trail to the two divers.

"This is my buddy, Mike," said Degraffenreid. "We'd like to take you up on your offer."

"Follow us," said Franze. Cellini led the two Fish and Game captains back down the trail to the cove from which he and Franze had just come. Twenty yards from the beach, he turned to his right and waded into a thick patch of California wood ferns.

"Everyone, grab a limit," said Cellini, pointing to a pile of red abalones, all of them still alive and lying on their shells.

One by one, each man walked over and picked up four red abalones. Cellini led the caravan back up the steep cliff, stopping every twenty or thirty yards so Franze could catch his breath. Reaching the top, they headed toward their respective cars. Degraffenreid and Wade immediately grabbed their badges and officer IDs, then walked over to thank the unsuspecting divers for their generosity.

"One more thing before we leave," said Wade. "The next time you decide to give away abalones, don't give them to a couple of game wardens." Wade and Degraffenreid pulled out their IDs. As Wade described the scene, many years later, "Their jaws dropped and they just about loaded their pants."

While Captain Wade stayed with the two violators, Captain Degraffenreid grabbed a burlap sack from the undercover truck, walked back down the trail, and retrieved the remaining eight abalones still hidden under the wood ferns.

Before leaving, Anthony Franze walked over to Degraffenreid and said, "Have you ever met anybody as dumb as me?"

The veteran Fish and Game captain paused for a second or two. "No, I can't say that I have," said Degraffenreid. "Not because you gave your illegal abalones to two game wardens, but because greedy guys like you and your partner over there are going to ruin it for everybody."

Although Franze and Cellini had no criminal record of fish or wildlife violations, Wade and Degraffenreid suspected that this wasn't the first time these two opportunists had grossly exceeded the bag and possession limits. This case was a small sample of the abalone violations taking place on the North Coast at the time. Both violators received $1,250 fines and were ordered not to take abalone or any other ocean species for a period of one year.

During the weeks and months that followed, Fish and Game officers, under the leadership of Captains Wade and Degraffenreid, continued to monitor the California coastline for the unlawful take and possession of abalone. As a result of their efforts, a number of historic commercial cases were made—some involving five hundred or more unlawfully taken abalones and organized criminal conspiracies.

Poaching remains a tremendous drain on California's fragile abalone resource. Dedicated wildlife protection officers have done everything possible to stem the tide of rampant exploitation, but warden numbers have remained far too low, while the price of abalone steaks continues to skyrocket (recently $125 a pound). California's only remaining abalone fishery lies north of San Francisco Bay, where a limited and highly regulated sport take of red abalone is still allowed.

Deer Meat for Mr. Big

———◆———

ONE FALL EVENING DURING the late 1980s, Fish and Game Warden Dave Szody and I planned a full night of working spotlighters. This was an enforcement activity that every inland Fish and Game warden engaged in at some point during his or her career—the frequency depending on how many deer occupied that particular warden's patrol district and how accessible those deer were to the local outlaws.

People have been spotlighting deer from cars and trucks since the automobile was invented. Deer are easier to find at night, and law-abiding citizens who might object to this unlawful activity are generally home in bed. So-called spotlighters will drive around shining their headlights or handheld, high-powered spotlights into the surrounding countryside until a pair of green eyes shines back. *Bang!* The deer is thrown into the trunk of a car or the bed of a pickup, and away they go.

Using an artificial light to assist in the taking of any game bird or mammal is a violation of Section 2005 of the California Fish and Game Code. Wildlife officers have always viewed spotlighting as a serious offense, as well as a repugnant, unsportsmanlike behavior; they will expend many hours trying to catch violators in the act. More often than not, a spotlighting detail turns out to be a long night of sitting in the dark, seeing nothing and hearing nothing. Wardens who double up at least have someone to talk to. By 3:00 a.m.—if they last that long—the officers will have discussed fifteen different subjects, solved most of the world's problems, and finished off a couple pounds of peanuts. If one of the wardens is a coffee drinker and the other one isn't, the coffee drinker will generally end up talking to himself by the end of the detail.

***

IT WAS ABOUT 9:00 p.m. on a weeknight in late October when Warden Dave Szody picked me up at my home and we began our patrol.

"Where do you want to go?" asked Szody.

"I don't know," I said. "Where do you want to go?"

"I asked you first."

"Why don't we head out Meadowview Road and see what Skipper Shanahan is up to. I heard he and his buddies have been terrorizing the neighbors again."

"What did they do this time?" asked Szody.

"Apparently one of them was driving Skipper's pickup while Skipper and another of his buddies stood in the bed of the pickup, howling at the moon," I said. "Either Skipper or the other guy took an ax handle to the neighbors' mailboxes as they drove down the road."

"Did they call the sheriff?"

"No! Everybody living on that road is scared to death. It's the same reason nobody will come forward about all the deer Skipper and his friends are supposed to be killing."

No place in Shasta County could match the beauty of Meadowview Valley in the springtime. Bordered on both sides by rolling green hills and sprinkled with brilliantly colored California poppies, the valley was cleaved by a salmon spawning stream that meandered right down its middle.

The Shanahan family owned most of the land in the valley. They had passed it down from generation to generation since the mid-1800s. Grandpa Shanahan was still around, but his son Nate operated the ranch. Nate had a twenty-year-old son everyone called Skipper. Skipper liked to drink and carry on with his rowdy friends, so the family moved him from the main residence to an isolated shack on the outskirts of the property.

When he wasn't cutting wood, poaching deer, or up to some mischief, Skipper did his best to stay in shape. He kept an old weight bench and a collection of rusted-out barbells under the giant valley oak that shaded his cabin. On occasion, Warden Szody and I would patrol up Meadowview Road and pass by while Skipper was out under the tree pumping iron. Skipper would usually give us a curious stare and continue with his workout. That wasn't the case if his friends happened to be around. Emboldened by their presence, Skipper would shout a couple of four-letter words in our direction, waving at us with the middle finger of his right hand.

Turning off the highway, Szody and I drove a mile or so down Meadowview Road and pulled onto a rocky, unpaved trail that led through a grove of blue oaks and into a shallow side canyon. With the patrol truck well hidden, we gathered our gear, put on our coats, and began walking.

"We may not even need these flashlights," said Szody, in a barely audible voice. "With this full moon, it's almost like daylight."

"Don't forget your binoculars," I replied.

Walking for more than a mile, we climbed two or three fences and traversed several hillsides before finally coming to a knoll overlooking Skipper's cabin. From our vantage point high on the hill, we could see most of Meadowview Road and would be able to tell if anyone was operating a spotlight.

"We should have brought a couple of lawn chairs," I said.

"Yeah," said Szody. "How about some popcorn?"

Skipper's pickup was parked outside and a light was on inside the cabin: it appeared that the subject of our stakeout was home. For the next three hours, Warden Szody and I sat on the cold, hard ground, paced back and forth, and watched bats chase mosquitoes. Skipper walked out to his pickup once or twice, but never left. When the lights went out in his cabin, we walked back to our patrol truck and headed east.

"That was a waste of time," said Dave. "Let's go up by the park. There's lots of deer right now and I got a call about somebody running a light up there the other night."

"Sounds good to me," I said. "Where'd you hide those peanuts?"

It was about midnight when we pulled off Highway 44 onto Road A17. From there we skirted the south edge of Lassen National Park and crossed a dozen or so logging roads.

"Just past Manzanita Creek, there's that little road that goes down in the flat. Let's sit there for a while and see if anyone comes by," I suggested.

By 2:00 a.m., not a single car had passed. We were both falling asleep, so Dave turned the radio to an all-night oldies station.

"Great station," I said.

"Name the five greatest singing groups of all time," said Szody.

"Let me think …. There's the Everly Brothers, the Beach Boys, the Drifters, the Statler Brothers, and Gary Lewis and the Playboys."

"Gary Lewis and the Playboys? You've got to be kidding!"

I began laughing. "Okay, who would you pick? Wait a minute. Let me guess—the Beatles, the Rolling Stones, Chicago, the Grateful Dead, and the Who."

"That's about right," said Szody. Just then, Del Shannon's "Runaway" came over the radio.

"Turn that up," I said, opening the passenger door and stepping into the cold night air. "Great song!"

"What are you doing?" shouted Dave.

"I had climbed to the hood of the truck and begun doing an amateurish version of the Twist. "Nothing like a great song to wake us up," I shouted back.

With our enthusiasm restored by a good laugh, Dave and I pulled back onto the main road and headed west. "I can't believe you did that," he said.

***

A month or so had passed since our all-night spotlighting detail. I was doing paperwork in the regional office squad room when the receptionist peeked in the doorway.

"Would you like to take a call?" she said.

"Who is it?"

"He wouldn't give me his name. He said he wanted to report a violation."

"Sure, put him through."

A few seconds later, the phone rang at my desk.

"Lieutenant Callan. May I help you?" No response. I could, however, hear a TV in the background. Finally the TV was turned down, and the caller began to speak.

"Yeah." It sounded like the voice of a younger man. "I know these guys who are sellin' deer meat."

"What can you tell me about them?"

"I don't wanna get involved in this, so I'm just gonna give ya a phone number."

"Can you give me any names?"

The caller hesitated for a minute or so, apparently deciding whether or not to answer my question. "One of 'em is called Skipper and the other one is Vince. The number is 762-4567. They shot a doe last night, and they're looking for a buyer right now."

"Do you know how much they're selling the deer for?"

"I heard they were getting thirty-five dollars a deer, unless it was a big buck; then they'd ask for fifty."

"Can I get your name or a number where I can contact you?"

I waited for a reply, finally realizing that the anonymous informant had hung up.

The caller could have been a friend, a relative, or possibly a work-related acquaintance who had overheard a conversation. Like so many well-meaning informants, he didn't approve of what was going on but feared retribution if he reported the violation. Whatever the scenario, when the caller mentioned the name Skipper, he commanded my complete attention.

I sat at my desk pondering the situation. Reaching into my desk drawer, I pulled out the cross directory and looked for the phone number I'd been given. As expected, it wasn't listed. For a brief moment, I toyed with the idea of dialing the number myself. *I'd like to buy some deer meat. Do you deliver?*

Much like drug dealers, those who engaged in wildlife trafficking generally dealt exclusively with people they knew and trusted. If the violator really was Skipper Shanahan, as I suspected, he might recognize my voice. I had contacted Skipper in the field on more than a few occasions. Just two weeks earlier, a CHP officer had stopped Skipper for illegally transporting firewood. Warden Szody and I had pulled over to provide backup while the CHP officer issued a citation. Chances were good that calling the number myself wouldn't work.

"I think I'll go by SNTF and see if George is available," I said to myself. George Whitmer was a veteran California highway patrolman on loan to the Shasta County Narcotics Task Force (SNTF). Since being assigned to the task force in 1986, Agent Whitmer had become the consummate undercover officer, so good at what he did that outside agencies frequently asked for his expert assistance. George had worked undercover cases for Fish and Game before. Coincidentally, he had a degree in biology and at one time intended to be a Fish and Game warden.

With long, scraggly hair and a graying Santa Claus beard, the forty-year-old professional undercover officer could easily pass for any number of Shasta County's stereotypical dope dealers. Whitmer claimed he looked so rough during his undercover years that he enjoyed shopping in the Sears tool section, just to see how many employees would follow him around.

As luck would have it, I caught Agent Whitmer between drug investigations. I explained the situation and included previous drug-related information we had learned about Skipper Shanahan. After receiving the approval of his supervisor, Agent Whitmer said, "I can give it a try right now, if you want."

"It's eleven o'clock," I said. "Yeah, let's try it. If they were out poaching deer last night, Skipper should be awake by now."

Whitmer dialed the number from his special undercover line at the SNTF office. "It's ringing," he said. The phone continued to ring for ten or fifteen seconds. "Do you want me to leave a message if a machine comes on or try to—"

"Hello," muttered a male voice, sounding half asleep.

"Yeah," said Agent Whitmer, "is this Skipper?"

"Who's this?"

"I met a guy in the bar up in Central Valley last night who told me you had a deer to sell. I might be interested if it's fresh."

"Who told you that?"

"I didn't get his name. We had a couple drinks and I told him I was in the market for some deer meat. He said you might be able to help me score some meth, too."

After a few more minutes of back-and-forth conversation, Skipper—or whoever it was on the other end of the line—agreed to meet Agent Whitmer late that afternoon at a residence on the south side of Anderson.

"He said he might have someone who could set me up with meth," said

Whitmer, after hanging up the phone. "This could turn out well for both of us." Agent Whitmer's supervisor was standing next to me and gave an approving nod.

Warden Dave Szody and I met Agent Whitmer and two other narcotics enforcement agents at the SNTF office about 4:00 p.m. Agent Whitmer was wired and it was agreed that Szody and I would provide backup, along with two narcotics agents. An additional benefit of working with SNTF was they had a wire and we didn't. I told the SNTF officers about a convenient hiding spot, south of Anderson River Park, where we could listen in on the nearby conversation and respond if necessary.

At approximately 5:00 p.m., Agent Whitmer located the designated meeting place. Driving a burgundy 1965 Ford Mustang with a dented right rear fender, he proceeded down a forty-yard-long gravel driveway to a run-down, single-story house. Parked in front of the house was a badly dented, older-model GMC pickup. Two men who looked to be in their early twenties were leaning against the pickup drinking beer. Whitmer noticed a Budweiser six pack sitting on the hood next to them.

Agent Whitmer pulled to a stop near the pickup and climbed out. "Hi, guys," he said. "I'm Dud Wiley. Would either of you be Skipper?"

"Yeah, I am," said the shorter of the two, taking a long slug from the beer he was holding. "You're not a damn game warden or some kind a narc are ya?"

"Do I look like one?" said Whitmer, chuckling. "Would you guys have an extra one of those?" Without saying anything, the taller man handed Whitmer a beer. "Thanks," said Whitmer. "What's your name?"

"Vince." He was later identified as Vincent Michael Chaney.

"Well thanks, Vince," said Whitmer, popping open the can and taking a drink. "This hits the spot."

A master of small talk, Agent Whitmer drenched the deer poaching suspects in meaningless blather while he sized them up and made a mental note of his surroundings. Both men looked like they'd been out woodcutting. Skipper Shanahan had sawdust in his hair and all over his faded blue jeans. Vince Chaney wore grease-stained overalls and smelled of chainsaw oil. Shanahan stood eye-to-eye with the five-foot-eleven-inch narcotics officer; Chaney was two or three inches taller, with forearms like Popeye's.

"What happened to you?" asked Whitmer, noticing a three-inch scratch across the side of Chaney's face.

"An oak branch hit me today, while we was cuttin' wood," said Chaney.

"You might want to put somethin' on that," responded Whitmer, continuing to look around and recognizing a splattering of blood on Shanahan's right pant leg. "So, where's this deer you're gonna sell me?" said Whitmer, finally broaching the purpose of his visit. Just then the narcotics agent noticed someone peeking at them through the house's screen door.

"Don't worry about that guy," said Vince. "That's my brother-in-law. He won't say nothin'."

Shanahan and Chaney pulled back a tarp in the bed of Shanahan's pickup and revealed a skinned-out yearling doe. "That's not much of a deer for thirty-five dollars," said Whitmer, not wanting to appear too eager. "How about I give you twenty for this one and you get me a bigger one next time?" While Shanahan and Chaney thought it over, Whitmer glanced over at the screen door of the house, where Chaney's brother-in-law was still watching.

"Okay, we'll take it," said Shanahan.

"I bet you guys are wondering what I'm gonna do with this deer," responded Whitmer.

"Don't matter ta me what you do with it," said Shanahan, reaching out and taking the twenty dollar bill from Agent Whitmer's outstretched hand.

"What are ya gonna do with it?" asked Chaney.

"I'm buying game for this guy who owns a fancy restaurant in the Bay Area," said Whitmer.

"What's the name of the restaurant?" asked Shanahan, suddenly interested.

"I can't tell you that … or the owner's name either," said Whitmer. "I call him Mr. Big. One of Mr. Big's specialties is venison."

"Isn't this Mr. Big worried about getting busted?" asked Chaney.

"No," said Whitmer. "He buys these domesticated fallow deer from some guy who raises them. I provide Mr. Big with wild venison when I can get my hands on it. No one knows the difference and he saves a little money."

Agent Whitmer's cock-and-bull story about Mr. Big and his fancy Bay Area restaurant was all it took to get Shanahan and Chaney all excited. "They thought their ship had come in," Whitmer would tell me later.

"We can get you all the deer you need," said Shanahan.

"You said you had a meth connection," replied Whitmer. "Can you help me score some?"

"Are you gonna be around here for a while?" asked Skipper.

"Oh, yeah," said Whitmer. "Here's my number. I'll be back up here in a couple days. Just call me when you've got something."

After leaving the two deer poaching suspects, Agent Whitmer turned the deer over to Warden Szody and me. We photographed the evidence and donated it to the local rescue mission.

"I think I know who your informant is," said Whitmer, as he drove away.

Two days later, Skipper Shanahan contacted Agent Whitmer by telephone. He told Whitmer he had another doe to sell and agreed to introduce him to his meth connection. Whitmer met Shanahan on an isolated road near Redding and paid him thirty-five dollars for the second deer. When Agent

Whitmer turned the deer over to us, we agreed to make one more deer buy, if necessary. That would give Whitmer and the SNTF boys time to identify Shanahan's drug connection and make the arrests.

The next day, Agent Whitmer met with Shanahan and Chaney at a Redding-area shopping center parking lot. Our deer poachers showed up in Vince's older-model Ford pickup. A highway patrolman by trade, Whitmer couldn't help noticing the expired registration sticker on Chaney's rear license plate.

"Let's take my car," said Whitmer, concerned about being stopped in Vince's truck and identified by one of the local police officers.

"Just start driving," said Skipper, jumping in the front passenger seat. "I'll tell ya where ta go."

"Did I tell you guys that Mr. Big was coming to Redding?" said Whitmer, turning west onto Cypress Street.

"No," said Skipper.

"Yeah," said Whitmer, "he'd like to meet you."

"What's he want ta meet us for?" asked Chaney, sitting in the backseat.

"Turn left after you cross the bridge," said Shanahan.

"I guess he just wants to know who he's dealing with," said Whitmer. "Which way from here?"

"Keep going," said Skipper. "I'll tell ya when to turn."

The meth connection turned out to be a thirty-plus-year-old, dark-haired woman with what Whitmer would later describe as the most unpleasant demeanor of any woman he'd ever met. Tall and unusually thin, Susan Jeanette Nagy skipped the pleasantries and said, "Are you a cop?"

"No," answered Whitmer. "These guys already asked me that." Nagy was anxious to make a quick deal, so Agent Whitmer bought one fourth of a gram of meth for $20. "If this is good product, I'll be back," said Whitmer.

"Could I have a quick pinch of that?" asked Shanahan, on the drive back to Chaney's pickup.

"I'd give it to you," said Whitmer, "but my girlfriend will know if any of it's missing."

"That's a bummer," said Shanahan.

"Hey, I meant to remind you guys that Mr. Big's gonna be here in a few days and still wants to meet you."

"When's that?" asked Chaney.

"I'll call you and we'll set up a meeting," said Whitmer, dropping Shanahan and Chaney off at Chaney's pickup.

Immediately after arriving at the SNTF office, Agent Whitmer began writing a search warrant for Susan Nagy's apartment. He also secured felony arrest warrants for Nagy, Shanahan, and Chaney. I advised Whitmer that we would file additional deer-related charges against Shanahan and Chaney after the planned takedown. Meanwhile, I had to find someone to play the role of Mr. Big.

Patrol Captain Rich Elliott happened to be in the Fish and Game regional office that day, so I asked him if he had ever had any dealings with Skipper Shanahan or Vince Chaney. Elliott joked that he had never had the pleasure. "Good!" I said. "You'll make the perfect Mr. Big." I explained to Captain Elliott that he would play the role of a Bay Area restaurant owner interested in obtaining a reliable supply of venison for his restaurant. Without hesitation, Elliott agreed to play the part. I phoned Agent Whitmer and gave him the go-ahead to set up the meeting with Shanahan.

"Where do you want to meet?" asked Whitmer.

"How about the library parking lot?" I said. "It's only a block or two away from the county jail, so that will be convenient."

"Okay," said Whitmer. "I'll make the call and get back to you."

Agent Whitmer telephoned Shanahan and set up a meeting for the following day at the Redding City Library parking lot on West Street. "It's important that you and Vince make a good impression with Mr. Big," said Whitmer, "so you might want to clean up a little."

"I don't know about that," said Shanahan, "but we'll be there."

After confirming the meeting with Shanahan, Whitmer telephoned Susan Nagy, Shanahan's drug dealer, and told her he wanted to buy an eight ball of meth. She said it would be ready the next day.

At three o'clock the following afternoon, Skipper Shanahan and Vince Chaney pulled into the Redding Library parking lot and drove to the rear, where Agent Whitmer and Fish and Game Captain Rich Elliott (Mr. Big) were waiting. Agent Whitmer was wired and several officers, including Warden Dave Szody and me, were listening from two blocks away. After introductions were made, Captain Elliott asked, "How many deer can you guys provide?"

"We can get ya four or five deer a week," replied Shanahan. "No sweat!"

"That sounds good," said Elliott.

"When the salmon are runnin', we can get ya them too," said Shanahan.

After about fifteen minutes of bargaining with the suspects, Agent Whitmer repeated the agreed-upon signal over the wire. Within seconds, the parking lot was filled with Fish and Game and SNTF officers. Herbert Lloyd "Skipper" Shanahan and Vincent Michael Chaney were arrested and booked into the Shasta County Jail, two blocks down the street. In addition to the felony drug charges, they were charged with unlawful sale of deer.

Immediately after the arrest, Agent Whitmer drove to Susan Nagy's apartment, where a search warrant and an arrest warrant were being served. When Whitmer walked into the apartment, Nagy was cuffed and sitting on the couch with her hands behind her back. Still unaware of Whitmer's true identity, Nagy jumped up and began chasing him around the room.

"You dirty snitch, I'm going to kick your ass," shouted Nagy.

Whitmer described the scene many years later. "I ran around the apartment in fear until my laughing fellow agents finally subdued the assailant."

All three subjects pleaded guilty to their crimes and were sentenced to serve time in the Shasta County Jail. Agent Whitmer continued to work narcotics for four more years before cutting his hair, shaving his beard, and going back to writing speeding tickets on the freeway. He spent the last four years of his highly productive law enforcement career assigned to the Department of Justice's Bureau of Narcotics Enforcement before retiring in 2000.

Warden Nick Albert with waterfowl from his San Francisco duck case (1975).

The Desert Rats 1980: Front row: Jim Reynolds, Tom Harrison, Jim Worthington, and Dave Blake. Back row: Steve Callan, Reggie Zavala, and Dave Szody. Working the desert along the Colorado River was one of my most enjoyable experiences as a Fish and Game officer.

Old friends: Dave Szody and me at Dave's home in Fortuna (circa 1982).

Lieutenant Steve Callan investigating a closed-season deer violation with
Warden Don Jacobs (circa 1982).

My Lab, Molly, and I are contacting fishermen at Potem Falls,
Shasta County (circa 1983).

Evidence from U.S. Fish and Wildlife Agent Joe Sandberg's golden eagle case
(circa 1985). Photo by Joe Sandberg.

This is the deer photographed by Steve Guill, as described in the chapter entitled "The Head Hunter." Steve Guill took this photo in 1992.

Dad and me at the Redding Fish and Game office (1995).

Evidence from Warden Larry Bruckenstein's rockfish/lingcod case (2005).
Photo by Larry Bruckenstein.

Smuggled marijuana bales discovered by Warden Ryan Hanson on California's
Central Coast (2012). Photo by Ryan Hanson.

Old friends enjoying retirement at Lassen Volcanic National Park:
Steve Callan and Dave Szody (2010).

Eighty-eight-year-old retired Fish and Game Lieutenant Gil Berg at one of my book
signings in 2013. What a thrill it was to see Gil after all these years!

My father, retired Fish and Game Inspector Wally Callan, and I return to Plaskett Meadows after forty-three years (2013).

My father and me, early 2015.

END OF AN ERA

THE 1990S AND BEYOND

The Headhunter

---◆---

THE ALARM WENT OFF at 3:45 on Tuesday morning, December 15, 1992. Thirty-nine-year-old amateur photographer Steve Guill rolled out of bed as he'd been doing on his days off in December for the past thirteen years. Guill had been photographing wildlife since high school, when he gently released the shutter on his first Nikon. Since 1979, he had made the 200-mile drive from Redding to Tule Lake National Wildlife Refuge 175 times, snapping between 3,000 and 4,000 wildlife photographs each year.

It was exceptionally cold that December morning in 1992. The weather forecast called for snow in the mountains by the end of the day. Steve didn't care: extreme weather often created ideal conditions for photographing wildlife, particularly the majestic Rocky Mountain mule deer that congregated inside the refuge.

By daylight, Guill had made his way up Highway 299, past the tiny community of Lookout, past Timber Mountain, and into Lava Beds National Monument. With his trusty camera on the seat beside him, he remained ever vigilant for that perfect shot of a mountain lion, a fox, an eagle, or a herd of deer. As Steve described it, "In those days it wasn't unusual to see several hundred deer in a single outing."

It was about noon when Guill entered Tule Lake National Wildlife Refuge and slowly proceed north along Hill Road. "There was already a foot of snow on the ground, and by one o'clock that storm they predicted was quickly moving in," said Guill. "I was trying to get outta there, but I kept seeing deer. I noticed this one particular buck standing about thirty yards off the road."

"What was it about this buck that attracted your attention?" I asked.

Guill explained that it looked like a typical five-point buck, but when he counted the little cheater points protruding from the deer's antlers, it turned out to be a seven-pointer: six points on one side and seven on the other.

As was the case with most of the deer on the protected winter range, this buck showed no sign of alarm. Guill continued to take photographs from the window of his car while the stately animal casually munched on the sparse vegetation. "It was right at the end of the drought and there wasn't much to eat," said Guill. "This big boy looked pretty thin in the hindquarters. The snow really started coming down, so I finally put my camera away and skedaddled for home."

LATE ON THE DREARY, overcast afternoon of December 17th, 1992, a late-model Ford pickup slowly cruised north on Hill Road, inside Tule Lake National Wildlife Refuge. Thirty-seven-year-old bartender Travis Danner was at the wheel. A cocky little man with a big mouth, Danner was well-known among the Tule Lake bar scene as a braggart, prone to exaggeration and eager to take center stage.

As Danner scanned the countryside, he glanced to his right and spotted a large buck foraging on the limited vegetation that grew along the lake. "There's that big five point," said Danner, fumbling for his binoculars. Alerted by the sound of Danner's squeaking brakes, the deer raised its head and displayed its magnificent antlers with an imperial, almost regal air. Danner shivered with excitement, his simple but devious mind contemplating what to do next. He studied the road ahead; refuge headquarters was still two miles away. He scanned the lake, looking for signs of any nearby duck hunters; there were no boats or hunters in sight. Finally, he turned and pointed his binoculars back down the road from which he had just come. The coast was clear.

Confident that no one else was around, Danner reached for the driver's-side door latch, opened the door halfway, and squeezed out onto the snow-covered road. The truck motor continued to run as he braced the back side of the bench seat with his left hand and released the latch with his right. The seat slowly sprang forward, revealing a leather rifle case. Danner would later admit to a bar customer that he was so nervous about being caught, he almost wet his pants. Standing on his tiptoes, the would-be deer poacher peered across the cab and out the passenger window. "Still there!" he whispered, ducking back down.

Danner unzipped the rifle case and pulled out a bolt-action 30.06 rifle, with scope attached. Turning sideways, he quietly jacked a live cartridge into the firing chamber and locked the bolt. Slightly bent over, Danner looked to his rear, then peeked around the open driver's-side door. There was still no sign of anyone approaching, and as quiet as it was in the freshly fallen snow, he knew he'd be able to hear a car coming from miles away. "It was so quiet,

I could hear that damn deer chewing while I hid behind the truck," Danner would later tell a bar regular.

Carefully sliding across the bench seat, Danner slowly lowered the passenger-side window. With the stately buck forty yards away and still foraging, he rested the rifle barrel on the window frame. Centering the buck's muscular right shoulder in the scope's crosshairs, Danner placed his finger on the trigger and began to squeeze. The buck must have sensed danger: he suddenly jerked his head upward and stared back at the pickup. Bolting for the woods, the fleeing deer startled his pursuer, causing an errant bullet to rip thorough the deer's hindquarters. Reeling from the earsplitting sound of a 30.06 going off inside the pickup, Danner exited the truck and ran after the deer. *Boom!* came a second resounding blast. This time the bullet entered the buck's massive heart and dropped the terrified animal to the ground.

Danner ran back to the truck, hid the rifle behind the seat, and climbed into the bed of the pickup. He opened an attached toolbox and pulled out a meat saw. Blood still coursed through the deer's veins as Danner grabbed its antlers with his left hand and began sawing with his right. Within seconds, he was scampering back to the pickup, carrying the deer's bloody head and antlers. Danner wrapped the deer head and antlers in a green canvas tarp he also kept in his toolbox. The twenty-four-inch-wide antlers wouldn't fit inside the toolbox, so Danner placed the blood-soaked tarp and the deer head on the floorboard of his truck and took off.

ON THE MORNING OF December 19, 1992, Bob Clements, a U.S. Fish and Wildlife Service refuge employee, was driving south on Hill Road when he spotted a large concentration of birds. "There must have been fifteen eagles, eight or ten vultures, and a half-dozen ravens fighting over that carcass," said Clements. Investigating the avian frenzy, Clements discovered a large, partially eaten buck lying in the snow, its head and antlers missing. Horrified by what he'd found, Clements raced to the refuge headquarters and telephoned California Fish and Game Warden Al McDermott.

"Where's the carcass now?" asked McDermott.

"It's about two miles south of the refuge headquarters, on Hill Road," said Clements. With all the birds around that headless carcass, you can't miss it."

"Headless!" said McDermott. "Not another damned headhunter." Warden McDermott was referring to unscrupulous wildlife traffickers who killed trophy bucks for their antlers and sold them to wealthy collectors and crooked taxidermists on the black market. "I'll meet you there in a half hour."

Warden McDermott parked his patrol rig next to the Fish and Wildlife Service pickup and followed Clements out through the snow to where the deer carcass lay. For every two steps Clements took, the broad-shouldered veteran warden took one. McDermott was in full uniform, wearing a moss-green wool coat with Fish and Game patches on each shoulder.

"Looks like the son of a bitch shot it in the hindquarters first, then had to shoot it again," said McDermott, in his deep yet soft voice. "Too bad we've had all this snow the last few days. We might have found some footprints."

Warden McDermott examined the carcass for slugs that might be lodged in the body. Unfortunately, there were entrance and exit holes at both sites and no slugs or bullet fragments to be found. Based on the fresh condition of the carcass and the fact that scavengers had just begun to feed, McDermott guessed that the deer had only been dead three or four days. He took blood and tissue samples, then walked back to the patrol rig to get his camera.

While photographing the carcass, it dawned on the wildlife officer that even without its head, this deer looked familiar. "I think this is the same deer I photographed four or five days ago," said McDermott, staring down at the buck's narrow hindquarters. "Yeah, it has to be the same deer. He was standing right here by the road and didn't pay any attention to me."

"Do you have the photograph?" asked Clements.

"It's still in the camera," said McDermott. "I'm almost at the end of the roll. Here, smile. I'll take your picture."

Within minutes of Warden McDermott and the refuge employee leaving the scene, bald eagles swooped in from nearby perches, followed by an assortment of ravens, magpies, and vultures.

A FEW DAYS LATER, WARDEN McDermott held the developed photograph in his hand. It had been taken with a standard-issue Pentax pocket camera, which worked well for evidence purposes but had its limits when it came to zeroing in on a subject from any distance. In this case, the buck had been thirty or forty yards away when McDermott snapped the photograph. McDermott could see that the large, seemingly undernourished buck had five distinctive points on the right side and four on the left. He noticed some smaller protrusions on the antlers, but due to the distance factor and the angle of the photograph, couldn't quite make them out. "This is all I've got for now," said the determined warden. "It'll have to do."

The community of Tulelake had a human population of approximately 1,000 in 1992, and it hasn't changed much since then. Like any small town, not much happened without somebody hearing about it and spreading the word. Warden McDermott was filling his patrol vehicle with gas when a fifty-year-old acquaintance named Lyle Tibbetts walked up.

"Hey, Al," said Tibbetts, "I hear someone killed a big buck down on the refuge and cut the head off."

"Oh yeah," said McDermott, "where'd ya hear that?"

"Word gets around," said Tibbetts. "How long ago did this happen?"

"About three weeks ago. Why?"

"That's just about right," said Tibbetts.

"Lyle, you're actin' like you want to tell me something. What is it?"

Tibbetts explained that he had been in one of the Tulelake pubs a couple of weeks before, when the bartender started bragging about a big buck he had supposedly killed during the season. "I thought it was kinda funny that he would wait to bring that up two months after the season closed," said Tibbetts. "I been in that bar a dozen times during and after the season, and he never mentioned it before."

"Did he describe the buck?" asked McDermott.

"He said it looked like a five pointer, but it had some o' them little nubbins stickin' outta the antlers that made it a seven pointer."

"Where'd he say he shot it?"

"Porcupine Burn, wherever that is."

"What's this bartender's name?"

"He calls himself Travis Danner, but here's the kicker …."

"What's that?"

"I went in there the other night and he was gone. The owner of the bar said he just up and left town."

"What's this Danner look like?"

"Well, he's probably pushin' forty, about my height, kinda on the skinny side."

"What color hair?"

"I don't think he's got any. I've never seen him without some kinda hat on."

Warden McDermott finally had a suspect, but now he had to find him. He drove to the pub where Danner had worked.

"Strange thing," said Bill Beckwith, the bar owner. "He just up and left without tellin' me or bothering to leave a forwarding address. I still owed him for a couple hours tendin' bar."

"What's this Danner's middle name?" asked McDermott.

"I'm embarrassed to say I don't know," said Beckwith. "I never asked him for it."

"How long'd he work here?"

"Oh, about six months or so."

"And you didn't know his middle name? How'd you pay him?"

"I probably shouldn't tell you this, but I just paid him cash from the register."

Warden McDermott contacted the Siskiyou County Sheriff's Department and ran a records check on the name Travis Danner, with these associated qualifiers: approximately forty years old, five feet nine inches tall, approximately

150 pounds. Without a middle name or anything else to go on, three Travis Danners popped up in the computer: two lived in Los Angeles, and one lived in Palmdale. None matched the description McDermott had provided.

Warden McDermott let it be known around Tulelake that he was looking for Danner as a possible suspect for the killing and beheading of one of the refuge bucks. Most of the good citizens of Tulelake were very protective of their local deer and frowned upon the idea of one being poached during closed season. The fact that the poacher had cut the head off and left the carcass to rot added fuel to the fire of their acrimony. Within a week, McDermott received word that Danner had moved to Alturas, in nearby Modoc County. By doing a little more digging, the skilled investigator came up with an address.

Cal Albright was the veteran California Fish and Game warden for the Alturas Patrol District. He had been the warden in Alturas for over twenty years and had his finger on its pulse. He knew just about everything that happened there. When McDermott telephoned Albright and told him about Travis Danner, Albright said, "Come down tomorrow and we'll go see him together. By the time you get here, I'll be able to tell you what Mr. Danner's been up to."

A little more than a month had gone by since the headless deer was found lying in the middle of Tule Lake National Wildlife Refuge. It was about 10:00 on a crystal-clear Sunday morning in late January when Wardens McDermott and Albright approached a small, single-story stucco house on the outskirts of Alturas. "It's that gray-colored house about halfway up the block," said Albright.

"Let's walk from here," said McDermott. "I don't want him to see us pull up and start hidin' things."

When McDermott and Albright stepped out of McDermott's patrol truck, they were assailed by the bitterly cold, thirty-mile-per-hour north wind that blows down from Goose Lake in the wintertime and chills Alturas's 2,800 residents to the bone. "Damn!" said McDermott. "I think it's colder here than it is in Tulelake."

"You get used to it," said Albright, laughing as McDermott's hat blew off.

As McDermott and Albright approached the front door, they passed a picture window. "Do you see what I see?" said McDermott, knocking on the door.

"Are those your antlers?" said Albright, peering through the window at the opposite living room wall.

A middle-aged, sandy-haired woman, still in her bathrobe, answered the door. She stared up at the towering warden with a look of complete surprise on her face.

"I'm Warden McDermott, with the Department of Fish and Game. Are you Mrs. Danner?"

"No."

"Does Travis Danner live here?"

"It's my house. Richie Danner lives here with me."

"Richie?"

"Travis is his middle name."

That explains why we couldn't find him through NCIC [National Crime Information Center], thought McDermott. "May we come in for a minute and talk with you?"

"Yeah, I guess. Come on in and get outta this wind."

Wardens McDermott and Albright stepped into the living room. McDermott's hard-soled, size-sixteen boots caused the wood floor to creak and groan as he eased his way toward the hanging antlers. Albright stood next to the front door and watched for any sign of the suspect.

With a five-by-seven-inch photograph in his right hand, Warden McDermott studied the plaque on which the deer antlers had been unprofessionally tacked. A plastic inscription read:

Mule Deer
Porcupine Burn
1992

McDermott remembered what Lyle Tibbetts had said to him several weeks earlier. *This is our man*, thought McDermott. *Hopefully he's around here somewhere.* Just then a slender, shirtless man, about Warden Albright's height, appeared from the hallway with a towel wrapped around his waist. "What's goin' on?" he said.

"Richie, these men are with the Fish and Game," said the woman.

"I'd like to talk to you about these deer antlers," said McDermott, his deep voice echoing through the room."

"I shot that buck legal," said Danner, water dripping off his bare legs onto the wood floor.

"I'd like to see your deer tag," said McDermott.

"I don't have it," said Danner. "It musta got lost. It says right there I killed it on Porcupine Burn."

Warden McDermott reached up and removed the plaque and deer antlers from the wall. "Well, we're going to take this to the lab and have some experts look at it," said McDermott. "I'll write you out a receipt for the time being. Do you have some identification?"

"Sally, where's my wallet?" said Danner.

"I guess it's in the bedroom on the dresser."

"Would you mind getting his wallet for him?" said McDermott, looking at Sally. Wardens McDermott and Albright had the slick deer poaching suspect right where they wanted him and didn't want to give him the opportunity to get dressed and duck out the back door without producing identification. "Are you working?" asked McDermott, waiting for the woman to return.

"Not at the moment," said Danner.

Warden McDermott copied information from Danner's California Driver's License. While he continued to discuss the issue with Danner and his girlfriend, Warden Albright walked back to the patrol truck and ran a warrant check on their suspect. Danner had no outstanding arrest warrants, so the wardens provided him with a receipt for the antlers and left.

Late that same afternoon, Warden Al McDermott sat down at his home desk and began documenting what had transpired earlier in the day. Questions began popping up in his mind: *I'm sure that's the same deer, but is a jury going to be able to convict this guy using my limited-quality photograph? Is the Fish and Wildlife Lab in Ashland going to be able to secure enough DNA from the antlers and skullcap to make a case?*

As the warden sat there contemplating his next course of action, he glanced over at a recent copy of *Tracks* magazine resting on a stack of papers at the corner of his desk. *Tracks* was a hunting publication put out by the California Department of Fish and Game. On the front cover was a full-sized photograph of the exact same deer that had been poached on the refuge. McDermott put his own photograph up next to it and compared the antlers. "That has to be the same deer!" said McDermott. "And this is a much better photograph."

Monday Morning at exactly 8:00, the phone rang in the Fish and Game office of Region I Information Officer Paul Wertz.

"Paul Wertz."

"How ya doin', Paul? This is Al McDermott."

"Are ya freezing your ass off up there?"

"No, it's nice up here," said McDermott, laughing. "It's a balmy five degrees this morning. Hey, Paul, I need to ask you something."

"Shoot."

"This *Tracks* magazine the Department puts out ... who does all the work on that?"

"You're talking to him. What do you want to know?"

"Where did the deer photograph on the front cover come from?"

"That was taken by my friend Steve Guill."

"How do I get in touch with him?"

Warden McDermott contacted Steve Guill that same afternoon and learned that Guill had photographed the poached buck on December 15—four days before it was found dead. Much to Warden McDermott's delight, Guill had taken close-up photographs of the deer from several different angles. Guill said he would gladly testify to that fact in court, should the case go to trial.

The next day, Warden McDermott delivered the antlers and Guill's photographs to the U.S. Fish and Wildlife Forensics Laboratory in Ashland, Oregon. One month later, the lab contacted McDermott, saying the detailed photographs he had provided matched perfectly with the antlers; their forensics experts would have no problem testifying to that fact in court. Warden McDermott completed the arrest report narrative he had begun almost two months earlier and immediately filed a criminal complaint with the Siskiyou County District Attorney's Office against Richard Travis Danner. A warrant was issued for Danner's arrest.

I would like to be able to tell you that Danner was arrested the next day, fined $5,000, and sentenced to nine months on the county rock farm. As is often the case with misdemeanor wildlife offenses, it didn't quite turn out that way. When McDermott and Albright went back to Danner's Alturas residence, they learned that Danner's girlfriend had booted him out and Danner was once again on the lam.

Determined not to let Danner get away with his blatant act against nature, Warden McDermott continued to follow up on this investigation for the next three months. He ran repeated record checks and contacted Danner's previous acquaintances. One day an unidentified man telephoned McDermott, saying he had received a telephone call from his old drinking buddy. "You know, I wouldn't have said anything if he had poached that deer because he needed the meat," said the informant. "But he killed it just so he could brag about the antlers, and that really bothered me."

"Did he say where he was?" asked McDermott.

"He said he was tending bar in some little town south of Bishop. Big Pine or Little Pine—something like that."

"Lone Pine?"

"That's it," said the caller. "I think Travis likes livin' in mountain areas so he can kill deer. He's kind of a nut when it comes to them big bucks. That's all that guy ever talked about."

"Did he tell you the name of the bar?"

"No, and I didn't want to ask him that 'cuz he might get suspicious. That's all I got." The caller hung up.

Warden McDermott immediately contacted the warden in Lone Pine and asked him to check the area bars for Richard Travis Danner. It took about a week to finally locate him; Danner was taken into custody and allowed by the Siskiyou County Court to post and forfeit $1,000 bail. Warden McDermott would have preferred to have Danner return to Siskiyou County, appear before a judge, and receive an extended jail sentence, but the court decided otherwise. When the $1,000 bail was forfeited, the case was closed—no jail sentence, no probation conditions, nothing further. Danner was never heard from again.

Al McDermott retired in 2000 after nine years as a deputy sheriff and twenty-one years as a dedicated warden for the California Department of Fish and Game. He now lives in the wilds of Wyoming.

The Terror of
Humboldt Bay

———◆———

HIS REAL NAME WAS Harlan Regis O'Lander, but every California Fish and Game warden who worked in or around Humboldt County during the 1990s knew him as Butch. In his early thirties and strong as an ox, Butch O'Lander loved to hunt, fish, and fight—not necessarily in that order. One of his favorite fighting tactics was using his incredibly hard head to beat his unfortunate opponents into submission.

The warden who knew O'Lander best was Jon Dunn. Tall, good-looking, and personable, Dunn had a gift for gab that served him well in the Eureka community. If anyone was violating fish and wildlife laws, it didn't take long before Warden Dunn heard about it.

"During my twenty-plus years in Humboldt County, Butch O'Lander was discussed as frequently among the hunting and fishing community as the weather," said Dunn. "If I was checking brant hunters on Humboldt Bay, he'd be there. I could be working deer or bear hunters in the National Forest; there was Butch. During waterfowl season I could count on running into him sooner or later—sometimes during the day, other times after shooting hours. When the salmon were running in the Eel River or up on the Mattole, it was just a matter of time before I'd receive a call. The conversation would go something like this:

'There's a man down on the sandbar snagging the hell out of the salmon.'

'What does he look like?'

'He's about six-two, husky build, long dark hair, with a two-week-old beard.'

'I have a good idea who that is. I'll be right out.' "

***

LIKE MANY FISH AND Game wardens, Jon Dunn enjoyed hunting and fishing himself. In November of 1995, he had arranged to take two weeks' vacation for a previously planned deer hunting trip to Colorado. Dunn was at home packing for the next day's trip when the phone rang.

"Hello," said Dunn.

"Jon, this is Jerry."

"I'm on vacation and getting ready to go to Colorado, Jerry. Call the office."

"No, Jon, I'm not calling to report a violation. You said you wanted me to let you know when the brant hunting was good out on the South Spit."

Brant season was open, and these ocean-going geese had been flocking into Humboldt Bay since the previous day. Dunn's personal friend Jerry Daniels maintained a waterfowl hunting blind at the south end of the bay.

"Where are you now, Jerry?"

"I'm getting ready to head out."

"Okay, I'll meet you there."

Every conscientious game warden knows that you're never really off duty when you're in the field or on the water. Along with his shotgun, ammunition, and chest waders, Dunn brought along a handheld Fish and Game radio and his duty weapon, a .357 magnum revolver, which he wore on his hip.

Dunn could see duck blind after duck blind, all occupied by hunters, as he slowly drove along Humboldt Bay's South Spit. Decoys were out and flocks of black brant geese circled in the distance. "Never fails!" he said to himself. "The best brant hunting all year and I'm gonna be in Colorado." Pulling off the road near his friend's blind, Dunn sat on the tailgate of his personal pickup and began putting on his chest waders. He could hear shotgun blasts coming from various blinds across the bay and loud shouting close by.

Excited about the prospect of bagging a couple of geese before leaving for Colorado, Dunn didn't pay much attention to the shouting. Brant hunting had become akin to a social event on the South Spit. Hunters from nearby Eureka and Arcata had become acquainted over the years and would call out from blind to blind, "Nice shot!" or "How'd you miss that one? My ten-year-old could have made that shot."

As he walked out to his friend's blind, it finally dawned on Warden Dunn that all the shouting was coming from one person—and it wasn't friendly banter, either: obscenities and angry threats hung in the air like heavy fog.

"What's all the shouting about?" asked Dunn, arriving at Jerry's blind.

"Butch O'Lander just killed a goose," said Jerry. "When he paddled out to retrieve it, his skull boat overturned and he went in headfirst. Everyone out here's been laughing at him, but you know Butch—he doesn't think it's funny."

As O'Lander sloshed his way back toward shore, pulling his skull boat behind him, he turned and looked in the direction of Jerry's blind.

"I'm gonna come down there and kick somebody's ass," he shouted.

Everyone on the spit knew how crazy Butch O'Lander could be and what he was capable of. You could have heard a pin drop when they all stopped laughing and a lone voice cried out, "Here he comes."

All too familiar with O'Lander's angry tone, Warden Dunn could tell he meant business. "All right, everyone, gather up your shotguns and unload them now!" instructed Dunn. They could hear Butch sloshing through the shallow water in their direction. Dunn began walking up the shoreline toward the oncoming recalcitrant. He intended to intercept O'Lander, calm his raging temper, and prevent the situation from escalating any further.

Butch was still coming hard, when Warden Dunn approached and was about to meet him halfway. "Somebody's gonna get hurt bad," shouted O'Lander, water dripping from his face and a crazed look in his eyes.

"Butch, let's settle down and talk about this," said Dunn, as he stepped directly into O'Lander's path and held out his arms.

O'Lander blew past the outstretched arms of the plain-clothes game warden like he wasn't even there, shouting, "I'm gonna find Jim Driscoll and kick his ass for laughing at me." Dunn had just come from the group and knew that Driscoll wasn't there that day.

"Butch," shouted Dunn, "Jim isn't even here. He couldn't have laughed at you."

"I heard him laughing and I'm gonna get him," O'Lander shouted back. Apparently there'd been some bad blood between Butch O'Lander and Jim Driscoll over the years, and O'Lander intended to settle their feud once and for all.

When Warden Dunn returned to Jerry's blind, he found an overturned skull boat that belonged to another friend. O'Lander had picked it up and was attempting to punch a hole in the bottom with a hardwood dowel. Since Butch wasn't really hurting the boat and his antics were expending energy, Dunn decided to leave him alone and let him blow off steam. While O'Lander continued to beat on the boat, who should walk up but Jim Driscoll.

"What's going on?" said Driscoll, just arriving for a day of brant hunting.

At the sound of Driscoll's voice, Butch O'Lander stood up, reared back, and hurled the wooden dowel at Driscoll—hitting him in the side. Before Dunn could react, O'Lander took three steps, and with a loud grunt, landed a powerful uppercut on Driscoll's chin. As Dunn described it later, "I've never seen such a blow, even while watching old fights between Mohammed Ali and Joe Frazier. Jim went stiff and his eyes rolled back in his head. His feet came off the ground and he fell backward onto the beach grass." That wasn't the end of it. With the speed of a cat, O'Lander quickly changed position and was about to kick Driscoll in the head, when Dunn and two others jumped on the would-be assailant.

With the strength of two men—derived from years of moving heavy objects all day—O'Lander quickly wriggled free and made a beeline for Driscoll's shotgun—the only gun that hadn't been unloaded. Dunn reached into his chest waders and drew his revolver, commanding O'Lander to drop the shotgun.

Now sixty-seven and long retired, the former warden described this potentially life-changing moment eighteen years later: "He was standing quartering away from me, with the shotgun at port arms. As I sighted my revolver on him, I remember thinking I wasn't going to be able to thread the bullet through his arms, through the shotgun, and hit him in the chest, so I changed my sight picture to his head and again demanded that he drop the gun."

Warden Dunn had been a Department of Fish and Game range master for many years and considered himself an excellent shot. He was sure that with his "rock solid sights," he could hit O'Lander right between the eyes if it came to that.

Butch O'Lander was irrational as hell, but not so irrational that he didn't recognize the look in Dunn's eyes. Instead of fear, which is what O'Lander expected, he saw confidence and steely determination.

Dunn knew if he shot this maniac, he would be answering questions and writing reports for the next six months. In the end, however, witnesses at the scene would surely testify to O'Lander's homicidal behavior, and the shooting would be ruled completely justified.

As crazy and irrational as Butch O'Lander was, he realized that if he didn't drop the gun, he would soon be dead. No more hunting, no more fishing, and no more drinking and carousing with his buddies. He would be as dead as the goose he had just shot. With that gruesome picture imprinted in his crazed mind, O'Lander dropped Driscoll's shotgun in the mud and proceeded to stomp on it.

O'Lander's anger didn't end there. He was about to go another round with Dunn and his two friends, when one of Butch's friends showed up and grabbed him by the arm. Warden Dunn immediately seized the opportunity by approaching O'Lander and advising him that he was under arrest. "I'm ordering you to go back to your blind and stay there until I come for you," said Dunn. Surprisingly, O'Lander complied with Dunn's instructions.

As Butch O'Lander walked back to his blind, Warden Dunn checked on his friend, Jim Driscoll. Driscoll was still groggy but able to stand with the help of his friends.

"Jim, are you all right?" asked Dunn.

"I'm not sure," mumbled Driscoll. "Are any of my teeth missing?"

"You guys stay here with Jim. I'm going to radio for a sheriff's unit," said Dunn.

Warden Dunn radioed Humboldt County Dispatch and requested that a deputy respond to the South Jetty and assist with a felony arrest for assault and battery. When the deputy arrived, he and Dunn walked out to O'Lander's blind. O'Lander was once again advised that he was under arrest. Without further incident, the deputy handcuffed O'Lander and transported him to the Humboldt County Jail.

That evening, Jon Dunn went home and typed an arrest report. He delivered it to the district attorney's office early the next morning, in time for O'Lander's arraignment. Waving goodbye to his friends and acquaintances at the DA's office, Dunn climbed into his personal pickup and headed for Colorado.

Harlan Regis O'Lander was charged and pleaded no contest to assault with a deadly weapon (the hardwood dowel), battery upon Jim Driscoll, and brandishing a deadly weapon in a threatening manner. The following May he arrived in court for his long-awaited sentence hearing. Seeing Warden Dunn in the courthouse hallway, O'Lander walked over and sat down beside him. "Were you really going to shoot me?" asked O'Lander. Before Dunn could answer, the bailiff called them into the courtroom.

Warden Dunn and the other witnesses to Butch O'Lander's abhorrent act of violence had hoped that O'Lander would receive a lengthy jail sentence for his crimes. Instead, the sentence read much like this: shall not be in possession of firearms, shall not commit assault on anyone, shall not hunt for three years, and shall pay a fine of $1,350. O'Lander's sentence was extremely lenient, considering his crimes and the damage he had done to Driscoll.

Jim Driscoll, a mild-mannered soul dedicated to family and wildlife conservation, didn't hunt brant again for many years after this incident. As for Warden Jon Dunn, he knew this wouldn't be the last time wildlife officers had to deal with Butch O'Lander. And he was right.

The Badger Mountain
Bait Pile

———◆———

HAVING SPENT A CAREER enforcing fish and wildlife regulations, I was always amazed by the extent to which some people would go to circumvent the law. Sometimes it took a couple of crack investigators, like the two in this next adventure, to expose the scofflaws and bring them to justice.

***

ON SEPTEMBER 7, 1997, California Fish and Game Warden Don Jacobs received a phone call from Lassen National Park Ranger Walt Baker. Baker said he had encountered a radio-collared blue tick hound inside an area currently closed to dog training and the pursuit of mammals.

"Were you able to get a look at the collar?" asked Jacobs.

"I couldn't catch the dog at first, but a couple of radio technicians came along and helped me corral him," said Baker. The name on the collar was Merle R. Sackett. I saw a hound rig earlier in the day and tried to get its license number, but the front plate was missing."

"Was the truck black, with a gray dog box in the bed?"

"That's it."

The fifty-year-old veteran warden had worked houndsmen out of his Burney Patrol District for eighteen years and could identify most of the area hound rigs on sight. "That's Sackett all right," said Jacobs. "I'm gonna need reports from you and your technicians, if you don't mind, describing what happened and including the date and time. One or two paragraphs is fine."

"You might want to talk to Greg Bettis at the Forest Service office in Old Station," said Baker. "I heard he's seen the same pickup in the area."

That afternoon, Warden Jacobs contacted Dennis Harding at the U.S. Forest Service office in Old Station.

"What's this about, Don?" asked Harding. Harding and Jacobs were on a first-name basis, since they both competed in local cross-country running events. Like Jacobs, Harding was tall, with prematurely gray hair and not an ounce of body fat.

"I heard Greg Bettis has seen Merle Sackett running his dogs in the closed zone," said Jacobs.

"That's the same guy I've been telling you about for the last three years, Don. I see him once a week goin' up and down Highway 44. Greg is working over at Manzanita Lake today. I'll get him on the phone for ya."

Greg Bettis told Warden Jacobs he and his engine crew had been checking lightning strikes off Little Bunch Grass Road on Thursday, September 4, when he saw a middle-aged man walking up the road, carrying some type of radio equipment. "We had to stop, because the son of a bitch had parked his pickup right in the middle of the road," said Bettis. "It was a late-1970s, black GMC pickup, with a gray dog box in back. I told the rest of the crew that I was pretty sure dogs weren't allowed in the area this time of year."

"What did this guy look like?"

"Five-eight or nine, butch haircut, skinny legs, and a pot belly."

"Yeah, that's sounds like Merle all right. Did he have a chipped front tooth?"

"I don't know. He wasn't smiling when we asked him to move his truck."

On the morning of September 8, Warden Jacobs received a phone call from an elderly man named Vic Schaffer. Schaffer said he and his son had found what they believed was a baiting area for bears.

"We was up near Little Bunch Grass Meadows, scouting for deer, when we came across this big pile o' grain," said Schaffer. "There was tracks and bear crap everywhere. I figured it had ta be one o' them hound-doggers tryin' ta bait the bears in." Schaffer was having trouble describing the location of the site, so Jacobs agreed to meet him and his son on Wednesday, September 10, at the Badger Mountain turnoff.

Warden Jacobs met the Schaffers on September 10 and followed them for several dusty miles past Little Bunch Grass Meadows to a dead-end road. The bait pile was located at the end of the road, just inside a Forest Service tree plantation—an area of plowed manzanita replanted with neat rows of pine trees that had grown to approximately thirty feet.

"It was right here in this area," said the younger Schaffer, pointing to scattered grain on the ground. "Most of it's gone now—probably eaten by the bears."

"The bears have definitely been here," said Jacobs, noticing fresh scat and bear tracks leading to and from the site. Warden Jacobs took photographs and collected samples of the grain and scat for possible future evidence purposes. California law prohibits …

> … the placing of feed, bait, or other materials capable of attracting a bear to a feeding area. No bait shall be used for the purpose of taking or pursuing a bear and no person may take a bear within a 400-yard radius of a garbage dump or bait [Title 14 California Code of Regulations, Section 365(e)].

Warden Jacobs returned to the baiting site several more times during the days that followed. On September 17, he walked to an area fifty yards from the original bait pile and found two hundred pounds of a freshly dumped grain mixture with a dark, fishy-smelling liquid poured over it. Jacobs again photographed the scene and gathered evidence samples. Before leaving, he encountered a half-grown, cinnamon-colored bear headed for the site. Seeing Jacobs, the bear bolted into the nearby woods.

A decision was made by Warden Jacobs and his captain to bring in a second warden and begin a surveillance detail prior to the opening of bear season on September 20. The obvious choice to assist Warden Jacobs was a husky veteran wildlife protection officer named Ken Taylor. Warden Taylor occupied Jacobs's neighboring Fall River Patrol District and had years of experience investigating illegal bear hunting activities.

On the afternoon of September 19, Wardens Jacobs and Taylor set out for the bait pile site, both wearing civilian clothing. Since the department did not have an unmarked undercover unit available at the time, Warden Taylor offered to drive his personal four-wheel-drive vehicle. Riding in the backseat were Taylor's wife and a female Fish and Game employee who happened to be visiting the Northern California Region from Sacramento Fish and Game headquarters.

Passing the tiny mountain community of Old Station, Jacobs and Taylor spotted three pickups parked near the Standard gas station payphone.

"What do we have here?" said Taylor, pulling in for a closer look. "Two of 'em are hound rigs."

"They all have Oregon plates," said Jacobs.

Warden Jacobs discreetly jotted down license numbers and descriptions of the three four-wheel-drive Toyota pickups: one beige, one gray, and one blue. The beige pickup and the gray pickup contained dog boxes with hounds on board. A camper shell was mounted in the bed of the light-blue pickup. When the beige pickup pulled onto the highway and headed south, Taylor and Jacobs followed.

Several miles down Highway 44, the beige pickup turned left toward Badger Mountain. "Well, they're headed in the right direction," said Jacobs.

The suspect vehicle continued on the dusty, unpaved road until it came to a stop on the north bank of Hat Creek, near Twin Bridges.

"They're stopping," said Taylor.

"Yeah, they're getting out," said Jacobs, watching with binoculars. "Looks like they're gonna water their dogs."

Taylor and Jacobs continued past the beige pickup in the direction of Little Bunch Grass Meadows and the illegal bait pile site. Without being obvious, Warden Jacobs wrote down brief descriptions of the two subjects. The passenger was an adult female, approximately forty years old, with medium-length brown hair; she wore a blue sweatshirt, green pants, and work boots. The driver was an adult male, in his late fifties or early sixties; he wore gray overalls, a long-sleeved blue shirt, and a big floppy hat.

When the wardens and their female companions had reached the end of the dead-end road, about one tenth of a mile from the bait pile, Warden Taylor said, "This is where Don and I get off, ladies. Come back and pick us up at five."

As the car pulled away, Jacobs and Taylor walked in the direction of the previously discovered baiting station. "They seem to have abandoned this first site," said Jacobs, pointing to some dried bear scat. "They're using the one farther back in the trees and away from the road."

Reaching the second baiting site, Jacobs commented that the bears had already eaten the pile of grain that had been left a few days earlier. "I see some of the grain scattered here in the dirt," said Taylor. "Look at all this bear sign!"

"How long do you think this site has been used?" asked Jacobs.

"If you look carefully, it's kind of like the spokes in a wheel," said Taylor. "Here, around the bait pile, we see tracks and bear scat everywhere. Some of the scat is fresh and some of it's old and dried up. Bits of grain are visible in the scat. As we walk farther out from the bait pile, the bear tracks and scat are fewer and farther between, but we begin seeing smashed-down vegetation where the bears have bedded down. See here, we've got bear trails heading in every direction. To answer your question, I think this site has been used for years. The only other place I've seen this much bear activity was at the Happy Camp Dump, in Siskiyou County."

An hour had passed and Warden Taylor was busy videotaping the scene when he and Jacobs heard a vehicle approaching.

"That doesn't sound like my rig," said Taylor. "Let's get outta sight!"

Not wanting to be seen, Taylor and Jacobs ran back into the trees and circled around to the dead-end road. They heard the suspicious vehicle stopping at the bait pile. The motor was shut off and doors were heard opening and closing. Taylor climbed a fir tree in hopes of videotaping the suspect vehicle and its occupants as they left. Seconds later, he got his wish. "Here they come," whispered Taylor. Jacobs was close by, hiding behind a patch of manzanita.

A black, four-wheel-drive GMC pickup with a gray dog box passed directly under Taylor's arboreal hiding spot. Warden Taylor immediately recognized the driver as Merle Sackett, a well-known houndsman and bear hunting guide. Seated in the middle was a smaller person, believed to be a woman. On her right was an older man wearing a big floppy hat.

"It was Sackett for sure," said Taylor, climbing down from the tree.

"Did you recognize the two people with him?" asked Jacobs. "The one in the middle looked like a woman."

"I'm not sure, but I think it was the same two people we just saw back at the bridge," said Taylor. "I'd recognize that big floppy hat anywhere."

When the two wardens returned to the baiting site, they found it freshly rebaited with two hundred or more pounds of the same grain mixture. Warden Taylor videotaped the bait and the fresh tire tracks left by Sackett's truck. At 5:00, Wardens Jacobs and Taylor returned to their car and left the area.

"What did you find?" asked Taylor's wife.

"Plenty," said Taylor. "As soon as Don and I grab something to eat and pick up our gear, we're coming back here for an all-night surveillance detail."

"I figured as much," said Taylor's wife.

"Ooh, that sounds exciting," said the female Fish and Game employee from Sacramento. "What a fun job you guys have!"

"Yeah," said Jacobs, laughing. "Lying on the cold, hard ground next to a smelly bait pile all night is lots of fun."

"Especially when the bears arrive for their evening meal," Taylor chimed in.

At 9:00 p.m. that evening, Warden Taylor followed Warden Jacobs back to the area of the illegal bait pile. Both wardens were driving marked patrol trucks. Taylor hid his truck far enough away from the baiting site so as not to be discovered. He then hiked a half mile into the baiting area, carrying his overnight gear and recording equipment. Warden Jacobs remained in his patrol truck and set up an observation point near Taylor's vehicle.

It was almost 11:00 when Warden Taylor approached the baiting site on foot. Well aware of the bag of tricks commonly used by illegal bear hunters, Taylor scanned the dirt road with his flashlight. Sure enough, he found where the road had been marked: both of Sackett's tire tracks had a line drawn through them, probably with a stick. Taylor knew that a vehicle wouldn't be able to pass without distorting the line. When the outlaws arrived, they would be able to tell if someone, possibly the game warden, had entered the area.

Clad in camouflage pants with a camouflage jacket over his uniform,

Warden Taylor set up an observation point forty yards from the bait pile, on the south side of the road. Lying on the hard ground behind a patch of crushed manzanita, Taylor glanced up at the stars. It was a sixty-degree night in late September. The air was still, the crickets were serenading, and a gibbous moon provided just enough ambient light to allow them to see a great horned owl soar overhead and land in a nearby pine tree. "It doesn't get any better than this," said Taylor, beginning to relax and settle in.

It was about 1:30 a.m. when Warden Taylor found himself nodding off. Pouring his last cup of coffee, he scanned the surrounding landscape in the remaining moonlight. *Why is it so quiet?* he wondered. Taylor suddenly realized that the reassuring sound of chirping crickets had been replaced by the unnerving, almost frightening sound of manzanita branches cracking and snapping on the ridge above. From the south side of the road, near the bait pile, came even more strange sounds: grunts, snorts, moans, and even a growl or two. "I'm surrounded by bears!" blurted Taylor. "Where did they all come from?"

For the next several hours, until daylight, Warden Taylor watched bears travel to and from the bait pile. Big bears, middle-sized bears, and a mama bear with cubs attended the party—all intent on eating their fill, leaving for a short time, and coming back for more. One exceptionally large bear walked within ten feet of the hidden warden, stopped and sniffed the air, then lumbered up the side of the ridge. *Someday I'll tell my grandkids about this,* thought Taylor. *For now, I better stay awake.*

Daylight came about 6:30 on opening morning of the 1997 bear season. Much to Taylor's and Jacobs's disappointment, there was still no sign of the suspects. At 6:55, Warden Taylor received a radio call from Warden Jacobs warning him that a vehicle was headed in. The first and only vehicle to arrive that day turned out to be occupied by a pair of elderly deer hunters; September 20 was also the opening day of deer season. The deer hunters drove to the end of the road, turned around, and drove away.

Discouraged and half asleep, Warden Taylor decided to walk over and check out the bait pile. Two-thirds of the grain that had been dumped the previous afternoon was gone. Taylor noticed something that had apparently been uncovered by the voracious bears—an orange feed sack tag that read: FARMER'S BEST, SWEET COB, Net Weight 70 Pounds; Ingredients: Flaked Corn, Steam Rolled Barley, Steam Crimped Oats, and Cane Molasses. Finding the tag helped renew the sleep-deprived warden's waning enthusiasm, so he quickstepped it back to his surveillance site and waited.

Whoever coined the phrase, "Patience is a virtue," must have been a game warden. Every good game warden knows that patience plays a major role in most successful investigations. Things don't always turn out as planned, and stakeouts, more often than not, don't bear fruit. This one certainly seemed to be going that way. Taylor and Jacobs stuck it out until 7:00 p.m., when Jacobs received a call from the captain.

"I want you guys to go home for the night and get some sleep," said the captain. "Resupply and come back in the morning."

At 4:00 the next morning, Warden Jacobs picked up Warden Taylor at his home and they again headed for the baiting site. Jacobs dropped Taylor off and Taylor returned to his previous surveillance point on the south side of the dead-end road, forty yards from the bait pile. Concerned about being too conspicuous, Taylor rolled a decaying log up against his right flank and another in front of him.

It was a few minutes before 7:00 when Jacobs came over the radio and advised Taylor that three rigs were headed into the surveillance area: the same beige Toyota pickup they had seen on Friday afternoon, Merle Sackett's black GMC pickup, and the same blue Toyota pickup they had observed on Friday afternoon. Warden Taylor, who lay on his stomach behind a flattened pile of dead manzanita and two hollow logs, mumbled, "Let the show begin."

The suspect vehicles came partway up the dead-end road and stopped. They were outside Taylor's range of sight, but he could hear engines idling on the road above. The engine sound grew louder as the beige Toyota pickup came into view. "Here they come," Taylor whispered into his radio microphone. Just then, he felt something crawling on the back of his right leg. "What the ..." he said under his breath. Glancing over his right shoulder, Taylor spotted a platoon of giant black carpenter ants marching, single file, over his right boot, up his pant leg, down the back of his calf, and back to the ground. He had apparently disturbed the semi-dormant insects when he moved the decaying logs.

Meanwhile, the beige pickup had passed directly in front of Taylor's hideaway. Taylor turned around just in time to see the female passenger and the male driver barrel out of the vehicle. The woman, later identified as Blanche Denise Riddle, wore the same clothes as before, along with a green stocking cap. Riddle walked directly to the bait pile, while the older man, later identified as Monte Edward Sewell, stayed with the three hounds perched on top of the dog box.

"There's that floppy hat," mumbled Taylor, watching Sewell with his binoculars. Sewell walked toward the bait pile. He stopped suddenly, then walked back and released one of the dogs. Riddle called the dog over to the bait pile. The two other hounds, still on top of the box, became excited and started baying. "Shut up!" said Sewell, in a hushed voice. He walked over and shocked both dogs with an electric cattle prod to make them stop. It was obvious to Warden Taylor that the two suspects did not want to make a lot of noise and alert people to the location of the baiting site.

Its tail wagging and its nose to the ground, the strike dog began its frenzied pursuit of a scent leading from the bait pile. Blanche Riddle followed closely behind, moving at a slow trot as the dog circled the immediate area and headed straight for Warden Taylor. "I knew I was caught," Taylor would tell me seventeen years later, "but the dog was so centered on the bear scent that he came within three feet, looked right at me, and kept on going. Riddle was right behind the dog and didn't even see me lying there on the ground."

"That must have been exciting," I said.

"My heart almost stopped," Taylor admitted.

The strike dog eventually lined out on the bear trail and headed south up the ridge and into the timber. Riddle followed from thirty yards behind. When the dog and Riddle were out of sight, Taylor turned his attention to Sewell. Sewell released the two hounds on top of the dog box and another dog from inside the box. All three hounds dashed off in the direction of the strike dog.

Sensing that someone else was on the road, Warden Taylor looked to his left and saw Merle Sackett marching toward the beige pickup. He walked right past Taylor and struck up a conversation with Sewell. A few minutes later, Riddle came running out of the timber. Warden Taylor watched as all three suspects stood next to the pickup, talking. Riddle explained to Sackett how the chase had begun, pointing in the direction of the bait pile, then in the direction the strike dog had gone. "You think they put the jump on the bear right over there?" Sackett was heard to say as he pointed at the bait pile.

Sackett had begun walking back toward his own pickup, when the hounds fired up like they had just treed the bear. "Looks like they got him now," he shouted back at Riddle and Sewell. Riddle and Sewell jumped into the beige pickup and sped away. "Wait until all three pickups have passed," said Taylor over the handheld radio. "Then come down and pick me up."

"Ten-four," answered Jacobs.

When Jacobs arrived, Taylor had removed his camouflage clothing and appeared in full uniform: Fish and Game shirt with identifying patches, badge, name tag, gun belt, and regulation duty weapon. "Enough surveillance," said Taylor. "It's time to get down to business."

Warden Jacobs drove his marked patrol truck back to Badger Mountain Road and followed the suspects' tracks south. The wardens had traveled only a short distance—a little over a mile—when four pickups appeared along the narrow dirt road. Warden Taylor immediately spotted Merle Sackett, who was on foot and headed up the adjacent hill with three hounds on a leash.

"I see the beige hound rig, but the woman and the old man aren't here," said Taylor.

"They're probably up at the tree," said Jacobs. "I hear the dogs sounding off, like they've got something cornered."

"Sackett is watching us," said Taylor. "Let's play dumb and act like we don't know what's goin' on."

"Maybe he'll let you follow them to the tree," said Jacobs.

"That's the idea," said Taylor. "We'll be able to tie a nice neat bow around this case."

When Warden Taylor climbed from the pickup, he greeted Merle Sackett as if it were a routine contact.

"What are you guys doin' here?" asked Sackett, obviously concerned.

"It's the opening weekend of deer season," replied Taylor. "We're just out checking deer tags and keepin' people honest. It sounds like you've got one treed."

"Yeah," said Sackett.

"Is this a guided trip?"

"Yes it is."

"Do you mind if I walk along with you?" said Taylor. "It's been a while and I'd like to see how it's done."

Sackett knew he couldn't stop Warden Taylor from walking to the tree, even if he wanted to. "Suit yourself," he replied.

Taylor could hear the dogs steadily baying as he and Sackett marched up the hill toward the tree. Stumbling along behind were Neal Pancake, one of Sackett's tagalong helpers, Frank Mills, a deer hunter friend of Sackett's, and Lewis Nichols, Sackett's middle-aged client from Stockton.

"Who else do you have at the tree?" asked Taylor.

"Uh, just a couple friends from Oregon," replied Sackett. "I'm pretty sure we don't have too many dogs out." Warden Taylor found it curious that Sackett would bring up the number of dogs: California hunting regulations allowed for only one dog per licensed hunter during the general deer season. "Yeah, I'm pretty sure we're okay," repeated Sackett. Without responding, Warden Taylor let him keep talking. Sackett claimed it was okay for him to have three dogs on a leash and they didn't count because they weren't really pursuing.

It was 8:30 when Warden Taylor and the houndsmen's entourage arrived at the tree. The hounds were going crazy, barking at the dark brown bear that maintained a death grip on the tree trunk, sixty feet above. With his body oriented upward, the frightened bear turned his head and stared at the chaotic scene below.

Taylor immediately spotted the woman he had previously seen at the bait pile, but the older man was mysteriously missing. Scanning the area, Warden Taylor began counting the number of hounds; they numbered ten, including the one Sackett had released from the road earlier and the three he still held on a leash.

Sackett introduced Blanche Riddle to Warden Taylor. "Where's your partner?" asked Taylor.

Riddle's back bowed, her chin dropped, and her eyes squinted back at Taylor. She didn't answer right away, but Taylor knew exactly what she was thinking: *How does this game warden know about my partner?* "Uh, he was here a minute ago," she said.

Taylor redirected his attention to the client, who was standing at the base of the bear tree, cradling a scoped 30-06 rifle. Wardens Jacobs and Taylor would later learn that Nichols had paid Sackett $1,500 for the guided bear hunt. "Is that your client?" asked Taylor, walking toward an unattended rifle that was leaning against a nearby tree.

"Yeah, said Sackett. "He came up from down south."

"Where's the other guy?"

"What guy's that?"

"The older gentleman who was riding with Ms. Riddle."

"Oh, don't worry about him," said Sackett. "He just doesn't like game wardens and took off when he heard you was comin.'"

"I'm not sure I like the idea of him being out there and possibly armed," responded Taylor, pointing to the rifle leaning against the tree. "Who does this belong to?"

"That's my backup gun," said Sackett, handing the rifle to Neal Pancake and shouting instructions over the ear-piercing barking of the hounds. "I want ya ta stand right over there. If the dude misses or wounds the bear and it comes down outta the tree, you kill it quick before it hurts my dogs."

"Do you have a bear tag?" asked Taylor, addressing Neal Pancake.

"Yeah, I do," said Pancake.

As Warden Taylor continued to address Sackett and Pancake, Warden Jacobs approached. Taylor began filling Jacobs in on the situation when Nichols's 30-06 rifle went off. Both wardens jerked their heads around just in time to see the bear crash through several branches and bounce on the hard ground.

"Shoot it again," shouted Sackett.

Nichols fired a second shot into the bear, rendering it lifeless. Wardens Taylor and Jacobs identified the bear as a full-grown male, weighing over 300 pounds. Sackett and Riddle took turns letting their respective dogs loose, allowing them to "worry" (chew on) the dead bear.

"How many of these dogs are yours?" asked Taylor, addressing Blanche Riddle.

"Four of 'em are mine and two belong to Monte," said Riddle.

As the hounds continued to gnaw on the dead bear, Taylor spotted Monte Sewell standing back in the forest, thirty feet away. Sewell didn't appear to be armed, so Taylor watched him move around in the background. When the hunting party began skinning and boning the bear, Sewell finally came in and participated. Taylor photographed the operation and noticed that Nichols, the client, was the only one who didn't get his hands bloody.

"With Blanche doing most of the work, I would have thought she was the guide," commented Taylor, watching Riddle and the others cut up the bear.

"Blanche and Monte came down from Oregon to work for me," said Sackett, laughing. "Ya might say this is a job interview."

It was 11:45 when everyone finally returned to the trucks on Badger Mountain Road. Wardens Jacobs and Taylor began the enforcement process by asking to see everyone's hunting license and bear tag. Sackett, Nichols, and Pancake were California residents. They all possessed California resident hunting licenses and bear tags. Blanche Riddle was a resident of Oregon. She possessed a non-resident hunting license but did not have a bear tag. Monte Sewell possessed neither a hunting license nor a bear tag, which explained his reluctance to participate in the hunt with two game wardens around. Sewell had been seen earlier, by Warden Taylor, releasing dogs at the bait pile. Hunting without the required non-resident hunting license would turn out to be the least of Sewell's problems.

The officers asked for and received verbal permission to search Sackett's, Riddle's, and Pancake's pickups. While searching Merle Sackett's black GMC pickup, Warden Taylor found three separate compartments located in the pickup bed: a tool box, a dog box, and what turned out to be a hidden compartment inside the dog box. Taylor examined the inside of the hidden compartment and discovered nine empty feed sacks. He also found a feed sack tag that was identical to the one he had previously found in the illegal bait pile. Hidden inside one of the feed sacks was a one-gallon jug of fish emulsion fertilizer, the same fishy-smelling substance that had been poured on the bait pile.

Wardens Jacobs and Taylor continued their investigation clear into early 1998 before filing criminal complaints against Sackett, Riddle, and Sewell. Merle R. Sackett was charged with eight conspiracy counts of unlawfully taking mammals (bear) for commercial purposes, placing bait for the purpose of taking a bear, and taking bear within four hundred yards of bait. He was also charged with running dogs in a closed area and using too many dogs during the general deer season. Upon conviction, Sackett received the following sentence: five years' probation, during which he was not allowed to hunt anywhere; $5,000 fine; and forfeiture of his hound rig. Riddle and Sewell were each charged with two counts of conspiracy to take mammals (bear) for commercial purposes, placing bait for the purpose of taking a bear, and taking bear within four hundred yards of bait. Sewell was also charged with hunting without a valid license. Riddle and Sewell received sentences similar to that of Sackett's, excluding the loss of vehicle.

Warden Don Jacobs was eventually promoted to patrol lieutenant and retired from the California Department of Fish and Game in 2004. Ken Taylor remained the Fall River Fish and Game warden until his retirement in 2008. The in-depth and highly successful Sackett Baiting Investigation is still being used as a training aid for California Fish and Wildlife wardens.

Fish Hogs

---◆---

I'VE KNOWN LARRY BRUCKENSTEIN for fifty-four years, so it's only fitting that I tell you a little bit about him before beginning the next story. Larry and I first met in 1960, the year my family moved to Orland. His father, Harry Bruckenstein, owned a dairy farm three miles west of town. During the winter months, Larry and I hunted ducks and pheasants in the fields and orchards within walking distance of the Bruckensteins' farmhouse. All summer we fished and swam in Walker Creek and the nearby irrigation canals.

Two outings with the Bruckenstein family will remain in my memory forever. Harry Bruckenstein coached our Little League team my first summer in Orland. He took several of us to see the Giants play in the then recently built Candlestick Park. I remember how excited Larry and I were, seeing Willie Mays in person for the first time. After the game, we stood by the players' entrance and watched all the stars come out and get into their cars. Mays never did come out, but much to our delight, Willie McCovey and Orlando Cepeda did.

The following summer, the Bruckensteins invited me to join them for a weekend trip to their family cabin on California's fabulously beautiful North Coast. The small, wood-frame cabin sat at the top of a rugged cliff, overlooking the Trinidad Coastline. With fishing rods in hand, Larry, his younger brother Tom, and I followed a narrow footpath down the steep embankment to the ocean below. From a rocky overhang, the three of us cast our lines into the surf. We waited a good hour before experiencing our first bite. By then we had lost or eaten most of the tiny salad shrimp we used for bait that day. When I least expected it, I felt a tug on my line and reeled in one of the strangest fish

I'd ever seen. It was mottled brown, with spines everywhere and a huge head. Harry Bruckenstein told me later it was a cabezon. He helped me prepare my five-pound trophy for that night's dinner. The flesh was actually green when raw, but after it was cooked, boy, did it taste good.

Entering high school, Larry and I chose different paths. I played baseball and basketball, while Larry became a star halfback on the football team. Being shy, I avoided dances and social functions, while Larry flourished and became one of the most popular students at Orland High School. After our graduation in June of 1966, Larry Bruckenstein would enroll in Shasta College before volunteering for the draft and spending twenty-one months, to the day, in the U.S. Army. The last twelve of those months were spent as an infantryman in the jungles of Vietnam. While in Vietnam, the lean, six-foot-one-inch soldier contracted a severe case of malaria that flared up from time to time long after his distinguished military service had ended.

Never forgetting his outdoor roots and love of nature, Larry Bruckenstein attended Humboldt State University after his tour of duty and was eventually hired as a warden for the California Department of Fish and Game in 1979. He transferred from the Merced Patrol District to the North Coast position of Garberville, California in 1985, where this story begins.

***

"GARBERVILLE WAS ONE OF the best patrol districts in the state," boasted retired California Fish and Game Warden Larry Bruckenstein. "Shelter Cove and the Lost Coast were to the west, with salmon, rockfish, and abalone. To the east were southern Humboldt County and Trinity County, rich with deer, bear, and lots of mountain activity. In the middle, I had three anadromous rivers: the Mattole, the Eel, and the South Fork Eel, all full of salmon and steelhead."

"How did you happen to spot those illegal fishermen way out in the ocean?" I asked, referring to a notable case that Warden Bruckenstein had made back in 2005.

"This was an example of being in the right place at the right time," said Bruckenstein. "That was often the story of my success as a warden, and it certainly was that day."

ON A BRIGHT, SUNNY afternoon in April 2005, Warden Larry Bruckenstein was patrolling the shoreline of Shelter Cove for abalone activity. He had been out since before daylight, investigating a possible deer violation in another part of his district. Since abalone season had just opened, Bruckenstein decided to check out Shelter Cove before working his way back toward Garberville.

With poor-to-nonexistent visibility in the tide pools, the usual morning rock pickers had given up and gone home. The beach and the parking areas were empty, with the exception of two pickups and a single boat trailer. Bruckenstein recognized one of the pickups as belonging to Frank Sorensen, a thirty-five-year-old suspected outlaw with a reputation for selling sport-caught rockfish fillets. Bruckenstein and the adjoining Fort Bragg warden had received several reports of Sorensen engaging in this type of illegal activity over the years.

Reaching for a pair of binoculars that sat on the bench seat beside him, Warden Bruckenstein scanned the ocean for any sign of a fishing boat. A large segment of the ocean off the coast of Shelter Cove was included in the North-Central Rockfish and Lingcod Management Area—closed to the take and possession of rockfish and lingcod at the time. All Bruckenstein saw, at first glance, was row after row of whitecaps bouncing up and down in the turbulent water. "Not much going on today," the sleep-deprived warden mumbled to himself. "It's too rough and windy out there."

Bruckenstein had placed his binoculars back on the seat and restarted his patrol truck when he caught a glimpse of something flashing in the distance. To the naked eye, it appeared to be a reflection of sunlight off a windshield. Turning off the ignition, he again picked up his binoculars and was able to barely make out a sport boat bobbing in the rough seas, a mile and a half offshore. Switching to a more powerful spotting scope, the newly energized warden immediately recognized one of the boat occupants as Frank Sorensen, better known around the docks as Skip.

"Hello, Skippy," Bruckenstein said aloud, as he adjusted the focus on his spotting scope. "I'd recognize those skinny legs anywhere. That looks like Pete Spencer's boat, but I don't see him.... Oh, there you are. Somebody else is on the bow. Not sure who that is." All three men were clearly fishing for bottom fish inside the closed management area. "Enjoy yourselves, boys," said the warden. "I'll be waiting to greet you when you come in."

It was two o'clock in the afternoon when Warden Bruckenstein parked his patrol truck out of sight in a location near the boat ramp. This veteran warden was no stranger to long stakeouts and was prepared to wait in the dark all night if that's what it took to catch a trio of rockfish poachers.

Sometime around 4:00 p.m., Warden Bruckenstein watched his subjects retrieving crab pots. "So that's your story," he said to himself. "You were just out there trapping a few crabs." It was legal to take crabs inside the management area, as long as the daily bag limit of ten Dungeness crabs per licensed fisherman wasn't exceeded.

Just before dark, the suspects' boat approached the launch area and began hauling out. With binoculars once again trained on the twenty-foot aluminum boat, Warden Bruckenstein identified the third fisherman as thirty-six-year-old Jimmy Burke, part-owner of an eating establishment up the coast.

"How did these three fishermen react when you contacted them?" I asked.

"They didn't know I was there until they saw me standing next to their recently trailered boat," said Bruckenstein. "By then it was too late. When they saw me, they all had that look on their faces that says, *We think we're screwed, but we're not quite sure yet.*"

Warden Bruckenstein relished the psychological challenge of dealing with serious violators in situations like this. Much like a cat would toy with a mouse, he initially engaged the poaching suspects in friendly conversation.

"Hey guys, how's it going?"

"We're doin' all right," said Sorensen, obviously nervous.

"How was the fishing? Did you have any luck?"

"We picked up a few crabs," replied Spencer.

"It must have been kind of rough out there. Did anybody get seasick?"

"I got a little queasy," said Burke.

"How does this North River boat handle in rough seas?"

"It handles all right," mumbled Spencer, anxious to drain the water out of his boat and leave. Folks around Redway and Garberville knew Spencer as a well-dressed real estate developer who made his living turning grassy meadows and redwood groves into strip malls and housing developments. On this day, he wore a hooded Gore-Tex parka with matching suspendered bibs.

"I like that outfit you're wearing," said Bruckenstein. "Did you find that around here or did you have to order it?"

"I ordered it," said Spencer.

Warden Bruckenstein looked in the direction of his patrol truck, then silently confronted each man with a discerning glance. "Well, since I'm here and you're here, do you mind if I take a look in your boat?"

Realizing that Warden Bruckenstein was going to search his boat anyway, Spencer gestured for him to climb aboard. Bruckenstein had watched the three fishermen engage in rockfish drifts in the closed area all afternoon. It was considered good form to ask first, but the skillful investigator knew he had all of the legal justification he needed to search Spencer's boat.

With his left foot on the trailer frame, Warden Bruckenstein lifted himself into the bow of the boat. The first item that caught his eye was a plastic garbage can filled with Dungeness crabs. "Have a few crabs," Bruckenstein muttered to himself, as he continued his cursory search. A large tote bag lying on the deck was jammed full of fish heads and carcasses, all of them rockfish and lingcod. "Crab bait?" commented Bruckenstein, continuing to search. Lifting the lid of a medium-sized ice chest, Warden Bruckenstein found it filled to the brim with fish fillets. A much larger ice chest was piled high with whole rockfish and lingcods.

After confirming that the three subjects had taken lingcod and rockfish in a closed area and possessed overlimits of crabs, Warden Bruckenstein climbed down from the boat and asked to see identification and California fishing licenses from all three fishermen. Removing a notepad from his coat pocket, he methodically recorded this information, as well as the CF number on the bow of Spencer's boat and license plate numbers from the two pickups.

With all three violators standing beside Spencer's boat wondering what was going to happen next, the disgusted warden turned to Spencer.

"Mr. Spencer, I would like you to pull your truck and trailer up to the cleaning table." It was getting dark, so Bruckenstein positioned his patrol rig to face the cleaning table and lit it up with his overhead spotlight.

"What do you want me and Jimmy to do?" asked Sorenson, sounding impatient.

"I want you to relax for a minute or two while I finish counting these crabs," said Warden Bruckenstein. "From the looks of it, you guys got a little carried away."

"What do you mean by that?" asked Burke, a diminutive figure wearing a lime-green stocking cap pulled down over his ears.

"Well," said Bruckenstein, "the limit is ten each and you guys have fifty-seven crabs. According to Mr. Herman, that's twenty-seven too many."

"Who's Mr. Herman?" mumbled Sorenson.

"Since these crabs are still alive, let's see if we can save a few of 'em," said Bruckenstein.

"Who's this Mr. Herman?" repeated Sorenson, a little louder.

"Oh," said Bruckenstein. He was my first-grade arithmetic teacher. After I take a few more photographs, I'd like Mr. Spencer to carry twenty-seven of these crabs down to the water and gently release them."

All of the unfilleted fish were counted next, including an assortment of rockfish species: blacks, blues, coppers, olives, and canaries. Among them were several large lingcod. Warden Bruckenstein was concerned about spoilage, realizing that if he filleted all the fish himself, he wouldn't finish until the wee hours of the morning. Determined to have this ill-gotten plunder go to a charitable institution, he looked down from the boat at the three fish hogs. "I'd like each of you to grab a fillet knife and get started," he said. "I'll provide the light."

As the fishermen filleted, Bruckenstein matched the carcasses with existing fillets inside the medium-sized ice chest. When the filleting was done, Warden Bruckenstein took one last photograph of the immense piles of fish heads and carcasses that blanketed the twenty-foot cleaning table. The carnage included 183 rockfish, two protected canary rockfish, twenty lingcods, and fifty-seven Dungeness crabs.

As all three poachers stood watching, each with a Michelob beer in hand, Frank Sorensen said, "We were just putting some fish in the freezer." The incredulous warden pondered the reason for Sorensen's seemingly shameless remark and air of entitlement: *This arrogant wharf rat claims to have salt water in his veins because of his "Norwegian heritage." Maybe he thinks he has a right to exploit the ocean and pillage its resources?* Shaking his head in disbelief, Warden Bruckenstein responded to Sorensen's ludicrous remark: "A criminal complaint will be filed with the Humboldt County District Attorney's Office. Each of you will be notified when to appear in court."

The next day, Bruckenstein drove to the Humboldt County District Attorney's Office and filed formal criminal charges against all three subjects. They were each charged with the following misdemeanors:

Take and possession of rockfish in the North-Central Rockfish and Lingcod Management Area during closed season;

Take and possession of lingcod in the North-Central Rockfish and Lingcod Management Area during closed season;

Joint possession of 153 rockfish over the legal limit;

Joint possession of 14 lingcod over the legal limit;

Joint possession of two protected canary rockfish;

Joint possession of rockfish fillets without the entire skin;

Joint possession of lingcod fillets without one-inch patch of skin;

Joint possession of 27 Dungeness crabs over the legal limit.

Frank Sorensen pleaded guilty to three of the eight charges. He was given a thirty-day jail sentence and placed on two years' summary probation. During the first year of probation, Sorensen was not allowed to fish. The other two defendants received minimal fines of $800 each and were instructed not to fish for one year. Disappointed but undaunted by the incredibly lenient disposition to this monumental case, Warden Larry Bruckenstein remained dedicated to the protection of California's fish and wildlife resources for the remainder of his long and productive career.

Handlines and Panga Boats

———◆———

I T WAS MID-AFTERNOON ON January 21, 2012. Fish and Game Warden
Ryan Hanson was patrolling the California coastline near San Simeon
in his four-wheel-drive patrol truck. *With this north wind blowing, it
should be clear enough to see the castle today*, Hanson thought. Hired by the
Department of Fish and Game two years earlier, the lanky Placer County
native was having the time of his young life and couldn't have asked for a
more adventurous first assignment.

As boarding officer of the Fish and Game patrol boat *Bluefin*, Warden
Hanson's primary duty was patrolling California's ocean waters from the
Northern Channel Islands to southern Monterey Bay. The sixty-five-foot
Bluefin was a state-of-the-art patrol vessel, designed to cruise up to 20 knots
and accommodate a crew of wildlife protection officers for two weeks at sea.
Threats to the resource were many, including abalone poaching, protected
rockfish violations, and a host of commercial fishing issues: failure to maintain
required records, overlimits, illegal gear, failure to offload, and hiding fish.
One of the newest and most important tasks was enforcing marine protected
area (MPA) closures and regulations.

For decades, resource managers have had major concerns about the
depletion of California's marine resources. In 1999, the Marine Life Protection
Act was passed by the state legislature, mandating that the California Fish and
Game Commission designate marine protected areas where fish, mollusks,
crustaceans, habitat, and other priceless marine resources are allowed to
recover. This statewide network was completed at the end of 2012, with
124 designated marine protected areas from the Oregon border to Mexico.
Among those marine protected areas were the Piedras Blancas State Marine

Reserve and adjoining Piedras Blancas State Marine Conservation Area, both inside Warden Hanson's patrol district.

When Hanson wasn't at sea on the *Bluefin*, he was responsible for patrolling the Central California coastline from Pismo Dunes to Big Sur. On this particular Saturday afternoon, he was joined on patrol by an enthusiastic twenty-two-year-old Cal Poly student named Brandon Wiley. One of the requirements of Wiley's criminal justice class was that he do a ride-along with one of the local law enforcement agencies and write a paper about the day's events. Since the athletic redhead had his heart set on being a game warden, Hanson was his obvious choice.

"There it is!" said Wiley. "I can see the spires from here."

"It's usually shrouded in fog or low clouds," said Hanson.

"One of my friends at school said he's seen zebras running around up there on the hill," said Wiley.

"I see them every once in a while," said Hanson, "sometimes right here by the highway. Two years ago, a couple of 'em apparently jumped the fence and were shot by the neighboring ranchers."

"Why did they shoot 'em?" asked Wiley.

"I guess the zebras were scaring their horses."

"Was Fish and Game involved?"

"No," said Hanson, "but anything involving the ocean or wild animals, even the exotic kind, usually ends up in my in-basket."

"I'd give anything to have a great job like yours," replied Wiley, a clipboard in one hand and a pencil in the other.

"Not everyone starts out in a beautiful place like this," said Hanson. "Most of the wardens I went through the academy with began their careers in L.A. or down in the desert somewhere."

It was 3:15 in the afternoon when Warden Hanson's cellphone rang. "Department of Fish and Game. Warden Hanson."

"Ryan, this is Mark. I'm in the undercover rig heading up the coast. I just saw two guys with handlines inside the Piedras Blancas Marine Reserve. They're just north of that old Piedras Blancas Motel that's on the east side of the highway."

"Do you have a vehicle description?" asked Hanson.

"Yes, it's a little red Honda sedan, parked in that turnout on the ocean side of the highway, just past the motel."

"I know right where that is. You must be just ahead of us."

"Where we going?" asked Wiley, itching for some action.

"That was my lieutenant," said Hanson. "Sounds like we've got some violators in the marine reserve."

"What marine reserve?" asked Wiley.

"Piedras Blancas."

"Isn't that where all the elephant seals hang out?"

"Yes, it is. If these guys are where I think they are, they're not too far from the seals' haul-out site."

When Warden Hanson and his ride-along arrived at Piedras Blancas, the red Honda sedan was still parked in the turnout on the west side of Highway 1.

"Okay, Brandon," said Hanson. "We don't want these guys to spot us, so stay low and follow my lead."

"I will," said Wiley. "Can I bring my binoculars?"

"Yes. Keep your voice down and don't slam the door when you get out."

Warden Hanson led his eager young apprentice down a narrow trail to a bluff overlooking the ocean. Peeking from a row of shrubs, Hanson spotted the two subjects walking on the beach, thirty yards away. The taller of the two, later identified as Zachery Aaron McCarty, was wearing a black, long-sleeved pullover shirt and a red baseball cap. The shorter and much heavier man, later identified as Edward James Rodriguez, wore blue jeans and a faded gray hooded sweatshirt.

"They look like they're about your age," said Hanson.

"I've seen that tall guy before," replied Wiley. "He plays a lot of three-on-three basketball down at the beach."

"Is he any good?"

"He's kind of a ball hog, but he's not bad. I heard he was going into the army."

"Interesting," Hanson said.

Breakers washed over the rocks as the two interlopers gathered crabs from the tide pools. "Eddie, watch out," shouted McCarty, barely audible over the roar of the pounding surf. On his knees and with his backside toward the ocean, Rodriguez was pummeled by a late-breaking wave that splashed onto the rocks and drenched him with the chilly fifty-degree water.

"Damn!" Rodriguez shouted back. "I didn't see that one coming."

"Here comes another one!" shouted McCarty.

"Do you think Mother Nature is trying to tell these guys something?" asked Wiley, laughing.

"Apparently they're not listening," replied Hanson. "It looks like they're using those rock crabs for bait."

Hanson and Wiley watched the two subjects retrieve three handlines, rebait them with small crabs, then toss them back in the ocean. All three handlines were made from white nylon tied to driftwood handles. At the business end of each line were two hooks and a makeshift rock sinker.

"That makes sense," said Hanson. "They're purposely using those primitive handlines instead of fishing rods so they don't get caught walking back to their car with fishing gear."

"That's pretty clever," said Wiley.

"I've seen people do this before," said Hanson. "My guess is they'll walk out with just the ice chest and leave all that junk lying on the rocks."

Rodriguez and McCarty continued to bait their lines with the small crabs they had caught by hand in the tide pools. About 4:30, Rodriguez walked over to one of the nearby tide pools and dropped to his knees. Reaching into a deep pool, he pulled out a half-dead cabezon and a large greenling. After placing the fish in his ice chest, he walked back to the same pool and retrieved two more fish: an even larger cabezon and another greenling.

"What did I tell you?" said Hanson, watching Rodriguez carry the ice chest up the beach, leaving a pile of twine and assorted litter lying on the rocks. With the tide coming in and waves washing over the rocks, Hanson knew it wouldn't be long before all that debris ended up in the ocean.

"Looks like they're moving to another spot," said Wiley.

From the same vantage point, Hanson and Wiley watched McCarty and Rodriguez carry three handlines, a small white bucket, and a package of squid bait down the beach to another assemblage of wash rocks, eighty yards away.

"Did you see them throw their lines out?" asked Hanson.

"I saw them set their gear down, but I couldn't tell if they threw their lines out or not," replied Wiley.

"Stay down!" cautioned Hanson. "They're coming back this way."

When Rodriguez and McCarty had reached the foot trail just below Hanson's and Wiley's vantage point, they picked up the ice chest and walked up the bluff toward their car.

"Too bad you got all wet," they heard McCarty say. "I wanted to see if I could catch another big cabezon."

"If the wind wasn't blowing, I'd stay," responded Rodriguez, "but I gotta get outta these wet clothes."

"Department of Fish and Game," announced Warden Hanson, stepping into view. "What have you gentlemen been up to?"

With an ice chest full of fish in his right hand, McCarty had no choice but to admit they'd been fishing.

"Are you finished fishing for the day?" asked Hanson, looking at Rodriguez.

"Yeah, we're done," said Rodriguez. "I got hammered by a wave and I'm freezing to death."

"I can see that," said Hanson. "Your lips are turning blue. By the way, where are your fishing rods?"

"We don't have any," said McCarty. "We used handlines."

"Oh? Where are they?"

"We lost 'em in the surf," said Rodriguez.

"Would you please open your ice chest for me?" instructed Hanson.

McCarty opened the ice chest, revealing several unopened beer cans and the four fish Warden Hanson had seen from the bluff. Hanson took out a measuring tape and quickly measured the smaller cabezon. It was an inch short of the required fifteen inches—a minor detail since all of the fish had been illegally taken inside the marine protected area.

"I'm going to ask you this one more time," said Hanson. "Did you fellas leave any fishing gear, empty beer cans, or other items down on the beach or out on the rocks?"

"No," said McCarty.

"What about you?" said Warden Hanson, looking directly into Rodriguez's eyes.

"I don't think we left anything," said Rodriguez, shivering.

"Let's all walk back down there, and you can show me where you've been fishing," said Hanson.

Rodriguez and McCarty led Warden Hanson to one of the areas where they had been seen fishing. Lying on the rocks was a section of nylon line with a hook attached. "Is this part of the fishing gear you guys were using?" asked Hanson.

"Yes," said McCarty, picking up the debris.

"Now show me where else you guys have been fishing."

McCarty pointed to another group of rocks where Hanson had seen Rodriguez retrieve the four fish. "We fished there for a little while," he said.

"Did you guys leave anything else down there on the beach or on the rocks?"

Both men again answered no.

"Let's assume that I've been watching you for the last forty-five minutes with these binoculars," said Hanson. "Would you like to change your story?"

Rodriguez and McCarty adamantly denied leaving anything else on the beach or on the rocks. Walking to the rocks where Hanson had seen Rodriguez pull the four fish from the tide pools, Warden Hanson discovered a large spool of nylon line, a package of hooks, and a plastic bag with live crabs inside.

After bagging up the evidence, Hanson led Rodriguez and McCarty eighty yards down the beach to the last location where he had seen them with fishing gear. With looks of impending doom on their faces, Rodriguez and McCarty watched Warden Hanson point out three handline rigs, a cardboard container of squid bait with squid still inside, an unopened package of fish hooks and leader, and another spool of nylon line. "Now, please collect your trash," said Hanson, "and follow me back to the highway. By the way, where are your empties?"

"What empties?" asked McCarty.

"Your empty beer cans?"

"Uh, we brought a few beers with us, but it was so cold we didn't drink any."

"Uh-huh," said Hanson, scanning the surf zone and the water's edge for washed-up cans. "Somehow I have a hard time believing that."

Back at the patrol truck, Warden Hanson asked Rodriguez and McCarty to produce fishing licenses. It came as no surprise that neither man possessed one. "All right," said Hanson. "I'd like you to listen while I explain the situation. You gentlemen have been fishing in the Piedras Blancas Marine Reserve, which is closed to the take of all marine life. You have left litter within 150 feet of state waters, an offense which is every bit as serious. All of those hooks and lines that you carelessly left down there on the rocks could easily become entangled with protected marine mammals and seabirds. Not too far from where you guys were fishing is one of the largest elephant seal rookeries on the Pacific Coast."

In addition to the charges of fishing in the marine reserve and littering state waters, Rodriguez and McCarty were charged with fishing without a license and failure to show their fishing gear on demand. McCarty had just turned eighteen, had recently enlisted in the military, and was scheduled for deployment. The court agreed to dismiss his case if McCarty contributed several hundred dollars to the Fish and Game Preservation Fund. Rodriguez spent the next year and a half paying off his own fine.

***

FOUR MONTHS AFTER RYAN Hanson made his first arrest at the Piedras Blancas Marine Reserve, the enthusiastic young warden would encounter a situation unlike anything he had ever experienced before. All over California, Fish and Game wardens were being diverted from traditional fish and wildlife issues to the ugly and pernicious world of illegal drugs. Inland, marijuana grows were springing up in wooded areas, fields, and on mountainsides—any place with available water nearby. Streams were being diverted, dewatered, and polluted. Wildlife habitat was being destroyed. Deer and other wildlife were being poisoned. Instead of routine hunting and fishing patrols, wardens were being assigned to marijuana eradication teams.

Near the ocean, Fish and Game wardens were encountering so-called panga boats. Panga boats are large, outboard-powered skiffs with unusually high bows. Under the cloak of darkness, these extremely seaworthy vessels were being used to haul cargoes of marijuana and other drugs from Mexico to isolated locations along California's southern and central coasts.

***

EARLY IN THE MORNING on May 24, 2012, Warden Ryan Hanson was on a routine low-tide patrol of the San Luis Obispo County coastline. The wind was blowing at twenty knots as Hanson approached the Piedras Blancas Marine Reserve. "What do we have here?" said Hanson, talking to himself. "That white travel van is parked at the same turnout where I caught those two handliners a few months ago."

Stopping to investigate, Hanson immediately noticed a red Nissan Xterra parked nearby, in a location not visible from Highway 1. Warden Hanson walked over to check out the Nissan, looking for any indication that the occupants might be fishing inside the adjacent reserve. Instead of telltale fishing gear, he found blankets and pillows in the backseat and absolutely nothing in the rear cargo area. Hanson radioed dispatch and ran a check on the license plate. The vehicle came back registered to someone out of the San Francisco Bay Area.

With binoculars in hand, Warden Hanson hiked down to the shoreline and began scanning the area for what he assumed would be illegal fishermen. Walking north, he spotted something unusual in the distance. *Is that a tent?* he wondered. *Whatever it is, it doesn't belong inside the marine reserve.* Walking a hundred yards farther north, Hanson again focused his binoculars on the object of his interest. "Oh, boy!" he blurted. "That's not a tent; it's a panga boat." The boat was sitting high and dry near the high-tide mark, with its two outboard motors propped up in the stern.

Warden Hanson was aware that smugglers using panga boats had been hitting Ventura and Santa Barbara Counties, but so far no enforcement officers had discovered one as far north as San Luis Obispo County. With cellphone service unavailable at his current location, Hanson ran back to his patrol truck and drove south to the Piedras Blancas Motel. From there, Hanson contacted two OSPR (Office of Spill Prevention and Response) wardens who happened to be working near Morro Bay at the time. Hanson relayed the location of the panga boat and requested that the assisting wardens immediately contact the appropriate enforcement agencies. The panga boat happened to be beached on state park property, so Warden Hanson radioed dispatch and requested additional assistance from the local state park ranger.

Racing north on Highway 1, Warden Hanson calculated where the beached panga boat would be located in reference to suspicious vehicles and the highway. When he believed he had reached that point, he made a sharp left turn across the highway and stopped in front of a primitive "cowboy gate." Pulling a vertical section of the two-by-four with his right hand and lifting the barbed wire loop with his left, Hanson quickly dragged the gate open and ran back to his truck. After squeezing his patrol truck through the narrow break in the fence, he closed the gate and drove 150 yards down a soft sand trail that dead-ended at a series of sand dunes.

With his M-1A duty rifle slung across his chest and binoculars in his right hand, Warden Hanson trudged through the soft sand to the top of the first dune. Dropping to his knees, he meticulously scanned the area ahead. Repeating the process with each dune, Hanson finally came to a bluff overlooking the beach.

Adrenaline rushed through the young warden's body as he crouched behind the bluff, contemplating what to do next. *Should I wait here for the cavalry to arrive or peek over the top and find out what the smugglers are up to?* Not sure if he had even calculated correctly, Warden Hanson decided to give his heart time to stop pounding, then take a quick peek. He laid his rifle in the sand next to his right hand and slowly raised his head from the prone position. "Oh!" gasped Hanson, again dropping behind the bluff. "They're right there!" The panga boat was directly in front of him, not ten yards away.

While lying flat against the bluff, Hanson glanced over his shoulder in the direction of the highway. *Backup should be arriving soon,* he thought. Just then a stiff wind gust whistled across the dunes, blowing sand in the warden's face. *I don't hear anything coming from the beach,* thought Hanson, clearing his eyes, *but with this wind and all that truck noise on the highway, I probably couldn't hear 'em anyway. They may have unloaded the dope during the night and left. But why would those cars still be there?*

The suspense was killing him. He had no choice but to take another look, this time from fifty feet north of his current position. Once again peering from the top of the bluff, Hanson was amazed by the size of the panga boat. *That thing must be thirty feet long,* he thought. *And it's stacked with gas cans. They must have needed all that gas to come from somewhere in Mexico.*

Warden Hanson surveyed the scene for another ten minutes before coming to the conclusion that whoever had been there was now gone. With his rifle at the ready position, he climbed down from the bluff and walked toward the beached panga boat. Approaching the bow of the boat, Hanson noticed fresh footprints in the sand leading toward an area of blown-out sand dunes and flattened shrubs, seventy yards away.

"What do we have here?" said Hanson, again talking to himself. With his finger extended, he quickly counted twenty-one bales of marijuana.

"Fish and Game thirty-three fifty-one, State Parks twelve twenty-two," came a voice on Warden Hanson's handheld radio.

Climbing to the top of the first bluff, Hanson was able to direct State Park Ranger Dave Mello to his location. From the same lofty position, Hanson spotted the previously inspected red Nissan Xterra slowly driving north on Highway 1. Much to his surprise, the Xterra pulled into a turnout near the cowboy gate through which Hanson had entered the state park property. With binoculars glued on the suspicious vehicle, Hanson watched the driver climb out of the car, walk twenty yards toward the beach, then pivot and return to the car. The same person spent three or four minutes at the rear of the Xterra, then drove back to the highway and headed north. At Warden Hanson's request, a BOLO (be on the lookout) was broadcast by the law enforcement dispatcher, but the Xterra was never found.

After spending an hour by himself at the scene of the crime, Hanson greeted officers from several area agencies as they began to arrive: State Parks, CHP, San Luis Obispo Sheriff's Office, and the U.S. Coast Guard. A thorough search of the area was conducted, on foot and by helicopter, but no suspects were located. The panga boat, two outboard engines, and 500 pounds of marijuana were taken into custody by the sheriff's department. The estimated street value of the marijuana was a half million dollars. Enough containers to transport 345 gallons of fuel were found in the boat.

Over a dozen panga boat incidents have occurred along the San Luis Obispo County coastline since Warden Ryan Hanson's initial discovery in May of 2012. Every time a Fish and Game warden finds a strange vehicle or boat in some isolated area along the coast, he or she must mentally prepare for possible danger. Warden Hanson has now assisted in the seizure of several tons of processed marijuana. While the sheriff's department and the U.S. Department of Homeland Security have ultimate jurisdiction over foreign vessels that come ashore carrying illegal cargoes, it's the California Fish and Wildlife warden who's most likely to encounter these dangerous criminals first.

"The possible threat is always on my mind now," says Hanson, "but I wouldn't trade this job for anything."

***

INTRIGUED BY THIS HAIR-RAISING event in Warden Hanson's life, I asked if the white travel van or the Nissan Xterra were ever located and checked out.

"I later heard that a woman walking her dog had reported a panga boat on the beach. She was probably the owner of the white travel van," said Warden Hanson. "I do remember seeing dog tracks, as well as human tracks, leading away from the panga boat that day. Almost two years after the panga boat incident, I saw the same red Xterra parked in the same area. I remember, because it was one of the rare days that it rained. I hiked out to the ocean and found a woman collecting seaweed for an art project."

Epilogue
Return to Plaskett Meadows

———— • ————

E ARLY ONE MORNING IN the fall of 2013, I picked up my eighty-seven-
year-old father at his home in Redding.

"Where we goin'?" he asked, climbing into the passenger seat and
fumbling for his seatbelt.

"You know how we've always talked about going back to Plaskett Meadows
someday?"

"Yeah."

"Well, today's the day."

"How long's it been?" asked my father.

"You tell me, Dad."

"I don't know … twenty years?" Dementia had raised its ugly head and
my father found it difficult to gauge time. He could still recall events from his
Fish and Game years, and even his childhood, but short-term memory had
become increasingly out of reach.

"Dad, it's been almost fifty years."

"Has it been that long?" he replied, sounding surprised.

An hour south of Redding, we crossed the Stony Creek Bridge.

"Kenny and I sure had a lot of fun down there," I said.

"Is that Stony Creek?" asked my father.

"It sure is, Dad. As kids, we spent so much time swimming and fishing in
that stream, by the end of summer we could walk on the hot rocks in our bare
feet. One of my best friends, Jim Pennel, lived right there on the other side of
this bridge."

"Orland was a great place to grow up, wasn't it?"

"Yes, it was. Did I ever tell you about the night Paul Martens and Mike Cauble got into the peanut butter fight?"

"No, I don't believe you did."

"Four of us were catfishing just downstream from here—Paul, Mike, Kenny, and I. Our original plan was to stay all night and sleep in our sleeping bags. When the bells on the ends of our fishing rods started jingling, we would get up, reel the fish in, and go back to sleep."

"Did you catch any fish that night?"

"I'll say we did! We were catching ten-inch bullheads as fast as we could throw our lines in the water. Occasionally, one of us would reel in a two-or-three-pound channel cat, but it was mostly bullheads."

"Bullheads were good eating," said my father.

"I know, but by nine o'clock we were out of bait."

"So, what did ya do?"

"We had brought a loaf of wheat bread and a giant-sized jar of peanut butter to eat for dinner. Paul was supposed to bring the jelly, but he forgot."

"Did you bring anything to drink?"

"I think I brought that old thermos of ours—the one with the red lid."

"Didn't your mother buy that with Green Stamps?"

"Anyway, the fishing was so good we didn't want to quit. We tried rolling the bread into little dough balls, but that only works with white bread. Mike decided to mix the peanut butter with the bread and squeeze it onto his hook."

"Did it work?"

"We never got the chance to find out. Mike's hands were all sticky from the peanut butter, so he thought it would be funny to wipe them on the back of Paul's shirt. Kenny and I started laughing hysterically, but Paul didn't think it was funny."

"What did Paul do?"

"He reached into the jar and pulled out a huge gob of peanut butter. By this time, Kenny and I were in stitches. Paul splattered peanut butter all over the front of Mike's shirt. The fight was on. Kenny and I laughed until our stomachs hurt while Mike and Paul smothered each other in peanut butter."

Talking about my brother Kenny was sometimes painful, but it felt good to laugh about the fun we'd had as kids growing up. As the game warden's sons, Kenny and I had shared more childhood adventures than most people experienced in a lifetime. Kenny passed away in September of 2010 from early-onset Alzheimer's. He was sixty-one years old.

Just as we had done a half century before, my father and I headed west from Orland on Newville Road. Fifteen miles out, we crossed the Burris Creek Bridge and approached the old Hamm place.

"Do you remember them?" I asked.

"Of course I do," said my father. "They used to call me once a week about somebody spotlighting deer out here."

"I see an old man standing by the mailbox up ahead."

"I think I know that guy!" said my father. "Let's stop and talk to him."

I pulled my ten-year-old Honda CRV to the side of the road and climbed out just in time to hear the elderly gentleman say, "Hello, Wally. I haven't seen you around in a while." It was like I'd stepped into an episode of *The Twilight Zone*. Fifty years had gone by, yet nothing seemed to have changed. I was sixteen again, patiently waiting at the car while my father chewed the fat with his old friend for the next half hour.

It was about noon when we reached Cold Creek. The stream had dried up after three years of drought, and the campground was no longer there.

"Do you remember this place?" I asked.

"Sure I do," said my father. "I patrolled past here a thousand times."

"Do you remember the time you fell in the creek trying to retrieve my lure?"

"I remember getting all wet. Wasn't that the same day we caught those two firemen up at Plaskett Lake with the overlimit of trout?"

"I think it was, Dad. With Cold Creek dried up, I'm wondering what Plaskett Lake is going to look like."

We arrived at Plaskett Meadows a little after 1:00. I stopped above the meadow to photograph my father with the upper lake in the background. As I peered through the lens of my camera, bittersweet memories flooded my mind: Dad and I had many adventures in this beautiful country when I was a boy, and now time had taken its toll. Who knew if we'd ever make it back this way again?

"Is the lake as you remember it, Dad?"

"It seems to be a lot smaller," he said.

"I think that's because of the drought. I see a picnic table over there. How 'bout a sandwich?"

"Good idea," said my father.

It was a little chilly that afternoon, so we donned our jackets and followed a steep footpath to the picnic table. My father's mobility had decreased considerably over the last few years, so it took a little longer than I expected to reach our dining destination. Dad still had the heart of a lion, and I knew he wouldn't ask for help, so I carefully monitored his progress.

Both of us sat facing the lake and eagerly dug into the delicious gourmet lunch I had prepared for the occasion: peanut butter and jelly sandwiches, oranges, and cookies. It was then that I noticed two old-timers fishing from the bank on the north shore of the lake.

"Whaddya think, Dad? Should we walk over and check their fishing licenses?"

My father laughed, the irony not lost on him. "They don't look like they're catching much," he said.

"Dad, have you heard from Bill Chilcote, your old fireman buddy from San Diego?"

"We used to write back and forth all the time," said my father. "But I haven't heard from him in three or four years."

"Remember when he tried to talk you into quitting your job and going to Australia with him?"

"How long ago was that?"

"It was right after you left the fire department and became a game warden."

"That turned out well for him," said my father. "He started all those Taco Bill Restaurants over there and became a millionaire."

"Do you ever regret not taking him up on his offer?"

"Bill asked me that very same question about ten years ago, when he came back for a visit."

"What did you tell him?"

"I told him in spite of all the money I might have made, I preferred catching poachers to selling tacos and enchiladas."

"That's pretty funny, Dad. We had great careers, didn't we?"

"If I had a chance to do it all over again, I'd do the same thing," said my father. "There were times when I almost felt guilty getting paid to do a job I enjoyed so much."

"I felt the same way, Dad. It was best job in the world."

Time had wrought its changes on both of us, but he would always be my father, and I would always be the game warden's son. By following in his footsteps with my own Fish and Game career, I had only made our bond stronger.

Walking back to the car, I suddenly stopped.

"What's the matter?" asked my father.

"I thought I heard one of those fishermen down there."

"What did he say?"

"I'm not sure, but I think he shouted, 'Fish on!' "

STEVEN T. CALLAN WAS born in San Diego, California, where he spent his early childhood. It was there that he first developed his love of nature, spending much of his spare time exploring the undeveloped canyons behind his house and learning to skin-dive in the nearby ocean. In 1960, Callan's family moved to the small Northern California farm town of Orland. Steve spent his high school years playing baseball, basketball, hunting, and fishing. With an insatiable interest in wildlife, particularly waterfowl, he never missed an opportunity to ride along on patrol with his father, a California Fish and Game warden.

Callan graduated from California State University, Chico, in 1970 and continued with graduate work at California State University, Sacramento. While studying at Sacramento State, he worked as a paid intern for the Sacramento County Board of Supervisors—using this golden opportunity to lobby for protected wildlife corridors in the county's general plan.

Hired by the California Department of Fish and Game in 1974, Warden Steve Callan's first assignment was the Earp Patrol District on the Colorado River. He was promoted to patrol lieutenant in January of 1978, leaving the desert and moving to the metropolitan area of Riverside/San Bernardino. While stationed in Riverside, Callan organized and led a successful effort to ban the sale of native reptiles in California. He also organized and led a successful campaign to stop a planned recreational development at Lake Mathews—establishing the lake and its surrounding wildlands as an ecological reserve for thousands of waterfowl and Southern California's largest population of wintering bald eagles.

Transferring north to Shasta County in 1981, Lieutenant Callan spent the remainder of his thirty-year enforcement career in Redding. While supervising the warden force in Shasta County, Callan created and coordinated the Streamside Corridor Protection Plan—working with city and county planners to establish development-free setbacks along the Sacramento River and its Redding area tributaries.

In 1995, Lieutenant Steve Callan and Warden Dave Szody conducted a three-year undercover investigation into the unlawful killing of California black bears for their gallbladders, possibly the most successful wildlife-related criminal investigation in California history at the time. Callan and Szody received the distinguished Frank James Memorial Award for their accomplishment.

Steve and his wife, Kathleen, a retired science teacher, are passionate about the environment. They are longtime members of no fewer than a dozen environmental organizations and actively promote environmental causes. They are avid bird-watchers, kayakers, anglers, and scuba divers. Steve is a wildlife artist, using photographs he takes while scuba diving for inspiration. Callan has played competitive softball throughout the United States since his college days and in 2004 was inducted into the National Senior Softball Hall of Fame.

Callan's first book, *Badges, Bears, and Eagles*, was selected as a 2013 "Book of the Year" finalist by *ForeWord Reviews*. Steve has also earned the 2014 and 2015 "Best Outdoor Magazine Column" awards from the Outdoor Writers Association of California.

You can find Steven online at www.steventcallan.com.